THOMAS HARDY
INTERVIEWS AND RECOLLECTIONS

Thomas Hardy

Interviews and Recollections

Edited by

James Gibson
*formerly Principal Lecturer
Christ Church College
Canterbury*

First published in Great Britain 1999 by
MACMILLAN PRESS LTD
Houndmills, Basingstoke, Hampshire RG21 6XS and London
Companies and representatives throughout the world

A catalogue record for this book is available from the British Library.

ISBN 0–333–24787–6 hardcover
ISBN 0–333–24788–4 paperback

 First published in the United States of America 1999 by
ST. MARTIN'S PRESS, INC.,
Scholarly and Reference Division,
175 Fifth Avenue, New York, N.Y. 10010

ISBN 0–312–22582–2

Library of Congress Cataloging-in-Publication Data
Thomas Hardy : interviews and recollections / edited by James Gibson.
   p. cm.
Includes bibliographical references and index.
ISBN 0–312–22582–2
1. Hardy, Thomas, 1840–1928 Interviews. 2. Hardy, Thomas, 1840–1928—Friends and associates. 3. Authors, English—19th century Interviews. 4. Authors, English—20th century Interviews 5. Authors, English—19th century Biography. 6. Authors, English—20th century Biography. I. Gibson, James, 1919–   .
PR4753.T495 1999
823'.8—dc21
[B]   99–15266
                                                                          CIP

Selection and editorial matter © James Gibson 1999
Text © the various copyright-holders where applicable - see acknowledgements

All rights reserved. No reproduction, copy or transmission of this publication may be made without written permission.

No paragraph of this publication may be reproduced, copied or transmitted save with written permission or in accordance with the provisions of the Copyright, Designs and Patents Act 1988, or under the terms of any licence permitting limited copying issued by the Copyright Licensing Agency, 90 Tottenham Court Road, London W1P 0LP.

Any person who does any unauthorised act in relation to this publication may be liable to criminal prosecution and civil claims for damages.

The editor has asserted his right to be identified as the editor of this work in accordance with the Copyright, Designs and Patents Act 1988.

This book is printed on paper suitable for recycling and made from fully managed and sustained forest sources.

10 9 8 7 6 5 4 3
08 07 06 05 04 03 02 01 00

Printed and bound in Great Britain by
Antony Rowe Ltd, Chippenham, Wiltshire

Contents

Acknowledgements	vi
Preface	viii
Abbreviations	xiii
1 The First Thirty Years 1840–1870	1
2 The Nine Years 1871–1879	7
3 The Ten Years 1880–1889	12
4 The Ten Years 1890–1899	28
5 The Final Years 1900–1928	62
Part I From the Boer War to the Great War, 1900–1918	62
Part II The Post-War Years, 1918–1928	125
Index	245

Acknowledgements

The author and publishers wish to thank the following for permission to use copyright material:

Mrs Joane Atkins
Carcanet Press for material from Robert Graves, *Goodbye to All That*, 1929
The family of Mr John Cave
Gerald Duckworth and Co. Ltd for material from Vere Collins, *Talks with Thomas Hardy at Max Gate*, 1928
Mrs Lucy Dynevor
Godfrey, Lord Elton
Ms Valerie Haig-Brown
Mrs Aileen Hawkins
David Higham Associates on behalf of the Estate of the author for material from Ford Maddox Ford, *Mightier than the Sword*, Bodley Head, 1938
Miss Vanessa Austin Hinton
Mr Michael Hurd and The Rutland Boughton Music Trust
Mr Patrick and Miss Margaret Mann
Mrs Mary Mardon
John Murray (Publishers) Ltd for material from James Milne, *A Window in Fleet Street*, 1931
Peter Newbolt for material from Margaret Newbolt, ed., *The Later Life and Letters of Sir Henry Newbolt*, Faber & Faber, 1942
Mrs Christine O'Connor
Peters, Fraser & Dunlop Group Ltd on behalf of the estate of the author for material from Edmund Blunden, 'Notes on a Visit to Thomas Hardy', 1922
Mrs Dorothy Phillips
Random House UK and Harcourt Brace & Company for material from Virginia Woolf, *A Writer's Diary*. Copyright © 1954 by Leonard Woolf, renewed 1982 by Quentin Bell and Angelica Garnett
Mrs Diana Reed
Mrs Diana Rothenstein
Royal Literary Fund for material from Eden Phillpotts, *The Angle of 88*, Hutchinson, 1951
Meriel, Lady Salt
George Sassoon for material from Siegfried Sassoon, *Siegfried's Journey 1916-20*, 1945, and *Siegfried Sassoon's Diaries 1920–1922*

Acknowledgements

The Society of Authors as literary representatives of the estate of the author for material from John Middleton Murry, *Katherine Mansfield and Other Literary Portraits* and a BBC broadcast on 19 February 1955; as the Literary Trustees of the estate of the author for material by Walter de la Mare from an article in *The Listener*, 28 April 1956; and as literary representatives of the estate of the author and the Provost and Scholars of King's College, Cambridge, for material from E. M. Forster, *Selected Letters of E. M. Forster*, vol. 2, 1985

Raglan Squire for material from J. C. Squire, *Sunday Mornings*, Heinemann, 1930

Mrs Diana Toms

Tweedie & Prideaux on behalf of the Trustees of the Seven Pillars of Wisdom Trust for material from T. E. Lawrence, *The Letters of Lawrence of Arabia*, Jonathan Cape, 1964

Virginia Quarterly Review for material from an article by Llewelyn Powys in *Virginia Quarterly Review*, winter 1939

Miss P. E. G. Voss

A. P. Watt Ltd on behalf of The Royal Literary Fund for material from W. Somerset Maugham, *Cakes and Ale*, Heinemann, and G. K. Chesterton, *Autobiography*, 1936

Mr Hugo Wood Homer

Mrs Norrie Woodhall

Every effort has been made to trace the copyright-holders but if any has been inadvertently overlooked the publishers will be pleased to make the necessary arrangement at the first opportunity.

Preface

When Hardy's publishers, Macmillan, asked me to be the editor of the Hardy volume in their 'Interviews and Recollections' series, I knew what an arduous and difficult task lay ahead of me. He had lived for nearly ninety years. Unknown to the world for the first thirty years, 1840–1870, he became a famous novelist in the period 1871–1897, and a famous poet in the last third of his life, 1898–1928. With fame came many hundreds of new friends and acquaintances anxious to meet the Grand Old Man of English Literature, ask him for his autograph, and return home to write about meeting him. Some of these accounts, those of Virginia Woolf, Robert Graves, and T. E. Lawrence, for example, were already well known, but there were obviously many others waiting to be brought out into the open from the brooding shelves of the British Library.

My work proceeded slowly through the 1980s and was greatly extended by Michael Millgate's edition of *The Life and Work of Thomas Hardy* and by his editing with R. L. Purdy of the *Collected Letters of Thomas Hardy*, both of which led to new areas of investigation because of the enlarging of our knowledge of the circle of Hardy's friends and acquaintances. May I here acknowledge the debt I owe to Michael, not only for the widening of the field of research and for the immense value of the index and information contained in *Collected Letters*, but also for his generous offer of help when I first began my work on this volume.

The research might have gone on for ever if my publishers hadn't at last told me that the time had come to stop the research and begin the editing. Their patience has been quite remarkable and my thanks go to Macmillan, too, and especially to Tim Farmiloe and Charmian Hearne, even if their call to publication means that research into whether Hardy's friend the Marchioness of Londonderry, or his friends of the noble Portsmouth family, or a hundred others, kept memoirs or diaries in which they discuss meetings with 'Uncle Tom' and give us their descriptions of him must wait for the attention of some future PhD student!

Up to the moment when editing began, I had accumulated some three hundred interviews and recollections, enough material to fill at least two books of this size, and as the price of just one book was likely to be beyond the pocket of Chaucer's poor scholar, I found myself faced with problems of selection and presentation, a problem made worse by the fact that there was too little material for the early part of the life, and too much for the remainder. An early decision was made to save space by eliminating the multiplicity of notes which so often encumber academic books of this kind. I have assumed that my readers will be educated enough to look up for themselves any extra information they may need, and that they do not require to know every detail of the lives of those whose memories of Hardy are found here. It is Hardy that we are concerned with. The need for pruning the material available to me has meant many hours of agonising over what had of necessity to be omitted, but I hope that what has resulted is a book which is of interest in itself and which will prove to be a valuable source of information about Hardy.

In an interesting article in *Documentary Editing* (June 1989), 'Conversations with Victorian Writers: Some Editorial Questions', Patrick G. Scott and William B. Thesing discussed some of the problems faced by authors of a series such as this. They point out that 'interview texts... have in a sense two authors', and that an editor has a responsibility towards both of them. Delicate judgements have to be made and I have been well aware of this. Although a man of integrity and honesty (most of the time) in his private life, Hardy the professional writer did not regard himself as being on oath to tell the truth in his public life. He was, after all, a writer of fiction. It was understandable in a class-ridden society that he did not want his middle-class readers and his upper-class friends to know too much about his working-class background and he was always ready to conceal or even lie about the early years of his life and education. He was sensitive enough to be aware of the repeated descriptions of him as a 'peasant', and of the snobbery of many of his acquaintances. His public persona was something he worked hard at, particularly in the early years of his life as a writer. During those early years, as a novelist striving to earn a living, publicity, however much detested, was vital to him. He was willing to give interviews, and, better stlll, was quite ready to write most of the article about himself for a journalist to publish as his own work, just as later he would pretend that his wife, Florence, had written his autobiography. However, with the success of *Tess* (1891) and *Jude* (1895) he had more publicity than he desired, and now a wealthy man, there was a radical change in his attitude towards those who did not just want to interview him but were anxious to exploit him. There was the same sensitivity about his early life, and interviewers were warned repeatedly about interpreting the novels in an autobiographical way although Hardy must have known that there was very much of himself in the novels. Interviewers in those later years of his life were not allowed even to write down notes at the time of the interview, which must cast doubt on the complete accuracy of the whole sentences given as Hardy's own words. In these interviews Hardy is not above having his little joke. Bored to tears by one visiting American professor who came to Max Gate not through any liking of Hardy's works but because he was writing a book about British writers, Hardy asked him whether Harvard was 'a girls' school?' Horrified at his ignorance, the professor put it down to Hardy's 'advancing years', when, of course, it was just Hardy's ironic attempt to relieve the tedium. (see p. 198) The same misleading trait can be seen in Harold Macmillan's anecdote on p. 61. Hardy was not, then, a simple and easy interviewee. His deliberate obfuscations, his sometimes unrecognised irony, and the refusal to allow interviewers to take notes mean that caution is required in our acceptance and appreciation of what he said or is supposed to have said.

The same caution needs to be exercised in our interpretation of the second element – what the interviewers chose to report and the manner in which it was reported by them. If we accept that an interview is a formal meeting with the intention of writing an article for a journal and/or book, and a recollection is something written at some time later, possibly many years later, we have immediately an important difference. What value can we give to the memories of a maidservant employed by Hardy for a period of twelve months some seventy years before she wrote them down? How can we compare her memories with those of someone like A. C. Benson who wrote his recollections in his diary within a few hours of experiencing them but is obviously such a snob that the 'peasant' Hardy has little chance of a sympathetic hearing? And how do we assess Virginia Woolf's penetratingly observant but so coldly objective account of her short visit to Max Gate? What I have tried to do is to give as diverse a group of interviews and interviewers as possible and to give warning where it is needed.

Another problem which has to be faced with the interviewers is that professional writers like Graves and Newman Flower exploited their Max Gate visits to the full, often reproducing the same material, some of which was incorrectly remembered, again and again. Not infrequently this means that an article written in 1940 on the centenary of Hardy's birth has a somewhat different text from that written at the time of Hardy's death in 1928, and from that originally written in, say, 1919. In such cases one assumes that the earliest version is the one to choose. There is evidence to show that in the 1890s the material provided by one or two interviewers was 'cannibalised' by others in what were either syndicate arrangements or brazen plagiarism. This seemed to happen particularly in the United States, but the prize for pretending to know Hardy well and for exploitation of that pretence must go to Clive Holland, with a runner-up prize for Cyril Clemens whose article, 'My Chat with Thomas Hardy', in the *Dalhousie Review* (April 1943) has been dismissed as faked by both R. L. Purdy and Michael Millgate; 'it is largely an unscrupulous pastiche from other sources.' It certainly can't be said that 'Never will I forget the thrill that ran through me from head to foot when I held my first copy of *Desperate Remedies* in my hand! I was in a veritable seventh heaven for weeks thereafter' sounds like an utterance of the eighty-five year old Hardy. 'Clive Holland' who was really Charles James Hankinson (1866–1959) wrote numerous articles implying a close friendship with Hardy, a claim which was somewhat economic with the truth. After Hardy's death Holland wrote in 1933 a study of Hardy's life and work which Florence, Hardy's second wife, angrily denounced as being mostly copied from the two volumes about Hardy's life published by Macmillan in 1928 and 1930.

I have already indicated that my selection of material has had to be made in the knowledge that there is far too much of it for the space available and that deciding what to include or exclude has been difficult. As it is Hardy's work rather than Hardy's life that matters most, I have gone first for material in which he talks about books, his own and others. Next in importance is what we can learn about Hardy's life and character. And here I must declare an interest. In writing my *Thomas Hardy: a Literary Life* (Macmillan, 1996) I had available most of the material now contained in this book, and my research had convinced me that Hardy was anything but the miserly, miserable, reclusive man portrayed by some biographers. Most of those who actually knew him personally were charmed by his kindness, his hospitality, his vitality, his sense of humour, his modesty and his intense curiosity about life. That is confirmed in the reminiscences found in this book. But to be fair, I have included a representative sample of the small number who found something to criticise adversely. It is inescapable that Florence Hardy was more melancholy and moody than her husband, and her constant complaints about the loneliness of life at Max Gate are not borne out by the never-ending stream of visitors who wanted to see the Master, very few of whom were turned away from his door.

A work like this could not have been done without the help of a great many people, far more than I could possibly mention, but my gratitude goes to them all. First, I must mention my wife, Helen, whose secretarial help has been invaluable and whose patience has been remarkable. In addition I must specially thank James Stevens Cox who was responsible for the Monographs (Materials for a Study of Hardy's Life, Time and Works), and who, sadly, died as I was writing these words, and I appreciate too the cooperation of his son, Gregory. Help has been generously given by Vera Jesty whose work on the Hardys has made her an expert on local families and their history. Two libraries have been particularly valuable to me: the British Library and the Dorset County Library. In spite of the cut-backs and economies the library service in England is still among the very best in the world.

My thanks are due also to the very many people who have generously helped with information and advice, among whom must be mentioned: Miss Denison Beach, Mrs Olive Blackburn, Mr Richard de Peyer, Dr T. J. Differ, Professor John Doheny, Dr Graham Handley, Dr Timothy Hands, Mr and Mrs W. Jesty, Mr Trevor Johnson, Mr Ronald Knight, Mr George Lanning, Mr Edward Leeson, Sir Rex Niven, Mr Christopher Pope, Lt-Cdr B. Pople, Mrs Anne Powell, Mr P. Rushforth, Dr George Rylands, Professor J. Schwarz, Mr Furse Swann, Mrs Lilian Swindall, Dr Richard Taylor, Mrs Ann Thwaite, Mrs R. M. G. Voremberg, and Professor Keith Wilson.

Abbreviations

The following abbreviated references to books frequently mentioned have been used:

Life	*The Life and Work of Thomas Hardy*, by Thomas Hardy, edited by Michael Millgate.
CL	*The Collected Letters of Thomas Hardy*, edited by R. L. Purdy and Michael Millgate.
CP	*The Complete Poems of Thomas Hardy*, edited by James Gibson.
Monograph	*Monographs on the Life, Times and Works of Thomas Hardy*, edited by J. Stevens Cox.

1
The First Thirty Years
1840–1870

The best source of information about Hardy in his very early years is his own autobiography. Originally disguised as written by his wife, Florence (1879–1937), we now know that it is mainly his own work, and readers are referred to Michael Millgate's edition of *The Life and Work of Thomas Hardy* (hereafter *Life*) by Thomas Hardy (Macmillan, London, 1984) for Hardy's own recollections of his childhood.

For the rest we are dependent upon people reminiscing so many years later that memories are blurred and imaginations stimulated in a desire to be associated with the great. An unidentified and anonymous article by 'P' appeared in *Sunday at Home* in May 1915 (pp. 621–2). It is entitled 'My Famous Schoolfellows' and has paragraphs on Hardy and William Barnes among others. Michael Millgate tells me that he regards 'the "memoir" itself with considerable scepticism' but it is worth printing a little of it because of its mention of Hardy's relationship with his mother and of his intense interest in his surroundings:

> He and I went as lads to the same school in Dorchester, and our homeward ways lay the same also. The Hardys lived at Upper Bockhampton, a village perhaps four miles out of the town, and my parents' house was in that direction, though not so far. But as Tom and myself were close comrades at that time, I would often accompany him right to their little cottage, with the garden in front of it. A small gate which I can still see clearly in my mind's eye, led into the garden; and over this gate would hang Mrs Hardy on a summer evening, watching and waiting for Tom's coming... They thought the world of each other, Tom and his mother. He used to wear a brown knickerbocker suit about the time which I am now specially recalling, and his fair somewhat curly hair and bright eyes always attracted me. I can see us both as it were yesterday – he swinging his satchel over his arm carelessly – he scarcely ever had it across his back – and I trudging idly alongside him with my own bag containing nearly as many "trophies" of boyhood,

in the shape of nests, marbles, a hedgehog, etc., as it did books! ...

Sometimes on a Saturday, when there was no school, Tom Hardy and one or two of us would wander through Lower Bockhampton village, and stroll over the ridge beyond, till we came to the farmstead at Norris Mill. When I reflect today how often we have lounged about that farm, he and I, watching the cows, the dairy-work, the farmer, etc., and think of what Tom has made of all this since, whilst I seem to have done nothing with the many hours we spent there, I am fairly mazed, as they say in Dorset. I suppose he must have been getting the environment deep into his mind, even if unconsciously, on those very afternoons, though as lads it never struck us thus.

Another early recollection, probably more reliable than that of 'P', is that of Charles Lacey (1843–1931) who for many years worked for the *Dorset County Chronicle and Southern Times* and eventually became its proprietor. It was first published as 'Reminiscences of an Old Durnovarian' in *The Dorset Year Book* of 1930:

> I came in every day to attend the British School in Greyhound Yard, Dorchester, which is entered through a Tudor arch and is now used as an estate office. The master, Mr Isaac Last, was a severe disciplinarian, and would frequently chase a boy round the room lashing him with his cane until he was white in the face, the ink-pots flying in all directions as they leapt over the desks. One of the cleverest pupils was Thomas Hardy, who was always ready to help the other boys with their lessons. We used to carry our lunch with us to school, and, clad in our pinafores, we ate it under a S. W. railway arch. In South Street, where the Wesleyan Chapel now stands, was a little shop kept by an old woman known to us as Sally Warren. To enter the shop one descended a step. The boys sometimes threw Hardy's cap down into the shop, and when he entered to retrieve it the old woman belaboured him with a broom ...

About 1890 Hermann Lea (see p. 54) described talking to 'someone who had attended the same school as Hardy and who told him that Hardy had always seemed different to the other boys, seldom joining in their games, spending his play-hours with a book or standing apart from the others plunged in thought and seemingly oblivious to what went on around him. It was not that he was in any way unfriendly, but, to use my informant's own words, "somehow different from the rest of us boys, kind of dreaming, seeming to prefer to be by himself."'

Lacey's description of Hardy as a boy is supported by an interview which James Stevens Cox had on 6 December 1964 with Mr Ernest Harding. Mr Cox did invaluable work in the 1960s and 70s recording the recollections of people who had known Hardy, most of whom are now dead. The results of his labours are to be found in a collection of 72 'Monographs on the Life, Times and Works of Thomas Hardy' (hereafter *Monographs*). The interview with Mr Harding appears as Appendix 2 to Monograph No. 8 (Beaminster 1965), and Mr Harding is quoted as saying, 'I did not know Hardy personally, but I heard much about him from my late cousin, Julia Green née Harding, who was born at Stinsford, 22 February 1843, and knew Hardy well in her young days. She told me that she remembered when he was a boy at school, and that, "He always carried a satchel of books and was an odd looking little boy with a big head. I remember him well and often saw him when I was a girl – he was a solemn looking little boy."' Julia's sister, Louisa, was the girl referred to in Hardy's poem 'To Louisa in the Lane'. In the *Life* Hardy talks of an attachment to a well-to-do farmer's daughter named Louisa (p. 30), but, according to Ernest Harding, the Harding family 'regarded the Hardys as socially inferior... You see, to my family, Hardy was just a village boy, although it was recognised that he was an unusual type and different from the other village children in several ways, for instance he never played games, and was a quiet, studious child of a retiring disposition.' Even as a young man Hardy must have been made painfully aware of class sensitivities. Louisa Harding was no more for him than Maria Beadnell was for Charles Dickens. How could girls of such indubitable upper middle-class status be expected to marry men of lower class with so little prospect of advancement in the world!

Mr H. Shobbrook Collins wrote to *Scribner's Magazine* on 26 December 1934 and his letter was published in March 1935 (pp. 188–91). The facts which can be checked are sufficiently authentic to make the letter worth publishing. For example there was a Miss Pearmain at the College of Sarum St Michael at the same time as Mary. Some idea of the date of these recollections can be obtained from the reference to Hardy's article in *Chambers's Journal*. We know this to be his sketch 'How I Built Myself a House' which was published anonymously on 18 March 1865 (pp. 161–4):

> I was born and "raised" in the same little parish of Stinsford and went to the two schools – in due course – where he had gone. Of course knew all his family well. Remember hearing "Tom" warble that old English ditty "Dame Durden" at a Christmas party, where I as a youngster was the favoured "dancing partner" of his eldest sister Mary.

I have a vivid recollection, of being at his home one evening – I was about seven at the time – with Miss Permain [sic] (who had been at Salisbury Training College with Mary Hardy) and her sister. I well recall the enthusiasm with which "Tom's" mother displayed the first article that "Tom" had ever got printed! Of course, I was not perhaps old enough to ask questions about it, but subsequently learned that it was that little article in *Chambers's Magazine*.

Just after hearing you talk, I felt that you would like to hear from one who has practically all his life, been viewing "T.H." from a viewpoint quite different from the majority.

His Uncle James (one of the old Mellstock Quire) used to give me violin lessons.

There is one other early memory worth preserving. Llewelyn Powys (see p. 231) attended the unveiling of the Memorial statue of Hardy in Dorchester on 2 September 1931, and in Monograph No. 70 (1971) reported the following meeting:

Next to us was an old man – a typical Dorset farmer of the last century with side whiskers and a countenance of sturdy good natured cunning. I think, as we did, he resented the fact that our tickets did not allow for us taking our ease in the councillors pen...

I liked the appearance of this farmer and thought I would talk to him a little. I opened the conversation by asking if he could remember so wet a summer. He told me that 1868 was as wet and also 1876. Then suddenly ejaculated,

'I was at school with he.'

At first I did not grasp the fact that he was referring to Thomas Hardy, but when I did realize this I asked him to tell me what he remembered of him at school.

'He used to sit away by himself,' he said. 'He was always in a stud. I can see 'en now, a little nipper going off to school with a bag all a-coloured like Jacob's jacket.'

'What kind of a bag?' I asked.

'It were a carpet bag,' he answered. 'I do mind his father well. He were in a paltry way of business. He were a mason and he only had one man a working for 'en! Yet they were a kindly people. I do mind woon day I and another lad did have to take a pig to 'en to Bockhampton and the old ooman did give we two slices of bread and butter and one with sugar on't. T'were a tasty bit.'

I asked him what his name was and he said 'Locke.'

'I do mind so far back as to time of parson Moule at Fordington. I used to supply 'en with butter.'

As Hardy approached his thirtieth birthday in 1870, he wrote about a 'time of mental depression over his work and prospects' (*Life* p. 59) and he was conscious of how little he seemed to have achieved. Although reasonably successful as an architect he had not been able to get any of his poems published, and his one novel, *The Poor Man and the Lady*, had been rejected by Macmillan. In matters of the heart he had been no more successful, and it must have been in something of a sombre mood that he set out on 7 March 1870 for a small hamlet near Boscastle, in Cornwall, called St Juliot, where he was to make drawings for the restoration of the church. There, on that never-to-be-forgotten day, he met the vicar's sister-in-law, Emma Lavinia Gifford, fell in love and married her four years later. A year before she died in 1912 she wrote down in an exercise-book memories of her first meeting with Hardy. Her title for the book, first published in 1961, was *Some Recollections*. Here she describes Hardy as she saw him at that first meeting:

> It was a lovely Monday evening in March after a wild winter we were on the *qui-vive* for the stranger, who would have a tedious journey, his home being two counties off changing trains many times and waiting at stations – a sort of cross jump-journey, like a chess-knight's move. The only damper to our gladness was the sudden laying up of my brother-in-law by gout, and he who was the chief person could not be present on the arrival of our guest. The dinner-cloth was laid, my sister had gone to her husband, who required the constant attention of his wife. At that very moment the front door bell rang and he was ushered in. I had to receive him alone, and felt a curious uneasy embarrassment at receiving anyone, especially so necessary a person as the Architect. I was immediately arrested by his familiar appearance, as if I had seen him in a dream – his slightly different accent, his soft voice; also I noticed a blue paper sticking out of his pocket. I was explaining who I was – as I saw that he took me for the parson's daughter, or wife – when my sister appeared to my great relief, and he went up to Mr Holder's room with her. So I met my husband or rather he met me.
>
> I thought him much older than he was. He had a beard and a rather shabby great coat and had quite a business appearance. Afterwards he seemed younger, and by daylight especially. His beard was yellowish, and the 'blue paper' proved to be the MS of a poem, and not a plan of the Church, he informed me, to my surprise.
>
> After this our first meeting, there had to be many visits to the Church, and these visits of deep interest for both, merged in those of acquaintance and affection to end in marriage, but not until after four years. . . .

He [Hardy] ... came two or three times a year from that time to visit me. I rode my pretty mare Fanny and he walked by my side and I showed him some of the neighbourhood – the cliffs, along the roads, and through the scattered hamlets, sometimes gazing down at the solemn small shores where the seals lived, coming out of great caverns very occasionally. We sketched and talked of books; often we walked down the beautiful Valley to Boscastle harbour where we had to jump over stones and climb over a low wall by rough steps, get through by narrow pathways to come out on great wide spaces suddenly, with a sparkling little brook going the same way, into which we once lost a tiny picnic-tumbler, and there it is to this day no doubt between two small boulders.

Sometimes we all drove to Tintagel and Trebarwith Strand, where donkeys were onerously employed to get seaweed for the farmers Strangles beach also, Bossiney, other places on the coast. Lovely drives they were, with sea-views all along at intervals, and very dawdling enjoyable slow ones; sometimes to visit a neighbouring clergyman and his family. We grew much interested in each other. I found him a perfectly new subject of study and delight, and he found a 'mine' in me, he said; he was quite unlike any other person who came to see us, for they were slow of speech and ideas!

(No attempt has been made to correct her punctuation. A text of this, corrected and edited by Hardy, appears in *Life* pp. 72–4.)

2
The Nine Years 1871–1879

The 1870s were for Hardy years of steady progress as a novelist. It was a period in which he had seven novels published, including three of his finest: *Under the Greenwood Tree* (1872), *Far from the Madding Crowd* (1874) and *The Return of the Native* (1878). Although the literary world began to realise that here was an exceptional writer, the general public was not impressed and the first edition of *Under the Greenwood Tree* did not sell well, while the first edition of *Far from the Madding Crowd* and *The Return of the Native* were both remaindered. Hardy had yet to acquire the success which brings the journalist and the famous to visit and then record their visits. In this decade there is little more material available than there was previously.

Hardy's first published novel was *Desperate Remedies* (1871). It is probable that it would not have been published if Hardy had not been prepared to enter into an agreement with the publisher, William Tinsley, according to which he had to put up £75 – a considerable sum of money in those days – as a share of the expense returnable only if the first edition sold out. It didn't and Hardy lost £16 of his advance. Tinsley next published *Under the Greenwood Tree* (1872) for which he paid Hardy a miserable £30 for the copyright, and in 1873 he published *A Pair of Blue Eyes*. Years later, in 1900, Tinsley wrote *Random Recollections of an Old Publisher* (London 1900):

> I read a good many manuscripts almost every year during the time I was a publisher. One I read, and took an especial interest in, was Thomas Hardy's first novel, called *Desperate Remedies*. In fact, I read the work twice, and even though I never thoroughly made up my mind that it was the sort of work to be a great success, I certainly thought it contained some capital characters and character drawing. But Mr Hardy had dragged into the midst of excellent humorous writing almost ultra-sensational matter; in fact, incidents unworthy of his pen and the main portion of the work. Still, I quite thought that there was enough of the bright side of the human nature in it

to sell at least one fair edition. However, there was not, but for a first venture I do not think Mr Hardy had much to complain about.

I purchased the copyright of Mr Hardy's second novel, called *Under the Greenwood Tree*. In that book I felt sure I had got hold of the best little prose idyll I had ever read. By "little", I mean as regards the length of the book, in which there is not more that about four or five hours' reading; but, to my mind, it is excellent reading indeed. I almost raved about the book, and I gave it away wholesale to pressmen and anyone I knew interested in good fiction. But, strange to say, it would not sell. Finding it hung on hand in the original two-volume form, I printed it in a very pretty illustrated one-volume form. That edition was a failure. Then I published it in a two-shilling form, with paper covers, and that edition had a very poor sale indeed; and yet it was one of the best press-noticed books I ever published. But even though it is as pure and sweet as new-mown hay, it just lacks the touch of sentiment that lady novel-readers most admire. In fact, to my thinking, if Mr Hardy could have imported stronger matter for love, laughter and tears into *Under the Greenwood Tree*, the book would have in no way been unworthy of the pen of George Eliot.

I tried Mr Hardy's third novel, called *A Pair of Blue Eyes*, as a serial in my magazine, and in book form, but it was by far the weakest of the three books I published of his. However, a good deal owing to my praise of him, and the merits of *Under the Greenwood Tree*, Mr Hardy was engaged to write his novel, called *Far from the Madding Crowd*, in *The Cornhill Magazine*, and for that he found more readers than for any book I published for him. Of course, Mr Hardy was quite within his rights in not offering me his third [sic] book, although I had paid him rather a large sum of money for *A Pair of Blue Eyes*.

However, there is no doubt *The Cornhill* offer was a large one, and started Mr Hardy afresh on his career as a novelist, for just about that time it was by no means certain he would not return to his profession as an architect, from which he could then have obtained a good income. At all events, he told me, soon after I did business with him, that unless writing fiction paid him well, he should not go on with it; but it did pay him, and very well indeed. Since Mr Hardy has become a noted writer of fiction, I have seen it stated that I refused more than one of his books. I never refused one of them, nor ever had the chance of doing so.

The following item, presented as if it were an interview, appeared in the *Literary World* (Boston) in August 1878. It is almost certainly written mostly by Hardy himself, and was to be the first of several such occasions in his life when he passed off his own work as having been written by someone else. The classic example here is that of his autobiography which the world was encouraged to think had been written by Florence. The *Literary World* article reveals Hardy striving to impress the public by the details of his birth and education. It is all very human and understandable in someone in his mid-thirties who still needs to earn a living:

> Mr Thomas Hardy, the English novelist, was born in 1840, in a lonely old-fashioned house in Dorsetshire on the margin of a wood, in the rear of which stretched a heath for several miles. One is reminded of the spot by the opening scene of his latest story, *The Return of the Native*. In his seventeenth year he was articled as a pupil to an architect, who had an extensive practice in ecclesiastical architecture, it being about the time when the passion for church 'restoration' was in full vigour. Mr Hardy came in for a good share of this work, and under colour of restoring and renovating for a good cause was instrumental in obliterating many valuable records in stone of the history of quiet rural parishes, much to his regret in later years. His attention, however, during this period was not wholly devoted to architecture, literature receiving his attention to a considerable extent, and his higher education being looked after by an able classical scholar and Fellow of Queens' College, Cambridge. Mr Hardy first took up his permanent residence in London in 1862. His knowledge of Gothic art became greatly advanced by the opportunity this change afforded him of designing under the direction of Mr A. W. Bloomfield [sic], the well-known architect, son of a late bishop of London; but his interest soon turned more particularly in the direction of pictures, and he made use of every opportunity which the International Exhibition of that year and public and private galleries afforded to extend his knowledge of the various schools of art, ancient and modern. During this very year Mr Hardy wrote an essay on Architecture, which took the prize medal of the Royal Institute of British Architects; and some time later he was awarded the prize offered by the late Sir William Tite, M. P., for architectural design. These successes encouraged in him the purpose of becoming an art critic, and to fit himself for that office he undertook special studies; but his early taste for romantic literature having meanwhile revived, he sent a first attempt in fiction to a London magazine. It was at once accepted, and his career was determined; though his love of art has been by no means abandoned. Mr Hardy's first complete novel was *Desperate Remedies* (1871), which in some quarters was applauded and in others loudly

condemned. *Under the Greenwood Tree* followed in 1872, a story which, though well received on all sides, was some time in making its way into notice. Both of the foregoing were published anonymously. In 1873 appeared *A Pair of Blue Eyes*, which attracted a good deal of attention; and in 1874 *Far from the Madding Crowd*, the latter first running its course in the pages of the *Cornhill Magazine*. *The Hand of Ethelberta* succeeded this in the same periodical a few months later, and *The Return of the Native*, Mr Hardy's sixth novel, is now reaching American readers through the pages of *Harper's Monthly*.

One of the earliest signs of Hardy's growing recognition as an up-and-coming writer occurred in 1879 when he was invited to be a member of the Rabelais Club and attended its inaugural dinner in London. In the *Life* (p. 136) he describes himself as being 'pressed to join as being the most virile writer of works of the imagination then in London'. At the Rabelais Club dinners he met many well-known literary figures, including George Meredith, Henry James, 'who had a ponderously warm manner of saying nothing in infinite sentences', and Henry Irving. An American guest at the Club was Bret Harte who described Hardy as 'a singularly unpretending-looking man, and indeed resembling anything but an author in manner and speech' (Letter in Colby Library).

An idea of how little known Hardy was in the 1870s is shown by the fact that the only other recollections from this period which have been traced are both associated with Charles Kegan Paul (1828–1902), author, publisher and one-time vicar for twelve years of a Dorset village. Some editions of Hardy's early novels had been published by his House and in October 1879 Hardy had reviewed Barnes's *Poems of Rural Life in the Dorset Dialect* for Paul's magazine, *The New Quarterly*. In his *Memories* (London 1899, p. 314) Paul describes how while he was living in London a lady at his dinner-table asked Hardy where Egdon Heath was, and Hardy's reply was 'You must ask Mr Paul, as he is the one man in England who knows Dorsetshire as well as I do.' That lady may have been the novelist and writer, Jane Panton (1848–1923), who in her *Leaves from a Life* (London 1908, p. 206) describes a visit to Kegan Paul in the 1870s:

> Two more pictures before we go on to other matters; one is that of Kegal Paul's drawing-room in the seventies, an upstairs room in Kensington Square. Mrs Paul, herself an authoress, very delicate, very ailing, is sitting in a deep chair by the fireplace, and presently out of the gloom Mr Paul brings a short, frail-looking man and introduces him to us. It is Thomas Hardy, a name to be written in gold, to be placed next to Shakespeare's, and to be honoured as the greatest

writer of the time. Directly he knew I was then living in his native county we became friends. We both loved Dorsetshire and we talked and talked.

Jane Panton was a daughter of William Powell Frith (1819–1909), the distinguished painter of the Victorian scene in such paintings as 'Derby Day'. His short description of Hardy in his *My Autobiography and Reminiscences* (London 1888) brings us into the next decade of Hardy's life.

3
The Ten Years 1880–1889

These years, 1880 to 1889, produced five further novels, some of Hardy's finest short stories, and an important essay 'The Dorsetshire Labourer' (1883). With the publication of *The Mayor of Casterbridge* in 1886 and *The Woodlanders* in 1887 Hardy became far better known than he had been previously, and the number of people keen to meet him and record their meetings rapidly grew. Some of these meetings were in London but with Hardy's move into his 'country house', Max Gate, in June 1885, there began the first of very many visits from the famous and not so famous. Robert Louis Stevenson (1850–94) and his wife were there in late August 1885 and Hardy's long friendship with Edmund Gosse seems to date from the early 1880s.

Frith has this to say about Hardy in his autobiography (pp. 431–2): 'The author of *Far from the Madding Crowd*, *Under the Greenwood Tree*, *The Hand of Ethelberta* and *The Trumpet-Major*, and many other novels is a man of whose friendship anyone might be proud... For absolute truth to nature and a far sight into the depths of the human heart... no living author can surpass my friend...'

Richard Bowker (1848–1933) came to England in July 1880 as London representative for the American publisher, Harper and Brothers. Harpers were about to publish a European Edition of their successful American Magazine, *Harper's New Monthly*, in which, in 1878–9 they had serialised Hardy's *The Return of the Native*. Bowker was to be responsible for the European Edition and within two days of arriving in England he had called on Hardy and they became good friends. In his *Journal* for 23 July 1880 Bowker describes the visit:

> I was received in a pretty parlour by Mrs Thomas Hardy, with her Kensington-stitch work, and her pet cat; she is an agreeable youngish English lady, immensely interested in her husband's work, and we were at once good friends. Hardy presently came down, a quiet-mannered, pleasant, modest, little man, with sandyish short beard, entirely unaffected and direct, not at all spoiled by the reputation

which *Far from the Madding Crowd* and its successors have won for him. He was originally an architect and had little thought of writing novels. Told me he had the greatest difficulty in remembering the people and incidents of his own stories so that Mrs Hardy had to keep on the look-out for him. We three fell to discussing a title for a new story which he is writing.... Before I went, tea and cake were served. I came home, having made two pleasant friends, I think.

Eight years later, in June 1888, Bowker wrote an article on Hardy under the title 'Thomas Hardy: The Dorset Novelist' in *Harper's New Monthly Magazine*, pp. 8–9. Like the article in the *Literary World*, its style with its 'Born in Dorsetshire... of one of the many branches of the Hardy family' and 'He went up to London for wider study and opportunity...' and 'there distinguished himself by his architectural writings...' reveals it as an article based very much on notes supplied by Hardy himself:

He has now settled down in his native county, where, at Max Gate, near Dorchester, high on a hill which overlooks many of the real scenes of his 'Wessex' stories, he has planned and built for himself an interesting and characteristic house, with a cosy study where he may hide himself. This house, though it affords absolute isolation and the advantages which that offers for literary work, is but a short walk by foot-path from the railway which will deliver him in London within four hours, so that he is more often in the bustling world than would be inferred from the seclusion of his 'writing-box', as he calls this house. Every spring, moreover, after he has put the finishing touches on his winter's work, he comes up to London for a long vacation (unless, by way of change, he flits off to the Continent), lives pleasantly there in temporary quarters, and receives with Mrs Hardy on one day of the week, looks in at the Savile Club for letters and luncheon, and mixes freely in society. Mr Hardy, of whom it is difficult to get a really good portrait, is a quiet-mannered, pleasant, modest man, of small stature, with rounded brow and full head, entirely unaffected and direct in his ways, and quite unspoiled by the success which has followed him ever since *Far from the Madding Crowd* caused the critics to compare him with Charles Reade on the one side and George Eliot on the other. No one has so closely painted the English rustic or more carefully pictured English rural scenes; the fidelity of *Under the Greenwood Tree* is that of the old Dutch masters. This fidelity is the result of the strong impressions of youth, upon which he relies almost entirely. Indeed he hesitates to revisit places seen in childhood, and so fixed in his imagination, lest verification may disillusionize; thus he purposely kept away from the scene of *The Woodlanders* while writing it, though for most of the time he was within twenty miles of the place described. His rustics, in the same way, walk out from the chambers of memory through the gates of the imagination, to become real in his books, yet in their infinite variety the descendants and developments rather than the identities of the people he knew. His characters, in fact, do become entirely real to him, though for a long time he finds difficulty in making acquaintance with them, and particularly in calling them by name, so that Mrs Hardy, always his first reader and kind critic, sometimes has to suggest that this John Jones is really Daniel Smith. But soon the characters take possession of him and of the story, he comes to know what each will think and will do in given circumstances, and for this reason he never plots the final development, the latter half, of a novel, but lets the *dramatis personae* finish it for themselves, and literally work out their own salvation or the contrary.

In his working days he tries to begin work at once after breakfast, and sometimes succeeds in keeping steadily at work during the forenoon, but more frequently his work is done at fitful and irregular periods. In parts he prints from the first draft, and in other parts rewrites again and again, revising liberally in the proof also. He is seldom guilty of the little oversights which most writers have now and then to confess, as when Thackeray killed off a character in one number in his serial publication of a novel, and continued his conversation quite unconcernedly in the next. Yet I recall catching once in the proof a curious slip of the pen, by which Mr Hardy, having brought one of his people to the very summit of a hill, incontinently started him *up* again. On bringing it to Mr Hardy's attention he corrected it by a post-card of characteristic simplicity: "For 'up' read 'down.'"

Readers should decide for themselves how much of this is Bowker and how much Hardy, trying to impress his middle-class readers.

Dr Frederick B. Fisher (1854–1940) practised as a doctor in Dorchester from 1879 until 1910 and for much of that time seems to have been the Hardy family doctor. The following recollections appeared in the *Christ Church College (Cawnpore) Magazine*, Vol. XXIV, No. 3 in March 1930:

> I first made the acquaintance of the Hardy family about the year 1880 when they were still living in the romantic cottage so often described, and which is situated just off the heath pictured by Thomas in his novels. His old father was ill and nearing his end, lovingly tended by Mrs Hardy, whose cleverness I soon realised. Undoubt-

edly she was the fount of her son's genius. Her favourite book was Dante's "Comedia". The whole family, two sons and two daughters, could tell stories, and did so during the long winter evenings round the big fireplace, criticizing one another's efforts very freely. . . .

I may describe Thomas Hardy as a short, shy man of gentle speech and manners. He was indeed most unassuming and gave one the impression of being rather saddened by what he met with in his stern quest of Truth. He was under my care for a serious illness not long after his house, Max Gate, was built. I may say he was his own architect, having been brought up in that profession originally. On leaving him one morning he begged me not to let it be known he was ill for "his life would be made unbearable by torrents of telegrams from America." He made an excellent recovery and I do not think he was ever seriously ill again. . . .

I retired from practice in 1910 and lived in Devonshire, but on paying a visit to Dorchester during the War (1914–18) and passing Hardy's house I thought I would pay him a surprise visit, but the maid told me he saw no one. I then said: "Tell your master his old doctor is here." She soon returned and showed me in and my venerable patient came and had a happy chat with me.

He was in good trim for a man of his age (86), some three months before he died when I had tea with him, his wife, and some friends. It was a very wet, dark evening, so we sat round the table and as was appropriate, told stories. He entertained us with one about a Chinaman who had come all the way from China to consult him about what he ought to do as he had murdered his sister, and was full of remorse. Hardy knew nothing whatever about the man and was greatly embarrassed by his continually coming to see him. Of course the Chinaman had read some of the novelist's tragic stories and had concluded that the author was the one man in the world who could guide him.

Shortly afterwards I got up to go and Hardy came to the door to see me off. It was raining and very dark. He said: "Surely, doctor, you are not going out in this weather." "Oh yes," I said, "the walk will do me good. Anyway if anything happens to me I shall send for you." At which he burst out laughing, and so we parted for all time.

As Hardy's father did not die until 1892 and Hardy was 87 three months before his death, the doctor's memory is not entirely reliable. However, much of it rings true and Hardy in a letter to Dr Fisher of 13 April 1920 (*Collected Letters* VI, p. 13. Hereafter *CL*) does say, 'I remember the illness you speak of, which your skill pushed me through.'

Hardy and Emma moved to Wimborne in 1881 and lived there for two years. Montague Harvey, a long-time resident of that town, wrote down in 1978 some 'Miscellaneous Notes, Anecdotes and an Epilogue' (in the Priests' Museum, Wimborne), in which he tells us of an anecdote he heard from his mother. Her family had needed a cook and took in one who had previously worked for the Hardy household. According to his mother, 'She used to talk and laugh about Thomas Hardy, to her being a very strange man, who spent much time writing and who would go into the kitchen and stand about smiling and encouraging the domestics to talk to him. Suddenly he would go off into his study, the room behind the conservatory, and no more would be seen of him for the rest of the day.'

Another and more valuable reminiscence of the Wimborne period is provided by Sir George Douglas (1856–1935). He was a writer and landowner living at Kelso in Scotland and, as described here, he met Hardy in 1881 and became a life-long friend:

> It was in the autumn of 1881, at Wimborne, that I first met Thomas Hardy, and the circumstances of our meeting were perhaps sufficiently odd to justify recapitulation. I had gone to Wimborne to visit a brother who was studying land-agency there, and who, knowing my interest in books, lost no time in saying, 'By the way there is an author living here, and he seems to be a very good fellow, for he has lent me his stable, having no use for it himself, and he won't take a rent for it. His name is either Hardy or Harvey, I am not certain which.' 'Not by any possibility the author of *The Trumpet-Major*!' I said. 'The same,' remarked a fellow-pupil of my brother's, who was present, and I certainly cannot find words to tell how much this meant to me. For I cared for books above all earthly things, and for Hardy above all earthly authors. . . .
>
> Next day we called on Mr and Mrs Hardy, breaking in (for aught I know) on their routine, which even then was strict. Yet they received us with the utmost kindness and soon I was alone with the great man. Let me say at once that, in my own humble estimation, Hardy had even then reached the summit of his career as an artist – I don't say as a thinker or teacher or propagandist. He had already published *The Return of the Native* and *The Trumpet-Major*, and, than these great delightful books, he never in the department of pure art did finer work. . . .
>
> As I view him, then, Hardy was at his best and happiest about the year '81. Besides his work – ever with him the first consideration – there were, of course, other things to minister to his happiness – most notably his wedded life, and the unmistakable, though all

too slow, recognition by the public of his work. He was one whose appearance, in the over forty years during which I continued to see him, changed less than that of almost any man I have known, the groundwork, as I may call it, remaining consistently the same. And yet the Hardy of 1881 was a robuster figure than any I ever saw again, robuster and less over-weighted by care. His talk, too, was light and cheerful – mainly about literature; and, thinking of that day, I have since then considered that he did much less than justice to George Eliot as a storyteller. "A moral essayist who had mistaken her vocation," was his phrase. But these were, of course, the words of one who had *Daniel Deronda* uppermost in his mind, and who had himself in *Far from the Madding Crowd*, led the way in a movement in favour of sinking the personality of the storyteller and allowing his characters to act out their drama without comment or assistance. . . .

I have the pleasantest recollections of the welcome extended to me by the Hardys, together with warm gratitude for the trustfulness with which they received into their intimacy a young man who came to them unrecommended save by a sincere admiration of Mr Hardy's work. Henceforth we met with fair frequency, oftenest in London, where the Hardys would take lodgings during the season, choosing every year a new quarter of the town for their abode. Thus, I remember them in Pelham Crescent, Hamilton Terrace, and a street out of Oxford Street, where they would exercise a pleasant hospitality in the form of little luncheon parties and larger teas. We also walked in the Park together, and attended social functions, though to me more interesting than any of these things were the expeditions which I was sometimes privileged to make with the novelist alone, to visit less-known parts of London – the "slummier" the better – or, for example, to inspect the registry signed by Shelley and Mary after their marriage, or to call on friends of one or other of us. There was never a man who was less of a professional talker than Hardy. He never by any chance talked for effect. All the more interesting, then, was his conversation, ever quiet in tone, and absolutely spontaneous in form and substance, which one felt to be a true "growth of the soil." This was, however, sometimes disappointing to the lion-hunters. "Oh, I liked him well enough," said one of these, "but he made no splash!" "No, no, of course not," said a bystander, *"that's* for the little great men only!" (From *Gleanings in Prose and Verse*, Galashiels n.d., pp. 28–9.)

In the autumn of 1885, shortly after the Hardys had moved into Max Gate, they were visited by Robert Louis Stevenson (1850–94) and his wife, Fanny. Shortly afterwards she wrote two letters, the first to W. E.

Henley, describing Hardy as 'a most loveable creature', and the second to a Mrs Williams:

> The first day we went to Dorchester, and stayed a couple of days. Here Hardy the novelist, author of *Far from the Madding Crowd* and other books, came to see us. I suppose you would like to know what he is like. He is small, *very* pale, and scholarly looking, and at first sight most painfully shy. He has a very strange face, quite triangular, with a nose that bends down very suddenly at the point. His wife, he is lately married, is *very* plain, quite underbred, and most tedious. ...
>
> In the meantime I had the literary man quite to myself, and we had a most charming talk – on his side, I mean. Louis was as delighted with him as I was. There was something so modest, gentle, and appealing about the creature that one remembers him as a quiet, pathetic figure.

About the same time she wrote to Stevenson's mother:

> Did I tell you that we saw Hardy the novelist at Dorchester? A pale, gentle, frightened little man, that one felt an instinctive tenderness for, with a wife – ugly is no word for it! – who said 'Whatever shall we do?' I had never heard a human being say it before.

No one has yet explained just what was wrong with 'Whatever shall we do'!

Henry Havelock Ellis (1859–1939) was both a distinguished psychologist and a literary critic who as early as 1883 had written an article on 'Thomas Hardy's Novels' (*Westminster Review*, April 1883, pp. 334–64) which so pleased Hardy that he wrote to Ellis on 29 April 1883 to thank him for his 'generous treatment of the subject' and his 'keen appreciativeness' (*CL* I, p. 117). In 1929 Ellis wrote an introduction to Pierre d'Exideuil's (see p. 229) *The Human Pair in the Work of Thomas Hardy* (London, 1929) pp. XIV–XVI:

> It was so that life was for Hardy. He interested himself a little in philosophy, and more in art; as the years went on he interested himself in fiction as an art, his own in particular, and even wrote suggestively about it. But, whether or not he was a great artist, he was not a philosopher. He was a natural and simple man as free from the pretentiousness of "high art" as from any other pretence, so modest and human as to feel hurt by the clamour of fools around his *Jude the Obscure*. ...

His modest, quiet, smiling simplicity was the dominant impression the man made, at all events in earlier days, when one met him. I only knew him slightly – a few meetings, an occasional letter – and my most vivid memory dates from a long afternoon spent alone with him as far away as some forty years, before he became famous. . . . Yet even so brief a meeting may suffice to furnish a key to a writer's work, and to reveal the quality of the atmosphere in which that work moves.

The tragi-comedy of life, its joy and its pain, most often have their poignant edge at the point of sex. That is especially so when we are concerned with a highly sensitive, alert, rather abnormal child of nature, with the temperament of a genius. Such we in part know, in part divine, that Hardy was, though always reticent about any autobiographical traits in his novels. Every reader of Mrs Hardy's *Early Life of Thomas Hardy* has noted the statement that "a clue to much in his character and action throughout his life is afforded by his lateness of development in virility, while mentally precocious. He himself said humorously in later times that he was a child till he was sixteen, a youth till he was five-and-twenty, and a young man till he was nearly fifty." The statement may be vague, but it indicates an element of abnormality such as we are apt to find in genius; some such element is indeed an inevitable concomitant of the special sensitiveness and new vision of genius, – the new vision of things seen at an angle slightly, yet significantly, different from that at which the average man is placed. For genius feels the things we all feel but feels them with a virginal freshness of sensation, a new pungency or a new poignancy, even the simplest things, the rustling of the wind in the trees or over the heather, which become, since Hardy has revealed them to us, an experience we had never before known.

Hardy's need to make a living by his pen meant that in the 1880s he was keen to have publicity. Journal articles over which he had some control and which did not pry too deeply into his humble background were welcomed especially if he could write most of the article himself. It has not been possible to identify the writer of the following, but from its style and detailed knowledge it seems very probable that it is either written by Hardy or is based largely upon notes supplied by him. Support to this is given by Florence's introduction to her *Early Life of Thomas Hardy* of passages from the article (see *Life* pp. 508–9). It appeared in *The World* on February 1886, pp. 6–7, and Hardy knew Edmund Yates, the journal's editor, sufficiently well to call him a friend in a letter of 24 July 1890 (*CL* I, p. 214):

CELEBRITIES AT HOME
Mr Thomas Hardy at Max Gate, Dorchester

Country-folk who, shortly after sunrise, plod along the narrow lanes stretching to the east of Dorchester, have their eyes frequently attracted by a crimson spot high on a distant ridge of landscape and so intensely coloured in the early sunlight as almost to resemble a drop of blood. Though this optical effect is produced at points in hill and dale too remote for distinguishing details of the thing seen, there are few who do not know it to be the residence of Mr Thomas Hardy, the novelist, or, as they express it, "the man that makes up books about we." ... The house is of recent erection, and was the design of its owner and occupant, who, before he definitively adopted the profession of letters, had served his articles with an architect, and, during the years of his residence in London, was considered a promising representative of the young gothic school that flourished contemporaneously with the pre-Raphaelite movement in painting, and was led by Sir Gilbert Scott, Messrs Street, Butterfield, Blomfield, and other well-known architects. At this incipient stage of his career Mr Hardy was awarded the medal of the Royal Institute of Architects and other art-prizes for his various productions.

From the white entrance-gate in the wall a short drive, planted on the windward side with beech and sycamore, leads up to the house, arrivals being notified to the inmates by the voice of a glossy black setter, who comes into view from the stable at the back as far as his chain will allow him. Within, we find ourselves in a small square hall, floored with dark polished wood, and resembling rather a cosy sitting-room with a staircase in it than a hall as commonly understood. ... The broad, heavy-framed window of the dining-room is so high as to afford little exterior outlook in that direction, an arrangement which imparts considerable privacy to the apartment; from a lower window at the side, however, we have a full view of the immense ramparts of Maiden Castle, which, to quote from one of this writer's stories describing the place, "rises against the sky with a Titanic personality that compels the senses to regard it and consider." Although the spot is more than a mile distant, the sentence does not exaggerate the strange force with which the magnificent earthwork impresses its presence upon the occupants of this room. From the same window we discern, high on Blackdon, the monument to Sir Thomas Hardy, Nelson's captain, a circumstance which reminds us that the author is the third of the Thomas Hardys, born and resident in this immediate locality, whose names have become known to the outside world; the first in point of date being the Edwardian Thomas Hardy, probably ancestor of the rest, who founded the

The Ten Years 1880-1889

neighbouring Grammar School and many notable charities in the county and elsewhere.

The drawing-room discloses a window so arranged as to form a frame to the imposing tumulus before mentioned, known on ordnance maps as Conquer Barrow, probably a corruption of some earlier name. Immediately on looking round the room we observe that Mr Hardy's collection of old china is of a very peculiar kind. In place of the regulation Nankin, crackled, and what not, we see groups of black urns and vases of various designs characteristic of Anglo-Roman work of the third or fourth century, vividly recalling the pots and pans in Mr Alma-Tadema's picture of the "Visit of Hadrian to the British Potteries." With some surprise we learn from our hostess that such urns as these abound in the earth beneath our feet, the specimens on the shelves having been dug up in excavating the foundations at the building of the house. Human skeletons were also discovered here, curiously interred in oval graves cut from the maiden chalk, each body lying on its right side, with the knees drawn up to the chest in a manner strongly suggestive of the chicken in the eggshell. With these venerable pieces of crockery lie an iron blade, the head of a spear taken from the side of one of the same interred Roman warriors; with a gilt-bronze fibula – similar to those in the British Museum – which Mr Hardy himself unfastened from the forehead of a skull discovered under his kitchen, proving that these clasps were used to sustain some sort of head-fillet, and not only the cloak or other garment, as usually supposed. . . .

Mr Hardy's writing-room is up-stairs, and to reach the door we pass under a small archway at the end of the landing. Behind the arch is a slyly-contrived passage and steep staircase, closed by a sliding-door. This species of adit affords, if necessary, a way of escape to one who is not a society man, when he is likely to be invaded from the front stairs. In the shadow of the arch hangs a drawing of weird and sombre effect – apparently a procession of Acherontic ghosts, pallidly emerging from black fog, but really the life-size profiles of various members of Mr Hardy's family, portrayed by himself on the principle of the silhouette reversed, and somewhat suggestive of the groups of family portraits by Ambrogio Borgognone in the National Gallery. We enter the writing-room – a long apartment, solidly furnished, without a single article in it that is not required for use, our author's indifference to *things*, as such, showing strongly here – and there rises from a writing-table to meet us a somewhat fair-complexioned man, a trifle below the middle height, of slight build, with a pleasant, thoughtful face, exceptionally broad at the temples, and fringed by a beard trimmed after the Elizabethan manner; a man readily sociable and genial, but one whose mien conveys the impression that the world in his eyes has rather more of the tragedy than the comedy about it, and that he is disposed to rate life, and what it can give, at no very extravagant value. Mr Hardy has been revising the proof-sheets of his *Graphic* story. "The Mayor of Casterbridge" and as we seat ourselves in Gabriel Oak's chair – a high-backed, willow-seated article of furniture seen in many of the Dorset cottages, and known, locally, as a 'shepherd's chair' – we listen to as much of this writer's experiences of authorship, and descriptions of his methods of work, as he is disposed to tell us. When he has a story in hand, he begins writing immediately after breakfast, and remains indoors until he has finished for the day, even a very little time spent in the open air before beginning proving fatal to any work till after nightfall. When not dictating, a practice he indulges in occasionally, but not frequently, he prefers working alone, holding, moreover, with his friend Mr Aubrey de Vere, that not only a solitary room, but an impregnable house, would be the most desirable place for complete literary performance. Many chapters of his stories have been printed without revision, precisely as written down in the first heat of conception; on the other hand, great portions – perhaps a majority of his pages – represent a second writing. Speaking as to the principles he observes in the art of fiction, Mr Hardy rather humorously expresses his wonder whether his literary principles will go the way of his architectural canons. When he was in a state of pupillage in that art, he was taught, and firmly believed, that, as there was one true God, there was one true style of architecture – the style of the thirteenth-century Gothic; that all other styles were flat, stale, and unprofitable; in a word, wrong. "Now, where has thirteenth-century architecture gone?" asks Mr Hardy. "We have danced adoringly down the vista of 'wrong' styles since then. So with fiction: today's meat is tomorrow's poison. Nevertheless, I have a view or two of my own, which I hope may not prove erroneous." In politics, he remarks that his principles are "those of Bob Sawyer, a kind of plaid." In the main, his books are written with an eye rather to a masculine than to a feminine audience, and to middle-age women rather than to girls in their teens. The older he gets, the more abundant do materials seem to become, cropping up in every daily incident. His sense of flagging is limited to the clerical labour that would be necessary to work all his conceptions out...

Across the intervening fields, in a south-easterly direction from Max Gate, at the foot of Loscombe Hill, nestles among its trees the thatched rectory-house, which has long been the home of Mr Hardy's friend and nearest neighbour, William Barnes, the Dorset Poet. While we stand discussing with the novelist the fidelity to nature of the peasantry in *Poems in the Dorset Dialect*, we note, low-lying about Maiden Castle, huge masses of cloud, now luminous with the splendour of sunset, anon livid with the tones of approaching night and tempest. In a few minutes, the white figures of innumerable seagulls, hastening inland from the not far-distant English Channel, rise above the ridge of hills in that direction – another intimation of imminent rough weather. So we take leave, and pass down the hidden line of headless soldiers of the Empire, whose shadowy forms come mingling in our mind-sight with the familiar shapes of Bathsheba shouldering reed-sheaves, and Gabriel Oak thatching ricks, like those in the field before us, amid the fury of such a storm as seems now to threaten the country-side.

Hardy was living in London in 1879 and in the *Life* (p. 131) mentions attending a Macmillan garden-party where there were 'A great many present.' This could well be the one mentioned in the following extract from a letter by Mabel Robinson who, as the sister of Agnes Robinson, a poet and critic of the time, would have had an *entrée* to such events. The letter was written on 17 December 1937 to Irene Cooper Willis, a barrister, writer and friend of Florence Hardy who was appointed one of Florence's executors in her will. Little is known of Mabel Robinson but as Florence had died on 17 October 1937 the assumption is that Irene Cooper Willis was returning some of Florence's books to their writers. If Max Gate was 'raw new' at the time of her week's visit then it must have been in 1885 or 1886.

> How kind of you, dear Miss Cooper Willis, to offer to send me back my novel. . . .
> I saw the second Mrs Hardy once only, but her beauty, distinction and charm made a great impression, and I was glad when she became Mrs Hardy, thus securing for Thomas Hardy the great happiness of a congenial marriage.
> Many, many years ago when my parents were alive and lived in London we saw a certain amount of Emma and Thomas Hardy during the "Season", for they came up to London each spring, taking a house or rooms for six weeks or so. Both were from the first day that we met (I *think* at a garden party at the Mac Millans [sic] at Clapham) very friendly. Thomas was then only on the skirts of fame, diffident of his talent which we all appreciated so highly that Emma wrote down several phases [sic] my Mother had used. Emma then had a little note book and pencil and when any one said something that struck what she thought the right note she inscribed it; and the

little book was used to cheer Thomas when a despairing fit overcame him (whether the kind intention encouraged or merely exasperated the poor man who can say, but at that time Emma was, very obviously, devoted to him.) Then came great success and the adulation of women, some lovely and rich, others just lovely, others influential. Hardy became the fashion. May-be the admiration of many accomplished women of the world turned his head a bit, and he came to see Emma as others saw her – rather plain, very countrified and scatter-brained. . . . Both she and he were always *very* kind, and I spent a delightful week at Max Gate, so clear in my memory that I could write pages about it, Dorchester, the larks on the downs, the Roman remains and the clerical gardens.

Max Gate was then raw new and I never thought it showed talent in the designer, but it was pleasant. Hardy showed me his beautiful manuscripts and after dinner Emma lit a bright fire in the drawingroom and he read aloud bits from the novel he was engaged on. He read very badly and was suddenly overwhelmed with a sense of the inadequacy of his words "No, no, Its not at all what I thought!" Much turning of pages "Let's try here, this is – etc etc, but neither was *that* what he expected, and he dipped elsewhere in the vain hope of touching his own heart. Sometime during that visit he told me that the only novel whose tragedy had ever made him weep while writing it was *The Mayor of Casterbridge*.

Towards the end of the 1880s the cooling off of Hardy's marriage to Emma is evidenced by his increasing interest in other women, many of whom were keen to meet him, some of whom hoped he might be able to help their own literary careers. Although he affected to be critical of aristocractic families such as the Portsmouths, whom he met in 1885, he obviously enjoyed being taken up by them. The snobby Emma was immensely proud of her association with Lady Jeune (1845–1931), later Lady St Helier, who was distantly related to her by marriage. She was a well-known hostess of the later Victorian period and the Hardys were often entertained at her London House. In her book *Memories of Fifty Years* (London 1909) Lady St Helier describes in a somewhat condescending way how it had become fashionable in the 1880s and 90s to invite writers and artists to their dinner-tables and she goes on:

For many years of his literary career Mr Hardy was very little in London, and society had no attractions for him. He was shy and retiring, and the adulation and interest which he awakened was a cause of annoyance instead of being any pleasure to him. He was a delightful companion, always glad to talk about his books, and the reasons and events which had influenced him in his different novels.... His delightful little house near Dorchester, of which he himself was the architect, seemed in its simplicity a fitting home for so great a genius.

During his flying visits to London he used to stay at our house, and I look back now on these delightful evenings when he and my husband and I sat around the fire listening to the stories, theories, and ideals out of which all his novels had developed. I think he is the most modest person I ever came across, and he hated the publicity which necessarily surrounded him, and shrank from it as much as the most timid woman. ...

His visits to me became few and far between, for he loves the world less than ever he did, and remains in the country, in his own home. (pp. 240–1)

In her *A Backward Glance* (New York 1934) Edith Wharton (1862–1937) writes:

Thomas Hardy, however, I met several times, and though he was as remote and uncommunicative as our most unsocial American men of letters, his silence seemed due to an unconquerable shyness rather than to the great man's disdain for humbler neighbours. I sometimes sat next to him at luncheon at Lady St Helier's, and I found it comparatively easy to carry on a mild chat on literary matters. I remember once asking him if it were really true that the editor of the American magazine which had the privilege of publishing *Jude the Obscure* had insisted on his transforming the illegitimate children of Jude and Sue into adopted orphans. He smiled, and said yes, it was a fact... He seemed to take little interest in the literary movements of the day, or in fact in any critical discussion of his craft, and I felt he was completely enclosed in his own creative dream, through which I imagine few voices or influences ever reached him. (pp. 215–16)

Agatha Thornycroft, the beautiful wife of the sculptor Hamo Thornycroft, described by Hardy as having a mouth which recalled more fully than any other beauty's the Elizabethan metaphor 'Her lips are roses full of snow' (*Life* p. 230), sat next to Hardy at a dinner given by Edmund Gosse on 2 July 1889. In a letter to her husband she described 'Mr Hardy' as 'most attentive and nice, not shy, as he sometimes is, and quite talkative. He wanted to persuade me to go with the Gosses to the dinner of the Society of Authors... He considered it was right I should be gay while you were away: fearful morals with which to corrupt an inexperienced and innocent person!' (Letter to H. Thornycroft 3 July 1889).

In a letter to Agatha of 8 May 1894, Hamo described how he had met Edmund Gosse at a private view of the Royal Academy, and Gosse had told him of a meeting there with Hardy. In the course of it Hardy said, 'I am better than I was earlier in the day for I have been cheered up by seeing the most beautiful woman in England, or rather her whom I think the most beautiful woman in England, her on whom I wrote *Tess*.' 'Who was that?' said Gosse. 'Why, it was Mrs Hamo Thornycroft,' said Hardy. On 21 September 1895 Hamo made the following entry in his diary:

> the new feature in our summer holiday was cycling... On one occasion we went into Dorset to Dorchester to see Thomas Hardy... Our surprise visit to Hardy was interesting. He and his wife were having tea at which we joined with much pleasure, for it was baking hot and we had been cycling over the hills around Maiden Castle. There is such a delightful reality about Hardy. He is so human and none of the literary dancing master about him. Agatha and he got on very well. She likes him exceedingly. We almost persuaded both him and Mrs Hardy to take to bicycling.

Gertrude Atherton (1857–1948), the American novelist, who described herself as being 'born without awe', met Hardy on a number of occasions in London about this time and described him in her *Adventures of a Novelist* (London 1932, pp. 170–2 and 258–9), as 'A small delicate-looking man, with an almost excessive refinement of feature, and an air of gentle detachment.' At some stage in the 1890s she recalls an occasion when at a reception at Stafford House she was sitting with the politician, journalist and editor of *T.P.'s Weekly*, Thomas Power O'Connor (1848–1929), when,

> Hardy drifted by, looking as little interested in his surroundings as usual. In his wake was an excessively plain, dowdy, high-stomached woman with her hair drawn back in a tight little knot, and a severe cast of countenance. 'Mrs Hardy,' said T. P. 'Now you may understand the pessimistic nature of the poor devil's work.'
> No doubt Hardy went out so constantly to be rid of her! It was not easy to think of any other reason, for he certainly never had the air of enjoying himself. One would see him at literary gatherings of every sort, some in rooms so small and crowded that it was quite impossible to move, and the chatter deafening. He never spoke unless addressed, and then as if his thoughts were far away.... He was anything but great in personality.

Readers of Gertrude Atherton's book will find that she has no doubt about the considerable size of her own personality.

When Gertrude Atherton first came to London in 1889 a party was given in her honour by William Sharp (1855–1905), a writer of verse and prose. At that party on 10 July there was present a young Irish writer, Katherine Tynan. In her *Twenty-five Years: Reminiscences* (London 1913) she talks about meeting Hardy. 'I remember him standing with his peculiar air of modesty, his head down-bent, while I told him that every good thing that happened to me brought joy to my father in Ireland, and that the story of my having met him would be a great joy.' (p. 301)

4
The Ten Years 1890–1899

The 1890s saw Hardy bring to an end his career of nearly thirty years as a novelist. It was a career that ended more with a bang than a whimper. *Tess of the d'Urbervilles* (1891) and *Jude the Obscure* (1895) were Hardy's two most outspoken and courageous attacks on Mrs Grundy and the Victorian Establishment. In his Preface to *Jude*, he said, he was attempting 'to deal unaffectedly with the fret and fever, derision and disaster, that may press in the wake of the strongest passion known to humanity; to tell, without a mincing of words, of a deadly war waged between flesh and spirit; and to point the tragedy of unfulfilled aims.' *Tess* and *Jude* were inescapably a criticism of Victorian prudery, morality and hypocrisy, an attempt, as Hardy wrote in his essay on 'Candour in English Fiction' (*New Review*, January 1890), to reveal what 'everybody is thinking but nobody is saying'.

The outcry against these two novels was predictable and confirmed everything that Hardy had been saying. *The Saturday Review* found *Tess* 'an unpleasant story' told 'in a very unpleasant way' and the *Quarterly Review* thought that Hardy had told 'a coarse and disagreeable story in a coarse and disagreeable manner'. *Jude* had the distinction of being burnt by a bishop, banned from the bookstalls by W. H. Smith, and renamed by one reviewer 'Jude the Obscene'. But, as is even more obvious a century later, all publicity is good publicity and Hardy the well-known novelist became Hardy the famous (and somewhat *risqué*) novelist. He was now more than ever in demand at receptions, parties and dinners, and he became the subject of countless newspaper and journal articles. From 1890 onwards the searcher after interviews and recollections of Hardy finds that he has far too much material, and the selection of items for a book of limited length becomes a problem.

This last decade of the nineteenth century also witnessed a substantial change in Hardy's attitude towards those who wished to interview him. Once fame had come and he no longer had to be his own publicist in order to earn a living, his natural reticence prevailed, and in the twentieth century interviewers were not encouraged and visitors to

Max Gate were usually forbidden to take down any notes or make any comments on his personal life.

Ford Madox Ford (1873–1939), novelist and critic, described in his *Mightier than the Sword* (London 1938, pp. 125–8) a meeting with Hardy which, if he really was eighteen at the time, must have taken place in 1891. Mrs Lynn Lynton (1822–98) was a novelist and reviewer who had been in correspondence with Hardy as early as 1888. In spite of Robert Gittings's warning that Ford was known to be one of the 'great literary liars', this amusing episode has enough authenticity (Hardy did know a great deal of the *Aeneid* exceptionally well) to be worth publishing:

> At the same time I was keenly aware of a Mr Hardy who was a kind, small man, with a thin beard, in the background of London tea parties... and in the background of my mind... I remember very distinctly the tea party at which I was introduced to him by Mrs Lynn Lynton with her paralysing, pebble-blue eyes, behind gleaming spectacles....
>
> So, out of a sort of cloud of almost infantile paralysis – I must have been eighteen to the day – I found myself telling a very very kind, small, ageless, soft-voiced gentleman with a beard, the name of my first book, which had been published a week before. And he put his head on one side and uttered, as if he were listening to himself, the syllables: "Ow ... Ow ..."
>
> I was petrified with horror... not because I thought he had gone mad or was being rude to me, but because he seemed to doom my book to irremediable failure....
>
> I do not believe I have ever mentioned the name of one of my own books in my own print... at least I hope I have been too much of a little gentleman ever to have done so. But I do not see how I can here avoid mentioning that my first book was called *The Brown Owl* and that it was only a fairy tale....
>
> And then suddenly, in Mrs Lynn Lynton's dim, wicked drawing-room, in face of this kind, bearded gentleman, I was filled with consternation and grief. Because it was plain that he considered that the vowel sounds of the title of my book were ugly and that, I supposed, would mean that the book could not succeed....
>
> And I could feel Mr Hardy feeling the consternation and grief that had come up in me, because he suddenly said in a voice that was certainly meant to be consolatory: "But of course you meant to be onomatopoeic. Ow – ow – representing the lamenting voices of owls.... Like the repeated double O's of the opening of the Second Book of *The Aeneid*..." And he repeated:

"'COnticuer' Omnes intentiqu' Ora tenebant
Inde tOrO pater Aeneas sic Orsus ab altO'" –

making me really hear the Oh ... Oh's of those lamenting lines. ...

Years and years afterwards when I was walking with him over the links at Aldeburgh, I reminded him that he had quoted those onomatopoeisms to me and he would not believe that he had ever thought anything of the sort.

Then he said:

"Oh, yes, of course.... And isn't it true? Because if you go on to the third line you get: 'Infandum, Regina, iubes renOvare dOlOrem ...' And then, 'MyrmidOnum, DOlOpumv' aut duri miles. Ulixi...'" ... But, on that distant day in Mrs Lynton's drawing room, I was struck as dumb as a stuck pig. I could not get out a word whilst he went on talking cheerfully. He told me some anecdotes of the brown owl and then remarked that it might perhaps have been better if, supposing I had wanted to represent in my title the cry of the brown owl, instead of two "ow" sounds I could have found two "oo's." ... And he reflected and tried over the sound of "the brooding coots" and "the muted lutes."...

And then he said, as if miraculously to my easement:

"But of course you're quite right.... One shouldn't talk of one's books at tea parties.... Drop in at Max Gate when you are passing and we'll talk about it all in peace ..."

Some years later Ford met Hardy once again at one of the house-parties which Edward Clodd (see p. 73) used to give at his Aldeburgh home:

And there he was – infinitely simple, extraordinarily self-effacing; as if ineradically a peasant, with a face varnished and wrinkled by the weather as the exposed roots of ancient oaks are gnarled amidst their moss ... and with amazing powers of perception in his keen, limpid, liquid, poet-peasant's eyes ... and as instinct with the feeling of escape as a schoolboy who had run out from his school ranks on some down and was determined on naughtiness....

I imagined Mr Hardy to have looked like that when, shaving off his elder-statesman's beard and waxing his moustache till it stuck out like that of the sergeant-major of a bantam regiment, he determined to abandon prose for poetry. ... He was a man obviously of free passions who had borne long disciplining with a silent patience and had now definitely retired from trade to take up his life's hobby to the exclusion of all else.

Of his verse, on the other hand, he was fiercely jealous. No one could have persuaded him to alter a word either in the interests of fluidity of metre or of the delicacies. The shocked *Cornhill* would have published *A Sunday Morning Tragedy* if he would have omitted some verses and changed others, and would have published "Who now remembers Almack's balls?" if he would have altered a word or two – though I can't imagine what words they could have desired to see altered... unless they are perhaps contained in the lines:

> Is Death the partner who doth moue
> Their wormy chaps and bare?

And I like to think that some of his lightness of heart during that Aldeburgh week-end was caused by the fact that he had at last at his disposal a periodical that would publish whatever he wrote exactly as he chose to write it.

It was, as it were, another escape.... And it was symbolic that at Aldeburgh he only once mentioned his novels... that being to say that until the publication of *Tess* he had made almost no money in the United States by his books because of the non-existence till that date of copyright for foreign authors.... On the other hand he talked – after sufficient pressing – by the hour about *The Dynasts*, going over page after page minutely in a nook on the beach, explaining why he had used here heroics, here Alcaics or Sapphics or ballad forms or forms invented by himself, explaining how such and such an incident had been suggested to him... and keenly delighting in his achievement. For you could trust that mercurial, simple old peasant to know what he had done and what a great thing that tragedy is.

(*Mightier than the Sword*, pp. 141–3)

On Hardy's death in 1928 Sir George Douglas once again drew upon his memories of the past. In the *Hibbert Journal* of April 1928 (pp. 385–98) he remembered in an article entitled 'Some Recollections and Reflections' a visit Hardy had made to his home on the borders of Scotland in 1891, not 1892 as he thought:

It was in the late summer of 1892 that Thomas Hardy and his wife, whom I had already known for fully ten years, paid me a visit in the Borderland. They had been in Scotland before, notably on the occasion when Hardy derived the suggestion of Donald Farfrae from a good-looking and ingenuous young cabman who drove him and Mrs Hardy about Edinburgh. But the Scott Country was new to them, so that we applied ourselves to visiting as many of the local shrines and other places of interest as could be conveniently overtaken by the old leisurely modes of locomotion of those pre-motor days. The romance of Melrose Abbey, the elegance of Jedburgh, the verdant seclusion of Dryburgh, all in turn appealed powerfully to the architect who was still so much alive in the novelist. But it was the Scott localities that moved him most – the scenes of the Wizard's infancy and young manhood at Smailholm and Kelso, the home of his maturity at Abbotsford, the tomb at Dryburgh. ... One moment of his visit dwells in my memory above others. We had been invited to lunch at Abbotsford, and after lunch were graciously allowed to wander as we chose. From the contemplation of the Raeburn portrait, from the grand library, I led my friend to the cabinet which Scott had called his "Speak-a-bit," where his death-mask is deposited, and there, pursuing a deliberate policy, I left him to himself. Returning when I fancied he had been there long enough, I caught a glimpse of a memorable sight which I shall not forget. The face of the living novelist – that wistfully expressive face – was bending above the effigy of that other novelist, long dead and entered into his glory, and yet so living still. In the spectator little imagination was required to picture the world of love, of reverence, of sympathy and speculation, that was centred in the living eyes. Fortunately my entrance into Speak-a-bit had been noiseless. And not less noiseless was my departure. ...

It would have been impossible, I fancy, to find pleasanter visitors than the Hardys proved themselves to be whilst under my roof. Country-house life was simpler in those days, and, beyond exerting ourselves to show them as much as possible of what seemed likely to be of interest, I'm afraid we had no great attractions to offer them, nor any specially sympathetic guests to ask to meet them. Hardy, by the way, was not generally very much interested in meeting people, even when they were something of notorieties – though he was always very nice to them – but Mrs Hardy, I think, was. She liked to know the people whose names are well known. Despite the homeliness of my interior, however, the Hardys threw themselves at once into the interests of our family life. A portrait of Mrs Opie by her husband hung in my drawing-room, suggesting to Hardy that I might read them one of her *Simple Tales* after dinner, which of course I was only too pleased to do. Then, next morning after breakfast, Mrs Hardy said at once, "Let's go and visit the horses," whereupon she and my sister provided themselves with lumps of sugar, and we trooped off to the stables, which thenceforth became a part of our routine. ... Mrs Hardy belonged essentially to the class of woman, gifted with spirit and the power of deciding for herself, which had attracted Hardy in his early manhood. She had the makings of a Bathsheba, with restricted opportunities. The trifles mentioned above are perhaps no more than goodwill or good manners would prescribe. But even at that day good manners were already giving place to easy ones. . . .

He [Hardy] was bringing out *Tess* at the time, and I recall his narrating to me the scene between Tess and Alec in Cranborne Chase, which, omitted from the serial publication as too strong meat, appeared separately in the *National Observer*. It was obvious that the author was a little anxious as to its reception by the public. A day or two later, walking with Mrs Hardy in the same part of the grounds, I referred to *The Trumpet-Major* as my favourite of the novels. "Ah, yes!" was the reply, "that's one of the pretty ones." The hopeless inadequacy of the description struck me, and it was not without foreboding that I looked forward to the speaker's attitude to the scene I had lately heard related. For Emma Hardy was always very much on the side, if not of the angels, at least of the proprieties. . . . The first Mrs Hardy was an assiduous critic of her husband's work, but not an uninvited one. For all who have had the opportunities of observing their life in common must have been struck by his unfailing desire, as far as possible, to "take her with him" in his pursuits – whether it was a question of reading books together, cycling, or sight-seeing or of associating her with his literary labours.

Possibly this may have been partly due to his sense of the danger of mental isolation which besets a man absorbed in lonely toil. But no less striking certainly were his unremitted deference and chivalrous consideration where his wife was concerned. . . . Absorption in creative work puts a sore strain on human ties. But then, in an affectionate nature such as his, deep sorrow readily assumes some of the features of remorse. My own impression was that for Hardy custom had never staled the charm of the sweetheart in his first wife. Whether her criticism of his work ever produced much actual result is of course a very different question, notwithstanding that he would invariably refer to it with a deference which, to speak frankly, it scarcely deserved, based as it was on preconceived notions. Of infinitely greater service was she to him in caring for him and in aiding him to recuperate from the reaction which, however temperately a man may live – and no man could well live more moderately than Hardy – must infallibly follow intense and prolonged application to imaginative work. In Hardy's case this reaction was apt to be of extreme severity, as Mrs Hardy told me, and, indeed, as the nature and quality of his work make it easy to conceive. And if it did him no serious or lasting damage, the credit of that fact – over which so many have cause to rejoice – must, I think, be divided between an excellent physical constitution and the care with which his wife watched over him. I have known good friends of theirs who held that the Hardys were not well matched, basing their conclusion on the opinion that Mrs Hardy was incapable of appreciating the grandeur of her husband's genius. Against this may be set the fact that, faithful and conscientious artist as he was, he didn't appreciate this himself, or, if he did, he failed to be impressed by it. It is with diffidence that I venture to offer an opinion on their suitability one to the other, but that opinion is that they were to the full as well assorted as most of the happily married couples that one comes across in life. Each had sacrificed something to the other, but their attachment was strong enough for each to be resigned to that sacrifice.

He was now famous enough to appear in a 'Spy' cartoon in *Vanity Fair* on 4 June 1892. Leslie Ward who was 'Spy' summed him up in his *Forty Years of Spy* (London, 1915, p. 291) as 'not talkative as a sitter, but he was pleasant. In appearance he did not present the idea of a typical literary man: his clothes had a sporting touch about them.'

Three journal interviews published in 1892 are worth mentioning. '"Hodge" as I knew Him' appeared in the *Pall Mall Gazette* on 2 January (pp. 1–2). It was almost certainly written by Ernest Rhys and is a strange mixture of what are supposed to be Hardy's own words and an extract verbatim from the essay on 'The Dorsetshire Labourer' which Hardy had published in *Longman's Magazine* in July 1883 (pp. 252–69). Here is part of the *Pall Mall* article:

> The ridge of a noble down, dark outlined against a pale green sky; a small red house standing in its own grounds close to the ancient town of Casterbridge – I mean Dorchester; a little drawing-room, the windows of which are flaming in the rays of the dying sun, and in which are seated two persons, Mr Thomas Hardy, the novelist, the exponent, the exploiter, I might say, of the agricultural labourer, and myself, a *quondam* country parson – the representative on this occasion of the *Pall Mall Gazette*. Two people, therefore, very fairly capable of discussing Hodge and his peculiarities, though Mr Hardy repeatedly assured me that he was himself no authority whatsoever on the subject:–
> "All that I know about our Dorset labourers I gathered," he said, "from living in the country as a child and from thoroughly knowing their dialect. You cannot get at the labourer otherwise. Dialect is the only pass-key to anything like intimacy. I would not preserve dialect in its entirety, but I would extract from each dialect those words

that have no equivalent in standard English and then use them; they would be most valuable, and our language would be greatly enriched thereby. Dialect is sadly dying out, and children down here in Dorset often have to ask their parents the meaning of a word. Conversation, therefore, is in quite a transition stage now in these parts...

"And now, Mr Hardy," said I, "how do you explain the deadly dulness of village life?" – "In these parts," he replied, "to the fact that the 'liviers' – people who held small copyholds for generations – are dying out. These people were not labourers, but small mechanics, little shopkeepers, who were the centre of village life. Nowadays people are all weekly tenants of the landlord, who take no interest in the place, who are not self-centred in any possible respect. Great credit is due to the parson, who, in my opinion, does much to keep up interest in these quiet villages. It would be a thousand pities that such men, educated, sympathetic, original-minded as many of them are, should be banished by looming difficulties of dogma, and the villages given over to the narrow-mindedness and lack of charity of some lower class of teacher."...

"Then the typical 'Hodge', in your estimation, is non-existent, Mr Hardy?" – "Certainly I have never met him. At close quarters no 'Hodge' is to be seen, it is a delusion. Rustic ideas, the modes, the surroundings, appear retrogressive and unmeaning at first. After a time, if you live amongst them, variety takes the place of monotony."...

"They are full of character, which is not to be found in the strained, calculating, unromantic middle classes; and for many reasons this is so. They are the representatives of antiquity. Many of these labourers about here bear corrupted Norman names; many are the descendants of the squires of the last century, and their faces even now strongly resemble the portraits in the old manor-houses. Many are, must be, the descendants of the Romans who lived here in great pomp and state for four hundred years. I have seen faces here that are the duplicates of those fine faces I saw at Fiesole, where also I picked up Roman coins the counterpart of those we find here so often. They even use Latin words here which have survived everything."

Louise Chandler Moulton (1835–1908) was an American novelist and poet who met Hardy several times on her annual visits to London. The following is from the *Critic* (New York, p. 24) of 9 July 1892:

A writer in the Boston *Herald* says that when Mrs Louise Chandler Moulton, who knows Hardy very well, was asked whether Hardy was cynical about women as his 'Group of Noble Dames' would imply, she replied: 'But he doesn't think that he is cynical. He thinks that he is photographic. I know no man who likes women better, and there is nothing that a woman could possibly do that would seem to him wrong.'

The article on Hardy which appeared in *Cassell's Saturday Journal*, 28 June 1892 (pp. 944–6), was one of a series called 'Representative Men at Home'. Again there are indications in the style and the close repetitions of passages from earlier articles known to have been written by Hardy that he is responsible for some of this. But, of course, then as now, journalists borrowed from each other's writings and the exact genesis of many of these articles is difficult to ascertain. Undoubtedly some interviews with Hardy were written by literary hacks who had never met Hardy but cannibalised the work of others. R. L. Purdy in his *Thomas Hardy: a Bibliographical Study* (London 1954, p. 300) thinks that this Cassell article is 'a genuine interview' even though the editor of *Cassell's Saturday Journal* referred to it in a letter to Hardy (3 February 1892) as 'your article on yourself'. Here are some extracts from it:

"I purchased the land from the Duchy of Cornwall," Mr Hardy was explaining at the dinner table five minutes later, "about five or six years ago. There was much difficulty in finding a suitable house when I returned hither, and I was obliged to build. But I was resolved, you see, not to ruin myself in building a great house as so many other literary men have done," added the novelist.

"And yet you have a very nice one," I replied, looking round the cosy dining room and thinking of the square softly lit hall.

"Well, everything is not as I would have it. I think I shall have to enlarge it. It is difficult to say exactly how a house should be until one has lived in it."

"Although one is an architect oneself?"

"Yes; I was studying architecture for some time on going to London when I was about twenty-one and until I was twenty-seven. Originally, you know, I was inclined for the Church, but somehow I abandoned that. My first public literary production was an essay on Coloured Brick Architecture which gained the medal of the Institute of British Architects. Then I wrote a sketch which was printed – the essay was read, but not printed – in *Chambers's Journal* called "How I Built Myself a House."

"And then you drifted into literature?"

"I suppose the impressions which all unconsciously I had been gathering of rural life during my youth in Dorsetshire recurred to me, and the theme – in fiction – seemed to have absolute freshness. So in my leisure – which was considerable – I began to write *Under the Greenwood Tree*, but after writing about half, laid it aside to write *Desperate Remedies*. This novel was a success soon after its publication, but under my contract with the publisher I made nothing out of it. However, it encouraged me to go on with *Under the Greenwood Tree*. I finished it as I began it, which I now regret, because I think much more could have been made of the story. The incident of the choir, for instance, was quite a true one. It actually occurred at a village not very far from here. I can scarcely remember such choirs myself, but it is not so very long since they were very general in the villages."...

"There is some reason, I should think, to regret the disappearance of these old choirs."

"Yes, it is almost a pity, I think, that they have been entirely superseded by the harmonium and the organ. To many an old worthy the loss of his occupation in the church must have been a sad blow. It gave them an interest in the services and share in the work of the church. I should think that, with better education in the villages and the diffusion of musical taste, the old choirs might well be revived. The old custom described in *Under the Greenwood Tree* of going round the parish on Christmas Eve, still survives to some extent, but it has ceased to be the important function it used to be."...

"Yes; sometimes I am described as the novelist of the agricultural labourer," said Mr Hardy, in answer to questions. "That is not inclusive, I think. It is not true of *A Laodicean, Two on a Tower, Desperate Remedies*, and a volume of short stories I published last year called *A Group of Noble Dames*. And in my books of rural life I have endeavoured to describe the village community generally."

"But your point of view has been so different from other novelists – and they are numerous enough – who have laid their scenes in the country."

"Yes, I have endeavoured to write from the point of view of the village people themselves instead of from that of the Hall or the Parsonage. I chose them because there appeared to be so much more dramatic interest in their lives. Their passions are franker, for one thing. And I have lately been attracted by an interesting feature in the Dorsetshire peasantry, and that is that many of them are descended from the squires of olden times. It was suggested by hearsay, and inquiry into the records, etc., has fully confirmed the probability"...

"Most of your characters are taken from life, I believe, Mr Hardy?"

"A good many of them certainly. And I always like to have a real place in my mind for every scene in a novel. Before writing about it I generally go and see each place; no, one can't do with a picture of it. Local colour is of such importance."...

"Do you agree with Mr Walter Besant regarding the neglect of literary men by the State?" I asked Mr Hardy, after an accidental reference to the Society of Authors, of whose council he is a member.

"I agree with him in principle," he replied, "but it is to be remembered that some of the greatest poets and others are actuated by the spirit of revolt. As you say, originality necessarily implies antagonism to conventionality, and I am not at all sure that the honours would include all the right men – the Swinburnes and William Morrises, say. With whom could you vest the selection?"

Raymond Blathwayt (1855–1935) was a journalist working for the magazine *Black and White*. His article entitled 'A Chat with the Author of *Tess*' was published on 27 August 1892. Yet again we find a direct quotation about Hodge from 'The Dorsetshire Labourer' included in the article as if for the first time, and particularly noteworthy is the sending up of Emma Hardy's snobbery about her connection with 'the higher order of the clergy', and Hardy's own attempt to impress by his exaggeration about London drawing-rooms and Continental hotels:

> Mr Hardy is in himself a gentle and a singularly pleasing personality. Of middle height, with a very thoughtful face and rather melancholy eyes, he is nevertheless an interesting and amusing companion. He is regarded by the public at large as a hermit ever brooding in the far-off seclusion of a west country village. A fond delusion, which is disproved by the fact that he is almost more frequently to be seen in a London drawing-room, or a Continental hotel, than in the quiet old-world lanes of rural Dorsetshire. His wife, some few years younger than himself, is so particularly bright, so thoroughly *au courant du jour*, so evidently a citizen of the wide world, that the, at first, unmistakable reminiscence that there is in her of Anglican ecclesiasticism is curiously puzzling and inexplicable to the stranger, until the information is vouchsafed that she is intimately and closely connected with what the late Lord Shaftesbury would term 'the higher order of the clergy.'...
>
> It was by the drawing-room fire that we sat discussing the frail but charming 'Tess.'
>
> 'You cannot imagine how many letters my husband received,' said Mrs Hardy, 'begging him to end his story brightly. One dear old gentleman of over eighty wrote, absolutely insisting upon her complete forgiveness and restitution.' 'And why did you not, Mr Hardy?' said I. 'Surely without any very great stretching of points Tess might have left with Angel when he returned to her, and so have avoided her last great sin, with its fearful punishment?'

Mr Hardy shook his head.

'No,' he replied, 'the optimistic "living happy ever after" always raises in me a greater horror by its ghastly unreality than the honest sadness that comes of a logical and inevitable tragedy.

'The murder that Tess commits is the hereditary quality, to which I more than once allude, working out in this impoverished descendant of a once noble family. That is logical. And again, it is but a simple transcription of the obvious that she should make reparation by death for her sin. Many women who have written to me have forgiven Tess because she expiated her offence on the scaffold. You ask why Tess should not have gone off with Clare, and "lived happily ever after." Do you not see that under *any* circumstances they were doomed to unhappiness? A sensitive man like Angel Clare could never have been happy with her. After the first few months he would inevitably have thrown her failings in her face. He did not recoil from her after the murder it is true. He was in love with her failings then I suppose; he had not seen her for a long time; with the inconsistency of human nature he forgave the greater sin when he could not pardon the lesser, feeling perhaps that by her desperate act she had made some reparation. She had done what she could. She had done exactly what I think one of her nature under similar circumstances would have done in real life. It is led up to right through the story. One looks for the climax. One is not to be cheated out of it by the exigencies of inartistic conventionality. And so there come the tears of faithful tragedy in place of the ghastly and affected smile of the conventionally optimistic writer. And it is the very favourable reception by the public of this sad ending to my story that has impressed me as a good sign. At one time a publisher would tell you that "a tragic ending" was always a failure. Now, however, people have studied more fully the fictions of all time, and are infinitely more artistic.'...

'I suppose, Mr Hardy, that most of your characters are drawn from life?' 'Oh yes, almost all of them. Tess, I only once saw in the flesh. I was walking along one evening and a cart came along in which was seated my beautiful heroine, who, I must confess, was urging her steed along with rather unnecessary vehemence of language. She coloured up very much when she saw me, but – as a novelist – I fell in love with her at once and adopted her as my heroine. Old Mr Clare was a Dorsetshire parson whose name still lives enshrined in the hearts of thousands. "Shepherd Oak", in *Far from the Madding Crowd*, I knew well as a boy; while "Bathsheba Everdene" is a reminiscence of one of my own aunts. Our family, you know, has lived here for centuries. "Joseph Poorgrass", "Eustacia", and "Susan Nonsuch" [sic] in *The Return of the Native* were all well-known local characters. Girls resembling the three dairymaids in *Tess* used to get me to write their love-letters for them when I was a little boy. I suppose,' he went on, replying to a question, 'that unconsciously I absorbed a good deal of their mode of life and speech, and so I have been able to reproduce it in the dairy at "Talbothays".'...

'But now Mr Hardy,' said I, 'I have to quarrel with you for your deliberate description of "Tess" as a *pure* woman.'...

'Very well,' replied Mr Hardy, 'but I still maintain that her innate purity remained intact to the very last; though I frankly own that a certain outward purity left her on her last fall. I regarded her then as being in the hands of circumstances, not morally responsible, a mere corpse drifting with the current to her end.' 'And then again,' said I, 'you appear to ignore the idea much put forward of late by certain very earnest people that purity is as binding on men as on women, when you depict that very odious young gentleman, Angel Clare, casting off his wife for an offence of ignorance, and yet the very next week proposing to elope with her friend. I grant that you are true to human nature. Sometimes its seems impossible for the most high-minded reformers to attempt to legislate for us *men*, as though we were angels. They doubtless are theoretically right, but practically they are hopelessly in the wrong. Nature herself is against them. Remorselessly she exacts a purity in woman which she does not demand from man; and you have shown this truth in "Tess" I think.'

Mr Hardy replied: 'Exactly. That is what I have striven to show. I have adhered to *human nature*. I draw no inferences, I don't even feel them. I only try to give an artistic shape to standing facts.'...

'And the ultimate result of your book, Mr Hardy, will be, I hope, that a greater freedom will exist for the decent, grave consideration of certain deep problems of human life.'

'Well,' replied Mr Hardy with a smile, 'that would be a very ambitious hope on my part. Remember I am only a learner in the art of novel writing. Still I do feel very strongly that the position of man and woman in nature, things which everyone is thinking and nobody saying, may be taken up and treated frankly. Until lately novelists have been obliged to arrange situations and *dénouements* which they knew to be indescribably unreal, but dear to the heart of the amiable library subscriber. See how this ties the hands of a writer who is forced to make his characters act unnaturally, in order that he may produce the spurious effect of their being in harmony with social forms and ordinances.'

The last paragraph seems to depend almost entirely upon Hardy's essay 'Candour in English Fiction', and the phrase 'things which everyone is thinking and nobody saying', is a direct quotation. Once again one wonders just how this kind of article was put together. Could Hardy have prepared a broadsheet of extracts from his works to hand out to these visiting journalists?

Frederick Dolman (1867–1923) was a journalist who seems first to have come upon the Hardy scene in November 1892. Hardy wrote to him on the 24th to tell him that Mrs Hardy would prefer not to have a photograph of herself published and with the letter he enclosed some facts provided by Emma for Dolman's proposed article in the *Philadelphia Home Journal*. (*CL* I, p. 289) That article about Emma eventually appeared in the *Ladies' Home Journal*, May 1895 (p. 5). In it Emma is described as being 'of the greatest assistance to her husband in his literary work' . . . she presides 'with grace and dignity over their charming home', and it ends, 'In appearance Mrs Hardy is striking: her hair is dark and slightly tinged with grey; her eyes are also dark. She is dignified and very graceful, and looks as though she might be the wife of some ecclesiastical dignitary.' Hardy must have felt some embarrassment in sending this to Dolman.

Dolman published 'An Interview with Thomas Hardy' in *The Young Man* (March 1894, pp. 75–9). In a letter dated 18 December 1893 to Florence Henniker (*CL* II, p. 44) Hardy refers to having been victimised by 'that interviewer. To my amazement instead of the *literary* review in *The Young Man*, which I conceded, I get a proof of a *political* convn. with Mr T. H. in the *Westminster Gazette!* Fortunately I have been able to correct it: but it consists of some careless remarks I made, after, as I thought, the interview was over. I find that these men, out of one visit, will make 4 or 5 interviews, for various papers.' This provides a valuable insight into what was happening in Hardy's life as a public figure at that time and into Hardy's lack of trust of the 1890s media. What would he have made of the 1990s media! When the *Young Man* interview came out three months later Hardy's irritation showed itself in his description of it as 'largely faked'. In fact, apart from a totally unbelievable opening when Hardy, who never smoked, says to Dolman: 'Do you smoke? You'll find some cigarettes in this box. I have given up smoking myself, and the consequence is that I sometimes forget my friends.'

Much of the rest of the interview rings true. Here are some extracts:

'So you are publishing another volume of short stories, Mr Hardy,' I begin, in allusion to his new book.

'Yes, a collection of these that have appeared in the magazines since the publication of *A Group of Noble Dames*, more than three years ago – about twenty in all. I like doing a short story occasionally, if only as a relief from the writing of three-volume novels. In the midst of a book one is chained to one's task, so to speak; even if you are not under contract to finish it by a certain time, the 'fever of composition' is upon you, and nothing can be enjoyed till the last chapter is written.'

'But it is sometimes said that a short story requires as great an effort.'

'Yes, I know; and since some promising young men write only short stories, there has been a theory that they require greater art. But to my mind that is absurd. With a short story you have simply one episode to deal with, and it cannot possibly call for as much effort or for more art than a number of incidents standing as cause and effect in their relation to each other.'

'In reading *A Group of Noble Dames*, Mr Hardy, I was greatly struck by the waste of good material. In one story you put the material, as far as plot goes, of a long novel.'

'Yes, I suppose I was wasteful. But there, it doesn't matter for I have far more material now than I shall ever be able to make use of.'

'In note-books?'

'Yes, and in my head. I don't believe that idea of a man's imaginative powers becoming naturally exhausted; I believe that if he liked, a man could go on writing till his physical strength gave out. Most men exhaust themselves prematurely by something artificial – their manner of living – Scott and Dickens for example. Victor Hugo, on the other hand who was so long in exile, and who necessarily lived a very simple life during much of his time, was writing as well as ever till he died at a good old age. So too was Carlyle, if we except his philosophy, the least interesting part of him.'. . .

'I suppose you are still fond of rambling about the country?'

'Well, I am not such a good walker as I was. At one time I thought nothing of twenty or twenty-five miles in a day. Now I am out of training, and could not do half.'. . .

We speak next of Mr Hardy's essay into dramatic authorship last year. His little play was one of a programme of five, a bad arrangement. Consequently, its run was a short one. . . .

'But shall you not write another play?'

'I don't know that I shall. In my opinion the drama is an inferior form of art, although there are, it is true, greater possibilities in it in one sense, appealing as it does so powerfully and directly to the feelings and emotions. But on the stage you can take such liberties with your characters, bringing about sudden changes in their temperaments and motives that would be ridiculous in a novel; while, on the other hand, you are seriously embarrassed by limitations of time and space. A play which the papers praise as really first-rate ranks in point of art, and, above all, character-drawing, no higher than a second or third-rate novel.'

'Then the author is so dependent on the actors and actresses.'

'Yes, they may put into or take out of the play almost as much as the author, not altogether in words, but in characterization.'...

'Are you fond of going to the theatre yourself, Mr Hardy?'

'Oh, my play-going is done in fits and starts. When I am in London or Paris I sometimes go and see two dozen plays in succession, and then perhaps I don't go to the theatre for a year.'...

'*Tess* is wonderfully popular.'

'Yes, but the frankness of the book has brought me some asperities, in the shape of letters and reviews mostly. In writing the story I expected such criticism, but the criticism has not come from the people I expected. There have been very few objectors really; in their secret hearts people know there is nothing honestly to object to. As a matter of fact, my tone has been the same in regard to moral questions for the twenty years or more I have been writing. From the very beginning I resolved to speak out. I remember that in the first edition of *Desperate Remedies* there were many passages exhibiting a similar plainness to *Tess*. Some of these were eliminated in the one-volume edition, in deference to my publishers; but I am sorry now that I did so, and if ever the book is included in the uniform edition of my works the old passages shall be restored.'...

Our talk about the clever books of the year led me to interrogate Mr Hardy about the younger writers generally.

'I think Sarah Grand,' said Mr Hardy, 'made the mistake of putting two distinct and independent stories into one book. She has explained to me that originally she had contemplated writing not one, but two novels, with the materials she has used in *The Heavenly Twins*.'

Of Barry Pain, he said: 'I prefer him in his serious moods; I don't care so much for his humour. Zangwill has made an excellent beginning with *The Children of the Ghetto*.'

'But he told me the other day that he did not care to continue writing about Jewish life.'

'Indeed, that's very curious, that a man should not care to continue doing what he can do so well. And I should think there's a fine field for such work. Up to the present there has not been a novelist of real Jewish life, for somehow or other I don't think George Eliot's Jews can be regarded as creatures of flesh and blood.'...

'It is the duplicate of one which they have in the British Museum,' explains Mr Hardy, as I examine the time-worn jewel [A Roman lady's fibula]. 'There it is described as a "cloak fastener". But this, I think, must be an error, for I took this from a female skull, where it had evidently fastened a band around the head.' Some of his prizes Mr Hardy has sent to the Dorchester Museum, the committee of which institution has the honour of numbering him among its members.

'Few people in Dorchester, I am afraid, think much of the memorials of the town's past. Some time ago a shopkeeper, in making some alterations, pulled down an old Gothic doorway, and it would have been carted away with other "rubbish", had it not been discovered in time. The stones were then taken to the Museum, but as it is only a small building, they were found to be in the way there and the question arose "What is to be done with them?" The committee interviewed the house-owner, and asked him to allow the doorway to be put back again in its original position. He agreed to this after some demur, on our agreeing to pay all the expenses.'

Rosamund Tomson (1863–1911) was a poet and writer who sent a book of her verse to Hardy in September 1889 and became one of the first of the women writers to entangle him emotionally as, unsatisfied in his marriage, he desperately and hopelessly looked around for some amorous experience. Photographs were sent to him and she engaged in that kind of flirting at a distance which Hardy was to meet more than once and which for him could lead only to frustration and disappointment. The relationship, if such it can be called, ended when Hardy took offence at a misstatement she published about his purchase of the land on which he built Max Gate. She wrote, under the pseudonym 'Graham R. Tomson', an article about Hardy which was published by the *Independent* (New York) on 22 November 1894 (p. 2). It is sufficiently informative to be worth quoting in part:

> Perhaps one of the most immediately striking characteristics of so eminent a man is his singular modesty; that, at least, was one of the qualities in him that struck me first. I would venture to affirm that the ordinary observer, ignorant of his identity, might pass a month with Thomas Hardy without suspecting his vocation, or that he was anything more than an extraordinarily interesting companion, who combined the two admirable functions of being a good talker and a good listener. Yet when he can be led to speak of his books and his method of writing, he does so with an unaffected frankness and an absence of self-consciousness that is positively charming.

'Oh yes!' I heard him say once, in answer to a passing query, 'I have no trouble in thinking of plots; indeed, I have so many novels in my head that I am afraid I shall never have time to write them all. But, you know, it is rather a terrible thing, in its way, this literary habit. It becomes a second nature: whenever I travel by train or omnibus, I find myself instinctively observing my fellow-passengers, and constructing the story of their lives from what I see in their faces.'

Almost as slow a worker as Flaubert, his average rate of production is about two pages a day; although, impelled by a fortunate mood, he will sometimes far exceed this quantity. Written with the greatest deliberation, the most careful choice of words, his manuscripts, covered symmetrically with small, clear handwriting, are patterns of precision and tidiness, with hardly an erasure or correction from the beginning to the end of a sheet.

While at work, a clean leaf of blotting-paper lies beneath his hand, under the last-written line, and travels downward, as the page is covered inch by inch during the long morning hours, his more habitual time for production. Yet the whole of the deftly-wrought fabric undergoes on completion the most uncompromising scrutiny and revision – for Mr Hardy is a perfect Spartan toward his brain-children, and holds no sacrifice too great, no pains too tedious for their ultimate weal.

G. K. Chesterton (1874–1936) described Hardy in *The Victorian Age in Literature* (1913) as 'a sort of village atheist brooding and blaspheming over the village idiot'. The following piece from Chesterton's *Autobiography* (London 1936, pp. 227–8) shows a far more sympathetic and understanding Chesterton:

The first great Victorian I ever met, I met very early, though only for a brief interview: Thomas Hardy. I was then a quite obscure and shabby young writer awaiting an interview with a publisher. And the really remarkable thing about Hardy was this; that he might have been himself an obscure and shabby young writer awaiting a publisher; even a new writer awaiting his first publisher. Yet he was already famous everywhere; he had written his first and finest novels culminating in *Tess*; he had expressed his queer personal pessimism in the famous passage about the President of the Immortals. He had already the wrinkle of worry on his elvish face that might have made a man look old; and yet, in some strange way, he seemed to me very young. If I say as young as I was, I mean as simply pragmatical and even priggish as I was. He did not even avoid the topic of his alleged pessimism; he defended it, but somehow with the innocence of a boys' debating-club. In short, he was in a sort of gentle fuss about his pessimism, just as I was about my optimism. He said something like this: 'I know people say I'm a pessimist; but I don't believe I am naturally; I like a lot of things so much; but I could never get over the idea that it would be better for us to be without both the pleasures and the pains; and that the best experience would be some sort of sleep.' I have always had a weakness for arguing with anybody; and this involved all that contemporary nihilism against which I was then in revolt; and for about five minutes, in a publisher's office, I actually argued with Thomas Hardy. I argued that non-existence is not an experience; and there can be no question of preferring it or being satisfied with it. Honestly, if I had been quite simply a crude young man, and nothing else, I should have thought his whole argument very superficial and even silly. But I did not think him either superficial or silly.

For this was the rather tremendous truth about Hardy; that he had humility. My friends who knew him better have confirmed my early impression; Jack Squire told me that Hardy in his last days of glory as a Grand Old Man would send poems to the *Mercury* and offer to alter or withdraw them if they were not suitable. He defied the gods and dared the lightning and all the rest of it; but the great Greeks would have seen that there was no thunderbolt for him, because he had not hubris or insolence. For what heaven hates is not impiety but the pride of impiety. Hardy was blasphemous but he was not proud; and it is pride that is a sin and not blasphemy. I have been blamed for an alleged attack on Hardy, in a sketch of Victorian literature; it was apparently supposed that talking about the village atheist brooding on the village idiot was some sort of attack. But this is not an attack on Hardy; this is a defence of Hardy. The whole case for him is that he had the sincerity and simplicity of the village atheist; that is, that he valued atheism as a truth and not a triumph. He was the victim of that decay of our agricultural culture, which gave men bad religion and no philosophy. But he was right in saying, as he said essentially to me all those years ago, that he could enjoy things, including better philosophy or religion. There came back to me four lines, written by an Irish lady in my own little paper:

> Who can picture the scene at the starry portals,
> Truly, imagination fails,
> When the pitiless President of the Immortals
> Shows unto Thomas the print of the nails?

The Ten Years 1890–1899

I hope it is not profane to say that this hits the right nail on the head. In such a case, the second Thomas would do exactly what Prometheus and Satan never thought of doing; he would pity God.

It has not been possible to ascertain when this meeting with Hardy took place, but it seems likely to have been in the mid 1890s.

Robertson Nicoll (1851–1923), a writer founder and editor of the *Bookman*, in his *A Bookman's Letters* (London 1913, pp. 5, 7 and 290) describes a meeting of the Omar Khayyam Club at Burford Bridge in Surrey in the summer of 1895. Among those present were George Meredith, Edmund Gosse, Theodore Watts-Duncan, George Gissing and Hardy:

> When we arranged ourselves for dinner, Meredith found his way to the right hand of the President, Mr Edward Clodd, and it became evident that something was in the wind. I have seldom been more interested than in gazing upon Meredith and Hardy as they sat near each other. Mr Hardy's features gave the impression of 'many thought-worn eves and morrows'; Meredith looked as if he had met and mastered life....
>
> Thereafter we had the scarcely smaller privilege of a speech from Mr Hardy. He expressed his gratitude to Mr Meredith for reading his first book which he described as 'very strange and wild.' Meredith here interrupted with the word 'promising'. Mr Hardy went on to say that if it had not been for the encouragement he then received from Mr Meredith, he would probably never have adopted the literary career.

There has been much discussion about the problems and sadness of the latter part of Hardy's marriage to Emma. Christine Wood Homer (1883–1975) was the daughter of a wealthy farmer and land-owner who lived near Puddletown, about five miles from Dorchester. The Wood Homers had become close friends of the Hardys, and Christine, whom I met in 1970 and who impressed me by her fairness and integrity, wrote a booklet called 'Thomas Hardy and His Two Wives':

> I first spoke to Mr Hardy when I was still a schoolgirl. In the 1890s he often visited my home, Bardolf Manor, with his first wife and they both used to go on cycling expeditions with my mother and Mr Hermann Lea. Sometimes Mrs Hardy's nephew and niece, Gordon and Lilian Gifford, would join the cycling party. They often used to stay with the Hardys for several weeks during the summer. When going on a cycling tour they would take food for a roadside picnic....

Mr Hardy was always very kind and genial to young people. His manner was rather shy. An unassuming man, he could interest himself in even the unimportant details of any subject that caught his interest. He was a learner during his whole life and was never ashamed to ask about anything of which he thought even a child might know more than he did. I remember him saying: 'Every person should know a great deal of *one* subject and a little about every other.' I always found him cheerful and not steeped in the melancholy that is so often ascribed to him, even by those who know him well. Mr Hardy was delighted to hear a bit of local gossip, especially about people he knew. He could gossip too. ... I once said to his sister, Miss Kate Hardy, after his death, 'People talk of your brother as though he were always sad, but I more often found him cheerful and laughing,' and she replied, 'Yes, that is true. Tom was always fond of his joke.' Hardy had a quiet chuckling laugh. I remember him during a conversation on literature, saying: 'I think I shall be remembered by my poems and not my novels.'

When we went to tea at Max Gate Mr Hardy was most hospitable in his welcome and after the visit he never failed to accompany his guests to the door to see them off.

The Hardys had not been a happy couple for a good many years before Mrs Hardy's death. I do not think Mr Hardy was to blame for this. Mrs Hardy never spoke unpleasantly about her husband to us; but I have heard from several people in Dorchester that she spoke unpleasantly about him to them. She was a peculiar woman and in many ways was like a little child, but despite her obvious defects we rather liked her, and as children we referred to her in private as 'Lady Emma'.

Mr Hardy suffered much from the behaviour of his wife, but was always polite to her. He would look at her in a rather quizzical but kindly way when she said something particularly childish. She was an increasing embarrassment to her husband. She sought an attention from the world which she never received. It may well be that she was deserving of pity and compassionate understanding rather than blame. At first she had only been childish, but she got steadily worse with advancing age and became very queer and talked curiously. In her younger days she had been pleasant, but never brainy.

When we went to see Mr Hardy after her death he spoke of her kindly and affectionately and said how lovely her golden hair had been in her youth. 'I have a curl of it still and will show it to you one day,' he said and one felt that he had forgotten and forgiven the many unbridgeable differences and insuperable difficulties which had spoilt so many years of their married life. ...

In 1914 Mr Hardy married Miss Florence Dugdale, chiefly, I think, because people criticised her living at his house as his secretary. She was devoted to him and did all she could to make him happy and he became very fond of her. After this second marriage Miss Kate Hardy visited Max Gate regularly and these visits Kate continued even after her brother's death in 1928. There had been a remarkable change of atmosphere from the days of poor Emma Lavinia.

Thomas Hardy was a devoted son, and during her life he visited his mother every week on Sunday. He was very fond, too, of his two sisters, Mary and Katherine (or Kate as she was always called). It had been a burdensome grief to him that the first Mrs Hardy had not cared for any of his family. (*Monograph* No. 18, 1964)

An 1895 visitor to Max Gate was George Gissing (1857–1903). His acquaintance with Hardy had begun in 1886 when:

Mr George Gissing, finding that Hardy was in London this summer, had asked if he might call upon him for some advice about novel-writing; which he did. Sending one of his own novels afterwards, Gissing writes at the end of June:

'It is possible you will find "The Unclassed" detestable. I myself should not dare to read it now; it is too saturated with bygone miseries of every kind. . . . May I add in one word what very real pleasure it has given me to meet and speak with you? I have not been the least careful of your readers, and in your books I have constantly found refreshment and onward help. That aid is much needed now-a-days by anyone who wishes to pursue literature as distinct from the profession of letters. In literature my interests begin and end; I hope to make my life and all its acquirements subservient to my ideal of artistic creation. The end of it all may prove ineffectual, but as well spend one's strength thus as in another way. The misery of it is that, writing for English people one may not be thorough: reticences and superficialities have so often to fill places where one is willing to put in honest work.' (*Life* pp. 188–9)

It is clear from these last lines that Gissing and Hardy had something in common, and Gissing was asked to stay at Max Gate and did so from 14 to 16 September 1895. He describes the visit in a letter dated 22 September 1895 which will be found in *The Letters of George Gissing to Eduard Bertz 1887–1903* (London 1961, p. 205).

Last week I accepted an invitation to go down to Dorchester, and stay for a couple of days with Thomas Hardy. Now Hardy is a man of far less intellectual vigour and distinction than Meredith. Born a peasant, he yet retains much of the peasant's views of life. He evidently does not read very much, and I grieve to find that he is drawn into merely fashionable society, talks of lords and ladies more than ordinary people. Most unfortunately he has a very foolish wife – a woman of higher birth than his own, who looks down upon him, and is utterly discontented. They have no children, and they travel about a good deal, but not to much purpose. I admire Hardy's best work very highly, but in the man himself I feel disappointed. To my great surprise, I found that he did not know the names of flowers in his own fields! A strange unsettlement appears in him; probably the result of his long association with such a paltry woman. Essentially, he is good, gentle, and poetically minded. But he sadly needs a larger outlook upon life – a wider culture.

This perhaps tells us more about Gissing than Hardy, who was, of course, immensely widely read but did not wear his knowledge on his sleeve.

Alfred Sutro (1863–1933) was a journalist and playwright who described himself as Hardy's 'sometime neighbour in Dorset'. The following is a passage in his *Celebrities and Simple Souls* (London 1933, p. 58). *Jude* was published in 1895.

To Archer, too, I owed an introduction to Thomas Hardy; he asked me to lunch, and I bicycled over from our cottage at Studland. There were only he and I and his wife – the first Mrs Hardy, of course – at the meal; it was about the time when *Jude the Obscure* had been published, and I was loud in my praise of that work. Mrs Hardy was far from sharing my enthusiasm. It was the first novel of his, she told me, that he had published without first letting her read the manuscript; had she read it, she added firmly, it would *not* have been published, or at least, not without considerable emendations. The book had made a difference to them, she added, in the County....

The position was awkward for me, and very embarrassing; Hardy said nothing, and did not lift his eyes from the plate; I was hard put to it to manufacture some kind of conversation, and it was a great relief when Mrs Hardy rose, and left us to our port. Even then Hardy's silence persisted, till I told him of a bird in our wood whose identity puzzled us; we had discovered at last that it was a corncrake. Hardy brightened at once, the cloud lifted, and we talked, talked birds and trees, evidently a favourite subject of his, till I left.

John Cowper Powys (1872–1963) published his first book, *Odes and Other Poems*, in 1896. It contained a poem about Hardy which resulted in the visit to Max Gate described here in Powys's *Autobiography* (London 1967, p. 227). Hardy's visit to Montacute in Somerset, home of the remarkable Powys family, probably took place in the same year:

> It was during my vacation at Montacute that I received a post card from the great Thomas Hardy himself, thanking me for the poem I had addressed to him in this apple-green volume [*Odes and Other Poems*] and inviting me to pay him a visit. . . .
> I gathered up my spirit within me and resolved to be worthy of the summons I was now obeying. Nothing could have been kinder than Hardy's reception of me. He took me into his study, the chief glory of which was, though it was yet unfinished, the great new *Oxford Dictionary*. He showed me the manuscript of *Tess*. He presented me with a paper edition of the same book. He gave me tea on his lawn. I remember telling how I detected in his work that same portentous and solemn power of dealing with those abstract-concrete phenomena, such as dawn, and noon, and twilight, and midnight, that Wordsworth displayed in his poetry. He accepted the comparison, I remember, as a just one, but he proceeded to animadvert in no measured terms upon Wordsworth's pious optimism. He called my attention to Edgar Allan Poe's "Ulalume" as a powerful and extraordinary poem. In those days I had never read this sinister masterpiece, but following up Hardy's hint I soon drew from it a formidable influence in the direction of the romantically bizarre. I invited Mr and Mrs Hardy to visit Montacute, an invitation which, to my delighted surprise, they accepted; and I enjoyed a second red-letter day in taking him to our church and to the Abbey Farm; though it was left to the son and heir of the squire himself to show these notable visitors over Montacute House.
> It was on this occasion that Hardy explained to me how the ancient builders of our church had deliberately left the chancel a little askew in order to represent the manner in which the Redeemer's head sank upon one side as he gave up the ghost; but I well recall how, as we issued forth from these symbolic meditations amid the tombs of Mr Phelip's ancestors, and I pointed out to our visitors the house where the most beautiful girl in our village lived, he gave a curious little start.
> 'We get back to humanity, back, back to humanity, Powys!' he chuckled. . . .
> I was already worrying in those days about the slaughter of animals for human food; and I remember, when I laid my scruples before him, how he said that in his opinion only very big animals ought to be killed, as in this way the flesh upon their bones would go farther.

John's younger brother, Llewelyn Powys (1884–1939) describes the same visit in the *Virginia Quarterly Review* (Winter 1939, pp. 426–7):

> It was, I believe, in these same holidays that Hardy and his first wife paid us a visit. They walked up from the station at Montacute, arriving at the Vicarage in time for luncheon. Hardy, I remember, wore a pair of tight snuff-coloured trousers which contrasted with the more sober colour of the upper part of his dress. My father had not read a word he had ever written, but he had heard rumours enough of the freedom of his thought to qualify his enthusiasm for this new hero that his eldest son had discovered. My mother's attitude was different. Her literary interests had always been so strong that any writer would have been honoured by her, and, as Mr Hardy's place was at her right hand, all went well. Hardy at the time must have been about fifty years old. His lips were pale and his face did not give the impression of good health; I remember my mother rashly predicted that he would not live to a great age. The first Mrs Hardy was a kindly woman whose forehead was adorned by two curls, which appeared to my irreverent little boy's fancy like the feathers at the end of a drake's tail. In the afternoon my brother took Mr Hardy over Montacute House and through the village, finally returning in time for him to write in the visitor's book of the Mabelulu, another garden playhouse my brother Bertie and my sister May and I had built, the words: 'Thomas Hardy. A Wayfarer.'

Another interesting visitor to Max Gate in 1896 was Mrs Patrick Campbell. In 1895 Hardy had been working on a dramatisation of *Tess* and Mrs Campbell was one of several well-known actresses who desperately wanted to be Tess. She visited Dorchester in January 1896 in order to reinforce her claim to the part and, in a letter to Mrs S. Coleridge dated 12 January 1896 (now in the Dorset County Museum), she writes 'It is lovely down here. This afternoon Mr Hardy has been playing old English dances on his fiddle and I have been dancing (improvised steps)! to them. It was a sight for London Town.'

Charles Lewis Hind (1862–1927) was a writer and editor of *The Academy* from 1896–1903. His visit to Hardy must have taken place in 1896 or '97, soon after the furore about *Jude*. This account is taken from his book *Authors and I* (London 1921, pp. 115–16):

> Once I found myself in Dorchester, and I thought, being younger then and bolder, that I would send a note to Thomas Hardy by messenger (we had been having, during the past year, an interesting correspondence) asking if he would allow me to be his companion

on his afternoon walk. Rightly I thought that a tramp through Wessex with Thomas Hardy would be something to tell my grandchildren. He replied that he would be glad to see me at 3 pm. On my way to Max Gate I called at a bookshop in Dorchester and inquired of an elderly, prim, and rather tart female if she had a copy of Thomas Hardy's *Jude the Obscure*, which had lately been published, and which had been received by what is known in England as the 'rectory public' somewhat superciliously. I think it shocked them. In response to my inquiry the prim female said that she had not a copy of *Jude the Obscure* in stock. 'What!' I cried, 'in his native Dorchester you have not a copy of the latest book by the greatest living English novelist.' She eyed me with hauteur, and, tossing her head, said: 'Perhaps we have not the same opinion of Mr Hardy in Dorchester as you have elsewhere.'

I withdrew. I was too amused to be angry. Indeed, so amused was I at this encounter with the 'rectory public' that when I reached Max Gate I told the story to Mr Hardy with glee. He did not smile: perhaps he looked a little sadder than usual. For it is a sad, tired face, very gentle, with much sweetness, yet alert as a bird's. He did not suggest a walk: we sat for an hour in his rather dim study, the trees swaying outside, I prattling literary gossip, and trying, craftily, to make him talk of his work and himself. I began to succeed. He told me that he was firmly resolved to write no more novels (*Jude the Obscure*, published in 1895, was the last, for *The Pursuit of the Well-Beloved*, published in 1897, had been issued serially five years before). I believe that he was about to tell me why he had decided to write no more novels, when Mrs Hardy entered the room. This was his former wife, niece of Archdeacon Gifford. Said Mrs Hardy to me – 'Oh, I want to show you my watercolours.' And I, being weak, and courteous to the nieces of archdeacons, was wafted away. So my interview with Thomas Hardy ended. Later, when I was about to depart, he came into the hall and looked at me with sad sympathy. He accompanied me to the garden gate, and as I was in the midst of bidding him a respectful adieu he said in his gentle voice – 'By the by, which shop is it where they are disinclined to stock my books?'

As the 1890s progressed it was not just the men of letters who wanted to meet Hardy and write about him. 'Spy' was soon followed by other artists who thought Hardy would make a good (and profitable) subject. One of the earliest was William Rothenstein (1872–1945) who asked Hardy to sit for him in March 1897. Hardy commented on 'the expression of the eyes in the drawing, " . . . he knew the look," he said, "for he was often taken for a detective." He had a small dark bilberry eye which he cocked at you unexpectedly. He was so quiet and unassuming, he somehow put me in mind of a dew-pond on the Downs.' (*Men and Memories: Recollections 1872–1938*, London 1978, p. 108). In the same book Rothenstein remarks that Hardy 'had much in common with painters like John Crome; indeed, Egdon Heath put me in mind of a landscape by Crome . . .' And later, 'He was pleased at my praise of his drawings in the *Wessex Poems*, and went upstairs and brought down the originals, together with some of his old sketch books full of touching little drawings of buildings and architectural details. There were big trees round his house and I remembered he had told me that he had planted these himself, and how they began to sigh directly the roots touched the soil.'

In 1898 a friendship began between Hardy and Hermann Lea (1869–1952) which, based upon shared interests and a love of animals, lasted until Hardy died. It is a measure of Hardy's regard for Lea that, although in earlier years he had refused to help anyone who proposed to publish a Wessex guide-book based on his novels, he very soon agreed that Lea could do so, and he gave Lea very substantial help in writing the book and in identifying the places which had 'suggested' the fictional locations. Hardy's help took the form of actually travelling with Lea to such places as Bulbarrow, and providing him with maps and detailed directions where the scenes in the book were too distant. This led to *A Handbook to the Wessex Country of Thomas Hardy*, published in 1905, and then to what became the standard work on the Hardy country, *Thomas Hardy's Wessex* published by Macmillan in 1913. It was fortunate that Lea was an expert photographer and the 1913 book contains 243 photographs. That Hardy trusted him so much and that all the evidence shows him to be a man of principle and integrity make his comments on Hardy of particular value:

> By this time (31/7/01) I had reached a sufficient stage of intimacy to realise Hardy's extreme kindliness of nature, his tolerance of the shortcomings of others, his sympathy with those who were striving towards all forms of self-expression . . .
>
> His kindness and friendliness was now (1910–1913) very marked, and we discussed many subjects of an entirely private nature, and which, although they are by no means forgotten, are too intimate to warrant inclusion in these memories.
>
> One evening in particular is indelibly written on my mind. It was April 8th, 1911, and I talked over with him a matter which was causing me considerable trouble and worry. Hardy was ever a good listener, and his comments and advice – all of which I found in later years to have been extraordinarily sound, and on some points verging on

the prophetic – wonderfully relieved my mind. At the end of our discussion he told me of certain incidents in his own past life, drawing parallels between my position then, and his own of years ago, and pointing out where he had made certain mistakes which had led to results such as his advice now sought to guard me from...

I had some curious experiences when I was journeying about gathering photographs and information for my guide book. One lady I applied to for permission to view a certain house replied with considerable heat: 'You're after that because of that Hardy who wrote about it. Lor', we're just pestered with people coming here ever since that book were wrote – I wish the man had hanged hisself afore he got it finished.' The book in question was *Tess of the d'Urbervilles*. T. H. was much amused when I related the circumstances to him later.

Another old lady to whom I put a few questions was still more comprehensive. 'Why the man could not try to do some useful work in the world beats me. Why could not he have done some building like his father, instead of writing a lot of rubbish that no one wants to read?'...

During 1914, 1915 and 1916 I had the privilege of taking Mr Hardy many thousand miles in my motor car. At first he seemed a trifle nervous, but this soon wore off, and, toward the latter part of 1916, he often assured me that motoring constituted his chief pleasure.

As a general rule he sat in front with me, while Mrs Hardy sat behind, either alone, or accompanied by a friend. Occasionally, on long journeys, he would change about from front to back, but as a general rule he seemed to prefer being in the front.

Many quite long journeys did we undertake, once going to Torquay and back in the day – nearly two hundred miles; but both he and Mrs Hardy frankly said that they thought eighty to a hundred miles was quite sufficient for one day, and longer than this proved tiring.

It always gave him intense pleasure to map out the route a day or two before we started, and many an hour have we spent over the ordnance maps spread out on the table at Max Gate planning each road, and so arranging that we took in any place he wanted to see, or to show Mrs Hardy, that lay not too far off the actual route. ...

Always generous to a degree, Mr Hardy always insisted on paying all the expenses incurred, even to the extent of hotel bills and refreshments. On this point he was adamant, and it was quite useless to want to share. Once, in a narrow lane in the eastern side of Dorset, we met with a slight mishap. A dairyman was coming home from market at a fast trot: he failed to see us as he rounded a corner, and although I blew both whistle and horn he continued to chat with his friends behind him. I drew in right to the side of the road and stopped the car. I shouted. Just as he was upon us he seemed to hear, turned his head towards us, lost his presence of mind, and *pulled the wrong rein.* The horse swerved right on to us, threw his weight against the rear of the car, and did some damage to the paint and mudguards. I got out and took his name and address, telling him I should expect him to pay the costs of repairs – some four pounds. He demurred, and a case in court seemed inevitable. It was an awkward predicament, for I certainly could not have called either Mr Hardy or the friends who were sitting behind as witnesses. Mr Hardy said at once, 'Have the repairs done and let me know the cost: that will be far less trouble than taking the case into court.' Here, however, I was too strong for him, since I absolutely refused to let him defray the cost. . . .

One memorable expedition was to Torquay to call on Mr Eden Phillpotts. We started in good time in the morning and reached Torquay about 3.30. Some three hours we spent at Mr Phillpotts' hospitable house and in looking at his notable garden, filled with plants from all the hemispheres and including some three thousand varieties. . . .

Another memorable outing was when we went to Plymouth. Mr Hardy's motive in going was to renew his recollection of Plymouth and its surroundings, to visit some relatives of the late Mrs Hardy's and to identify the tombs of some of those of the family who were buried here. . . .

During that time we took many walks together, cycled long distances on many occasions, and spent many days together in my car, visiting places in which Hardy had interests and occasionally stopping for the night here and there. I see from my diary that in 1915 we went for thirty-six tours in my car. During 1916, until I gave up the car owing to shortage of petrol, we had thirty-two such outings. He always insisted on paying all expenses on these trips. I find that during 1916 I visited Hardy fifty-four times at Max Gate.

It was in 1913 that I was able to rent and occupy the little house at Bockhampton which Hardy's forebears built and in which his brother and sisters lived until I went there. Immediately behind the cottage was the Heath, known to Wessex Novel readers as a part of Egdon, with its highest point described as Rainbarrow. And it was here, at his birthplace, that Hardy frequently paid me visits and walked with me on the heath. A footpath led across the heath to Puddletown, and once travelling this path, Hardy mentioned the many, many times he had trodden it as a boy, and how, when returning in the dusk of winter on this unfrequented path, he had often run fast to escape his fears produced by the sudden movement of a pony or deer, or a form that loomed in the half-light before being recognisable as a mere bush.

One day when Hardy paid me a visit he pointed out a tiny window at the back of the house that lighted the staircase. 'Smugglers,' he said, 'used to tap this window with their whips when passing at night, and when my father opened it a small keg of brandy used to be handed in.'

It was still in the days of his early childhood that it was his parents' practice to take him for a walk on the heath on Sunday afternoons, and their usual walk led them to Rainbarrow, from whence, with the aid of a telescope, his father would point out places of interest, houses and other buildings on which he was then working. Rainbarrow was a favourite spot of Hardy's later life, he always wanted to reach high points: 'and please don't forget your glasses,' he used to say to me when we set out for some high point, my binoculars having superseded the old telescope. But once, he told me, this ancient glass had enabled him to view Dorchester Gaol just at the moment when a body swung out from the gallows – the last hanging to take place there.

When his mother and his brother and sisters were still living in the cottage at Bockhampton it was his almost invariable habit to visit them on Sunday afternoons, and after his mother was dead and the others had removed to Talbothays he usually made that his Sunday afternoon goal. Sometimes we would walk to Stinsford churchyard and he would pause silent beside the spot where his parents were buried. Once I remember he turned to me with a smile and said "There is room for me here."

The above notes were jotted down over a period of several years for a biography of Hardy that Lea intended to write. They are taken from 'Monograph' No. 20, edited by J. Stevens Cox (Beaminster 1964).

James Milne (1865–1951) was a journalist who became Literary Editor of the *Daily Chronicle* from 1904 to 1918. Hardy recognised the value to him of knowing the leading editors of newspapers and journals. It enabled him in 1910 to bring pressure to bear on Milne to publish an article by Florence Dugdale which Milne had previously rejected. Milne called on Hardy at Max Gate on 23 August 1899 and an article 'Shall Stonehenge Go?' appeared in the *Daily Chronicle* on the following day. According to Richard Purdy in his *Bibliographical Study* (p. 306) 'this is largely Hardy's own composition... Hardy wrote out his reflections on Stonehenge in the form of a letter or article, which is here printed almost verbatim but cast by Milne in the form of an interview with the addition of setting, questions, and colloquialisms.' This may be the reason why Hardy was able to write to Florence Henniker (*CL* II, pp. 227–8) on 24 August and describe the whole affair as 'a quick business' as Milne was 'on our lawn at 3 p.m. and this morning about 1/2 past 10 the paper containing the interview was here.' The following extracts from that interview are taken from Milne's *A Window in Fleet Street* (London 1931, pp. 254–67):

> Stonehenge for sale! Stonehenge in the market! This was the rumour and alarm, one fine afternoon of the dying nineteenth century, and naturally it set the country agog. . . .
> If Stonehenge, a national relic, and now a literary monument, was in doubt, the one man to consult about it was Thomas Hardy, down there in Wessex, which he had rescued from history and made a new human kingdom for the world. So to Dorchester went I . . .
> He might, he smilingly agreed, fairly be called upon to speak about Stonehenge at such a moment. . . .

The writer goes on to quote from the Stonehenge chapter at the end of *Tess*, and then:

> Stonehenge in the market – after that! Thomas Hardy could not realise the possibility of its being carted out of the country by a rich American or anybody else. Nor was it, but there was much talk of the possibility and danger, and that led Hardy to a general observation about out national monuments. They always interested him, partly, perhaps, as a result of his training in architecture, more because his genius saw in them tokens of the rise and progress of mankind, especially Stonehenge in his own Wessex.
> 'A nation like our own,' he said gravely, bending towards me, one knicker-bockered leg thrown over the other – an attitude of his – 'should have a final guardianship of any monument which is of value to it as a page of history, even though the hieroglyphics of such monument or relic cannot be deciphered as yet. I don't know how this is to be brought about, but that the thing is right there should not be two opinions. We assume, in fact, that the owner of a property on which there happens to be a national relic is, in the larger sense, the custodian, for the nation, of that relic. It is possible to conceive circumstances in which this might be a hardship, only there it is.'
> Here was almost the one-time architect and born archaeologist speaking in the careful, estimated manner of such men, and indeed Hardy's novels often have that note. He was also practical when he told me

to suppose, for argument's sake, that the stones of Stonehenge were carried to America, or somewhere else, far from Wessex. What would happen?

They would lose all interest, because they would not be Stonehenge, and it would be the same with Stonehenge which was left. The relics being gone, the associations of the place would be broken, and all the sentiment would evaporate. It would, in a characteristic Hardy simile, be as if King Solomon had actually cut the child in two, leaving no child at all.

Hardy recalled, as an occasional personal experience, how the rain can come down on Salisbury Plain; in heavy, closely marshalled order, with drops that seemed to pass into one's body. It was a wonder, remembering the downpour of long centuries – and he shrugged his shoulders in realistic action of the thought – that Stonehenge had stood so well.

'Moreover,' he emphasised, stretching out his right hand, a rare gesture, 'apart from the effect of the water on the stones themselves, they are being gradually undermined by the trickling down of the rain they intercept, forming pools on the ground, so that the foundation sinks on the wettest side till the stone topples over.' Only three architraves remained on their proper pillars, and as these declined the architraves would slip off. The one way of protecting the ruin from driving rains, which must ultimately abraid and overthrow them, was by a belt of plantations.

'But the landscape,' said I. 'Yes,' answered Hardy, thinking, and then he examined this point in deliberate, constructive words meant to show how sentiment and practicability might be united.

Against tree planting, it could be urged that most people consider the gaunt nakedness of its situation to be a great part of the solemnity and fascination of Stonehenge. It was by no means certain, however, that the country immediately round it was originally bare and open on all sides. If it were enclosed by a wood approaching no nearer than ten chains to the bank of earth around the stone circle, the force of the disastrous winds and rains would be broken by the trees, and the duration of the ruin lengthened far beyond its possible duration otherwise. The objection to a plantation would be the less in that it would shut out the incongruities of cultivation and agricultural buildings, which had advanced across Salisbury Plain, so interfering with the eerie loneliness of Stonehenge...

'The size of the whole structure,' he said, 'is considerably destroyed to the eye by the openness of the place, as with all such erections, and a strong light detracts from its impressiveness. In the brilliant noonday sunlight, in which most visitors repair thither, and surrounded by bicycles and sandwich papers, the scene is not, to my mind, attractive, but garish and depressing. In dull, threatening weather, however, and in the dusk of the evening, its charm is indescribable. On a day of heavy cloud, the sky seems almost to form a natural roof touching the pillars, and colours are revealed on the surfaces of the stones whose presence would not be suspected on a fine day. And if a gale of wind is blowing, the strange musical hum emitted by Stonehenge can never be forgotten. To say that on moonlight nights it is at its finest is a commonplace.'

In a letter to the *Evening Standard*, written at the time of Hardy's death in January 1928, Rose M. Bradley, daughter of the Dean of Westminster, tells how in late June 1899 she had escorted Hardy and some friends round the Abbey by moonlight. She writes:

A solitary gasjet made a point of light among the ghostly statues of dead and gone statesmen, and the night-watchman's lantern glowed above the graves of the poets as he went to wind up his telltale clock in the South Transept.

Mr Hardy's appreciation, though expressed with the gentle courtesy habitual to him, was none the less intense. When we had groped our way up the dark staircase to look with our flickering light at the pallid faces of Queen Elizabeth, Nelson, and their companions among the waxworks, and had stood in the darkness before the Confessor's Shrine while Big Ben struck eleven, we wandered up into the comparative space and lightness of Henry VII's Chapel.

Here, under the thin tattered banners of the Knights of the Bath, Mr Hardy suggested that in this majestic silence, broken only by the distant rumble of horse-drawn buses, with the occasional clatter of a passing hansom, we should just sit down and enjoy it, which we did. His obvious and complete contentment was, I felt, that of the sensitive child or the poet who for the moment does not want to talk about it.

Twenty-eight years later Hardy was to lie there himself among the poets.

A. E. Housman (1859–1936), poet and classical scholar, probably met Hardy for the first time in June 1899. This meeting was followed by a weekend visit to Max Gate on 4 August where he had as fellow-guests, Edward Clodd and Arthur Symons. 'When they retired to their rooms for the night they found that Hardy had considerately placed by the bedside of each a selection of the other's works, so that by the next day they might have common ground of a literary kind for their better mutual acquaintance.' (From *A. E. H.* by Laurence Housman, London 1937, p. 86)

The publishers, Macmillan, were the most prestigious of English publishers during Hardy's lifetime, and it was probably for this reason that he submitted his first novel, *The Poor Man and the Lady* to them in 1868. It is a tribute to Macmillan's efficiency at that time that he had a reply written in Alexander Macmillan's own hand within a fortnight. Although he rejected the book, Alexander encouraged him to continue writing, but it was not until *The Woodlanders* (1887) and *Wessex Tales* (1888) that Macmillan began to publish his works. When Hardy asked them to become his main publishers in 1903 they responded enthusiastically, which was wise of them as he was to become the greatest of all their many writers and a superb earner of income for them ever since. As we have already seen, Hardy was friendly enough with the Macmillan family to attend their garden parties in the 1880s and on 21 April 1920 he was present at the wedding of Harold Macmillan to Lady Dorothy Cavendish (*Life*, p. 437). I met Harold Macmillan in 1984 when I first began work on this present volume and remember that he talked about Hardy's peasant background, his agnosticism which he (Harold), a firm believer in Christianity, could not understand, his shyness and reticence, his overriding sympathy for humankind, and his amusement and love of a joke. I was then told his favourite story about Hardy. It seems to date from about 1899. He had told it many times and the incidentals were often different but the substance remained the same. At some function (variously Hardy's cottage, at Wilton House, and at a 'crush' or party in London), a woman had come up to Hardy while he was talking to Sir Frederick Macmillan (Harold's uncle: 1851–1936) and asked him, 'What did Tess mean to you, Mr Hardy?' After a moment's reflection, Hardy turned to Sir Frederick and said, 'I don't know what she meant to you, Sir Frederick, but she was a good milch-cow to me.' No doubt the woman, failing to recognise Hardy's irony and her own insensitiveness in asking him such a question in a public place, went away convinced that Hardy was concerned only with money.

5
1900–1928
The Final Years

PART I FROM THE BOER WAR TO THE GREAT WAR, 1900–1918

Hardy was in his sixtieth year when the twentieth century began. The period 1900 to 1928 was to see the publication of another seven substantial books of verse, (*Wessex Poems*, the first, had been published in 1898), *The Dynasts* (1904–8), a final book of short stories (1913), and *The Queen of Cornwall* (1923). At a rough count Millgate and Purdy's superb edition of Hardy's letters has 580 pages of letters covering 1840–99 and 1620 covering 1900–28, a calculation which gives a rough idea of Hardy's growing correspondence with an ever larger range of friends, acquaintances and publishers. The sheer burden of Hardy's correspondence became such that in 1924 he told John Middleton Murry that for a time he had tried to answer every letter, but that now he had given up. 'He was sorry but it was impossible.' There had to be rationing, too, of those who wanted to meet him, and Hardy became ever more suspicious of anyone whose intention might be to exploit him by subsequently publishing their reminiscences of the occasion. With a few exceptions visitors were now not allowed to take notes, and on 1 July 1907, in a letter to Bram Stoker (*CL* III, p. 259) he writes, 'I thought I had better write direct and tell you that for a long time I have been compelled to refuse interviewing by any paper. I could give reasons but it is not worth while.' However, Hardy remained as hospitable as ever and Max Gate was visited by hundreds in those remaining twenty-eight years. More than one hundred people signed the Max Gate Visitors' Book in 1927, and there would have been others who failed to sign or relations who would not have been expected to sign. Florence Hardy, never slow to grumble, complained about the dullness of life at Max Gate in August 1923. In fact, in the previous four months, with Hardy aged 82–3, there were visits from Walter de la Mare, Newman Flower, the Granville Barkers, the Prince of Wales, Sir Sydney Cockerell, John Drinkwater, H. G. Wells and Rebecca West, while T. E. Lawrence had called on several occasions. As somehow, in spite of the ban on taking notes, visitors did manage to write down their recollections, there is from now on a veritable embarrassment of riches and selection and editing become much more difficult.

It was not just the British who were coming to Max Gate. On 9 September 1900, an American Professor, William Lyon Phelps (1865–1943), on holiday in England, came to Dorchester and called on Hardy. He describes what happened in his *Autobiography with Letters* (London 1939, pp. 390–5):

> On our bicycle tour in 1900, which had begun in London, we reached Dorchester in the moonlight Saturday evening, 8 September, and put up at the King's Arms. Sunday morning I walked to Hardy's house, Max Gate, and found a large sign on the front door, 'Not at home.' Accordingly, I knocked, and when I asked the maid if Mr Hardy were at home, she replied with another question. She pointed to the sign and asked if I could read. I asked in turn if she could, and if so, what were her favourite books? She was taken aback and perhaps thought I was insane. I explained that I knew I had no business to be there, but that I was an American who adored her master; and if she would explain to him that I was not a newspaper reporter, that I wished to see him only for a few moments, I should never forget her kindness. I never have. . . . Soon she returned and said Mr Hardy would see me at three o'clock.
>
> At three I was at the front door again and just in front of it was Thomas Hardy. He was sixty years old. Like me, he was clad in knickerbockers, with an aged jacket and a straw hat, the only Englishman I ever saw with that headgear. He was small and slight in stature and figure, looking rather frail and depressed, with grey face and grey moustache. We sat down on a bench in the open air. Although at this first interview he neither laughed nor smiled, he was, after the first moments, exceedingly gracious, kindly, and sympathetic. He was grave rather than sad. He spoke of the wickedness of shooting game birds, of killing any animals; 'wickedness' was the word he used. I reminded him of Emerson's poem beginning 'Hast thou named all the birds without a gun?' but somewhat injured the effectiveness of the quotation and my own reputation by confessing that I often went shooting in America.
>
> Discussing literature, I told him that I should have known by the structure of his novels that he had been a practising architect; even if he had not used architects as leading characters in *A Laodicean* and *A Pair of Blue Eyes*; that the structure of his novels was evidence enough, and that the manner in which buildings were described, as in *Two on a Tower*, revealed the architect. He said *A Laodicean* contained

more of the facts of his own life than anything else he had ever written. . . .

He said he thought the novelist ought always to *tell a story*; that a novel should be constructed with a definite plot.

He then asked me what I thought of his poetry; he had published his first volume of verse, Wessex Poems, only two years past, in 1898, with illustrations made from his own drawings. I wish I had then liked the poems as I do now; I could not believe they stood so much higher than the novels in his own estimation, that they were so close to his heart. He was evidently pained when I told him that of course I found them interesting reading, but that I felt they were not so great as his works in prose. He spoke quite strongly about this. He thought they were far superior to any of his novels and that many of his more discerning friends had told him so. I did not know then what I knew in later years, that he had ceased to care about his novels; he did not wish to discuss them. He wished to be considered and remembered only as a poet. Instead of a great novelist writing verse as an avocation, he wished to be regarded as an English poet, who had written some stories in prose. . . .

We talked for three-quarters of an hour. I had stood up to go after a few minutes, but he had urged me to stay. Finally, when I was taking leave, he asked, 'Is your wife with you?' and when I told him, he asked 'Why didn't she come?' I replied that she did not have the nerve. He cordially invited us both to tea with Mrs Hardy and himself the following afternoon at five o'clock. . . .

At five o'clock we walked into the gardens at Max Gate . . . Mr Hardy was almost covered with cats. Three or four cats were on various parts of his person, other cats were near at hand, and I noticed saucers of milk placed at strategic points in the shrubbery. 'Are all these your own cats?' 'Oh, dear, no, some of them are, and some are cats who come regularly to have tea, and some are still other cats, not invited by us, but who seem to find out about this time of day that tea will be going.' I said I was a fanatical cattist and was enchanted to have their company.

Mrs Hardy was an artist, and in the house she was kind enough to show us many of her pictures. I told her I thought her husband was the greatest of living English writers. She said she liked his earlier novels better, and did not care much for the latest ones. I suppose she had in mind *Jude the Obscure*. . . .

Mr Hardy was even more genial on this afternoon than during our conversation of Sunday. He was kindness itself, and seemed to be in almost radiant humour. We stayed two hours, and we shall never forget such kindness and hospitality.

In 1920 Professor Phelps sent Hardy an invitation to lecture at Yale University but it was courteously refused. Another visit to Max Gate took place in 1928 and a final one in May 1932 when they met Hardy's sister, Kate, 'a charming woman'. On that visit Florence told them that Hardy had the deepest conviction of the brotherhood of man, and during the 1914–18 War had taken a personal interest in the German prisoners, providing them with food and medicine.

Arthur Symons (1865–1945), poet and critic, was another journal editor with whom Hardy was on such friendly terms that there were several invitations to Max Gate. One of Symons's visits took place on the weekend of 4–6 August 1900. In a letter dated 6 August 1900 to Rhoda Bowser (MS. Columbia) he described Hardy as 'most simple and delightful', and Emma as 'nice, though homely'. The other weekend guests were Edward Clodd and A. E. Housman, and Hardy talked a lot about George Meredith who had once been so poor that he used to read aloud to a paralytic old lady. Hardy, Housman and Symons went for a walk in the moonlight to see an ancient barrow. 'What is nice about Hardy,' wrote Symons is that one can *be silent* with him so agreeably.' In another letter dated 10 June 1906 (*Selected Letters,* London, 1935, p. 178) written by Symons to Rhoda Symons, he gives an account of a visit made by Hardy and him to a private performance at the Literary Theatre Society of Oscar Wilde's *Salome* which had been banned by the Lord Chamberlain. '*Salome,*' said Symons, 'was gorgeous enough but Hardy saw instantly what was the play's weakness – that Herod swears his oath to Salome *before* she has danced, and not – as in the Bible, after...' Symons went on to say that Hardy told him 'that in his early stories he aimed at nothing more than pleasing the readers of the magazines for which he wrote them, and only gradually... came to take himself seriously'.

Writing to Florence Henniker on 15 February 1901 (*CL* II, pp. 279–80) Hardy mentions a visit to Max Gate by William Archer (1856–1924) 'about a week ago'. Archer, Hardy wrote, '... experimented on me in a new kind of interviewing: knowing him well I did not mind it at the time, but I have felt some misgivings since, and suppose I shall be thought to have prompted the production when it is printed. It is, however, only a discussion of abstract subjects: and the second person might have been anybody for that matter.' Indeed it might, but it helped no doubt that Archer had been a friend of Hardy's for several years, that he had seen in London several of Archer's translations of Ibsen's plays, and that he had declared himself 'drawn to your writings by their accord with my views'. The interview takes the form of a dramatic duologue and it was clear that Hardy had agreed to the interview on condition that he saw it before publication. In a letter to Archer written on 10 February 1901 (*CL* II, p. 279) Hardy wrote 'I return the copy and think you have been wonderfully faithful in your reproduction. It does seem rather long: if you abridge it I should like you to omit the more personal matters, such as those marked – this being nearest to the interview of years ago.' Archer's revision was first published in the *Pall Mall Magazine*, April 1901 (p. 257 *et seq.*). It was subsequently included with a few small changes in Archer's *Real Conversations* (London 1904, pp. 29–50) from which the following passages are extracted:

> **W.A.** I've often wondered what proportion, so to speak, of fact there is in your books.
>
> **Mr Hardy.** In several of my stories there is a very large element of fact, or tradition. For instance, the story of Napoleon's landing in person on the Dorsetshire coast – I don't know whether you remember it – is related as a fact.
>
> **W.A.** Do you yourself believe it?
>
> **Mr Hardy.** I cannot honestly say I do. But the incident in *The Trumpet-Major* of the people letting their cider run when Buonaparte was reported to have landed is a literal fact. Few of my longer books, however, are so closely founded on fact as *The Trumpet-Major*. On a single series of facts, that is to say. In other books, one situation will often be an amalgam of many real incidents. In that way, it seems to me, one may hope to get at what is fundamental in them – to present the typical incident. Just as, in character-drawing, several similar individuals will blend into one type.
>
> **W.A.** A sort of composite photograph, in fact? I wonder if you are properly grateful to the deities – the tribal gods of the West Saxons, I suppose – who have given you such stores of knowledge to draw upon, and have made you the historiographer of their ancient and delectable domain?
>
> **Mr Hardy.** I suppose it *is* an advantage, from one point of view, to be thoroughly at home in one region, however narrow. But think of the men who have been thoroughly at home in all!
>
> **W.A.** I believe if I were an artist, and had my choice as to the form of equipment I would prefer, I should choose intensive rather than extensive knowledge.
>
> **Mr Hardy.** It has been said that a man ought to know something about everything, and everything about something.
>
> **W.A.** Well, it seems to me that if ever man fulfilled the latter condition, you are that enviable mortal . . . You have history, local tradition, folk-lore, village gossip, all at your fingers' ends. You –
>
> **Mr Hardy** (*laughing*). Oh, one can't be such an encyclopaedia as all that! Perhaps some of what you take for my knowledge may be 'only my artfulness.' But it's true that my feeling for this county is that of

the countryman born and bred. Have you ever noticed the different relation to nature of the town child and the country child? The town-bred boy will often appreciate nature more than the country boy, but he does not know it in the same sense. He will rush to pick a flower which the country boy does not seem to notice. But it is part of the country boy's life. It grows in his soul – he does not want it in his buttonhole. I happened to live, too, in close contact with the people –

W.A. Haven't I heard you say that you used to write love-letters for the village girls?

Mr Hardy (*reluctantly*). Well – yes, to their soldier sweethearts in India – the East Indies, as it was called then.

W.A. That was part of Samuel Richardson's apprenticeship, too. He trained for Clarissa, you for Tess.

Mr Hardy. But I think you will find that Richardson's case was different. He was employed to compose the letters; I was only the amanuensis. Indeed, I was chosen on account of my tender years – because I could write, and read the replies, yet couldn't understand. They looked upon me as a mere writing machine, or a sort of phonograph to be talked into. And as a matter of fact I understood very little, and took very little interest in what I wrote and read; though I remember to this day one lover's address, as given in his letter: 'Calcutta, *or Elsewear.*'

W.A. I fancy many of those letters remained written in your mind in sympathetic ink, only waiting for the heat of creation to bring them out.

Mr Hardy. Possibly, in a sub-conscious way. The human mind is a sort of palimpsest, I suppose; and it's hard to say what records may not lurk in it.

W.A. Well, I can see that your country life goes far to account for your insight into rustic character. But how did you get your surface knowledge – your topographical mastery – of so large a region?

Mr Hardy. I don't know that my surface knowledge of the country is so intimate as you think. But, for one thing, when I was quite a young man, an architect's pupil, I used to be sent round to sketch village churches as a preliminary to their restoration – which mostly meant destruction. I feel very remorseful now; but, after all, it wasn't my fault – I was only obeying orders.

W.A. Ah, I had forgotten that you looked at the country not only with the novelist's but with the draughtsman's eye. That accounts for much. And these sketch-book wanderings must have brought you into many quaint nooks and corners. I suppose, now, you can yourself remember many of the old customs – the relics of paganism – that you have described?

Mr Hardy. Oh, yes. They survived well into my time. I have seen with my own eyes things that many people believe to have been extinct for centuries. For instance, the maypole was familiar to me in my childhood – the flower-wreathed pole, with what they called the garland at the top (that is to say, two intersecting hoops of flowers), round which the people danced. More than that, I have seen men in the stocks.

W.A. Is it possible?

Mr Hardy. I remember one perfectly – when I was very young. It was in the village I have called Weatherbury. I can see him now, sitting in the scorching sunshine, with the flies crawling over him, and not another human being near except me. I can see his blue worsted stockings projecting through the leg-holes, and the shining nails in his boots. He was quite a hero in my eyes. I sidled up to him and said good-day to him, and felt mightily honoured when he nodded to me...

W.A. Now tell me, as to rural superstitions – belief in witchcraft, and so forth – are they dying out?

Mr Hardy. On the surface, yes; in reality, no. People smile and say, 'Of course we don't believe in these things' – but their scepticism is only skin deep. You will find women to this day who will make an image of some enemy and either melt it before the fire or stick pins into it. The belief in the evil eye subsists in full force; also such ideas as that which I have introduced into one of my stories – that if you can draw blood from a witch, you render her powerless. ... I am most anxious to believe in what, roughly speaking, we may call the supernatural – but I find no evidence for it! People accuse me of scepticism, materialism, and so forth; but, if the accusation is just at all, it is quite against my will. For instance, I seriously assure you that I would give ten years of my life – well, perhaps that offer is rather beyond my means – but when I was a younger man, I would cheerfully have given ten years of my life to see a ghost – an authentic, indubitable spectre.

W.A. And you have never seen one?

Mr Hardy. Never the ghost of a ghost. Yet I should think I am cut out by nature for a ghost-seer. My nerves vibrate very readily; people say I am almost morbidly imaginative; my will to believe is perfect. If ever ghost wanted to manifest himself, I am the very man he should apply to. But no – the spirits don't seem to see it!

W.A. Yet you live in a graveyard, too, don't you?

Mr Hardy. A Roman graveyard – yes. We decapitated a row of five Roman soldiers or colonists in moving the earth to make the drive there.

W.A.   And wasn't there a lady as well?

Mr Hardy.   Yes. I think I showed you the little bronze-gilt fibula that had fastened the fillet across her brow. I took it from her skull with my own hands, and it lies in the corner cupboard yonder.

W.A.   Yet she hasn't haunted you? Well, that certainly establishes a very strong presumption against the spooks. I can only suggest that they don't think it worth while to appear to you, knowing that, if you recorded their visits, people would think you were romancing. 'What the novelist says is not evidence.'

Mr Hardy.   My mother believed that she once saw an apparition. A relative of hers, who had a young child, was ill, and told my mother, who visited her, that she thought she was dying. My mother laughed at the idea; and as a matter of fact she apparently recovered, and my mother went away to her home at some distance. Then one night – lying broad awake, as she declared – my mother saw this lady enter her room and hold out the child to her imploringly. It afterwards appeared (I need scarcely tell you) that she died at that very time; but the odd thing was that, while she was sinking, she continually expressed a wish that my mother should take charge of the child, though she had said nothing about it on my mother's visit.

W.A.   That seems to me a simple case of a very natural dream happening to coincide with a far from improbable event. But indeed I find it much easier to conceive the possibility of apparitions of the living – and the dying are of course living up to the last pulse-beat – than to conceive an apparition of the dead which should be other than a mere hallucination.

Mr Hardy.   Why should the one be more credible than the other?

W.A.   Simply because there seems to be ample evidence for the existence of forms of cerebral energy not as yet measured and catalogued; whereas in death, so far as we can see, cerebral energy ceases altogether. It may be hard to believe that even an active brain, fifty miles away, can instantaneously impress an idea or an image upon mine as I sit here; but if the brain has, to all appearance, ceased to act – nay, has mouldered into dust – the difficulty becomes infinitely greater. It is conceivable that, through some hitherto unrecognised property of matter, you, in Casterbridge, might be able to hear my watch ticking in London; but when my watch stops – when the mainspring is run down – you won't hear it ticking even if you hold it close to your ear.

Mr Hardy.   The spiritualist would maintain that the human watch, at the moment of its stoppage here below, is wound up afresh on another plane of being. But that, as I say, is precisely what, with the best will in the world, I can find no evidence for.

W.A. On the other hand, don't you think there is very fair evidence for the possibility of thought-transference, whether in the shape of words or of images?

Mr Hardy. No. In all the researches of the Psychical Society, I find nothing that carries conviction. I cannot get past the famous principle of Hume – wait a minute – I will get the book... Here it is, in the essay *Of Miracles*: the principle 'That no testimony is sufficient to establish a miracle, unless the testimony be of such a kind that its falsehood would be more miraculous than the fact which it endeavours to establish.' Like Hume, I am compelled to 'weigh one miracle against the other, and reject the greater.'...

W.A. And the pessimist holds, I take it, that the principle of evil is the stronger.

Mr Hardy. No. I should not put it precisely in that way. For instance, people call me a pessimist; and if it is pessimism to think, with Sophocles, that 'not to have been born is best,' then I do not reject the designation. I never could understand why the word 'pessimism' should be such a red rag to many worthy people; and I believe, indeed, that a good deal of the robustious, swaggering optimism of recent literature is at bottom cowardly and insincere. I do not see that we are likely to improve the world by asseverating, however loudly, that black is white, or at least that black is but a necessary contrast and foil, without which white would be white no longer. That is mere juggling with a metaphor. But my pessimism, if pessimism it be, does not involve the assumption that the world is going to the dogs, and that Ahriman is winning all along the line. On the contrary, my practical philosophy is distinctly meliorist. What are my books but one plea against 'man's inhumanity to man' – to woman – and to the lower animals? (By the way, my opposition to 'sport' is a point on which I am rather in conflict with my neighbours hereabouts.) Whatever may be the inherent good or evil of life, it is certain that men make it much worse than it need be. When we have got rid of a thousand remediable ills, it will be time enough to determine whether the ill that is irremediable outweighs the good.

W.A. And you think we *are* getting rid of the remediable ills?

Mr Hardy. Slowly – yes – very slowly.

W.A. War, for instance?

Mr Hardy. Oh yes, war is doomed. It is doomed by the gradual growth of the introspective faculty in mankind – of their power of putting themselves in another's place, and taking a point of view that is not their own. In another aspect, this may be called the growth of a sense of humour. Not to-day, nor to-morrow, but in the fulness of time, war will come to an end, not for moral reasons, but because of its absurdity.

W.A. It seems to me that the Press, with its thirst for alarmist news, and its gigantic exaggeration and reverberation of every international jealousy, suspicion, and rancour, is one of the great agents for keeping war alive.

Mr Hardy. I noticed that several people who answered that American editor's query as to the chief danger of the twentieth century, named the Press as the influence most to be feared – and I'm not sure that I didn't agree with them...

Other critics seemed to me to take unnecessary objection to my use of local Wessex words, which they declared to be obsolete. But they are not obsolete here; they are understood and used by educated people. And if they supply a want in the language – if they express an idea which cannot otherwise be so accurately or so briefly expressed – why may not one attempt to preserve them?

W.A. It is a beneficent act; but like so many other beneficent acts, it is apt to be met with ingratitude.

Mr Hardy. I have no sympathy with the criticism which would treat English as a dead language – a thing crystallised at an arbitrarily selected stage of its existence, and bidden to forget that it has a past and deny that it has a future. Purism, whether in grammar or vocabulary, almost always means ignorance. Language was made before grammar, not grammar before language. And as for the people who make it their business to insist on the utmost possible impoverishment of our English vocabulary, they seem to me to ignore the lessons of history, science, and common-sense.

W.A. I have been struck, in reading your books, with the large survival of pure Saxon in the Wessex speech.

Mr Hardy. Where else should you go for pure Saxon? It has often seemed to me a pity, from many points of view – and from the point of view of language among the rest – that Winchester did not remain, as it once was, the royal, political, and social capital of England, leaving London to be the commercial capital. The relation between them might have been something like that between Paris and Marseilles or Havre; and perhaps, in that case, neither of them would have been so monstrously overgrown as London is to-day. We should then have had a metropolis free from the fogs of the Thames valley; situated, not on clammy clay, but on chalk hills, the best soil in the world of habitation; and we might have preserved in our literary language a larger proportion of the racy Saxon of the West-country. Don't you think there is something in this?

Hardy met Sir James Frazer (1854–1941), the distinguished anthropologist and author of *The Golden Bough*, on a number of occasions on his visits to Edward Clodd at Aldeburgh. It may have been on the May 1901 visit that Frazer later remembered Hardy telling him that according to folklore the reason why certain trees in front of his house... 'did not thrive, was that he looked at them before breakfast on an empty stomach.' Before breakfast, it seems, there was a blasting influence in the eye that made them pine away.

Desmond McCarthy (1877–1952) was yet another of Hardy's editor friends. Beginning as a journalist he worked his way up to become editor of the *New Quarterly*, and then, after Hardy's death, contributed largely to the literary columns and reviews of the *Sunday Times* in the days when serious books were given full-page reviews. He made several visits to Max Gate, the first being in April 1902, and together Hardy and he walked or cycled around Dorset. The following extracts come from his *Memories* (London 1953, pp. 110–11):

> A good many years ago I had the pleasure of seeing Hardy sometimes, of talking with him, and sometimes bicycling with him. His simplicity of feeling was more impressive in him than anything he actually said. A few characteristic things, however, I remember him saying. He had been reading or re-reading *Tom Jones* and referring to that character – the poor trollop in Tom Jones' village, Molly Seagrim, about whose humiliations there are many jokes – he said 'It's a most extraordinary thing but Fielding seems to have forgotten she was a woman.' I remember thinking at the time – 'There speaks a man to whom village life is real in a very different degree to which it is to a writer of the squire class like Fielding; and how characteristic too of one who never in his work forgets the pain and seriousness of life.'
>
> Once when we were passing the scene of some incident in *Tess*, he said to me, 'If I had thought that story was going to be such a success I'd have made it a *really good book*'...
>
> Hardy's appearance is familiar from photographs and pictures. Two of the best known of his portraits, Augustus John's portrait of him and Strang's etching, do not seem to me like him. I do not recognise in the John portrait that startled and supercilious stare. There is far too much vigour and not nearly enough delicacy in the face, and the same comment applies, in my opinion, to the etching. There was something far more odd, winning and somehow twisted both in his features and expression; something agelessly elfin in him which neither artist has caught, and a glint in his eye which one might have associated with slyness in a mindless and insensitive man. He was very small, very quiet, self-possessed and extraordinarily unassuming. I

seem to remember that his laughter made no sound. As is usual with subtle people, his voice was never loud and a gentle eagerness which was very pleasing, showed in his manner when he wanted sympathy about some point. He would instantly recoil on being disappointed. I observed in him once or twice a look, a movement, too slight to be called a wince, but not unlike the almost imperceptible change one sees in a cat when a gesture has perturbed it.

Commenting on an unpublished letter she had received from McCarthy, Irene Cooper Willis, friend of Florence Hardy and executor of her will, quotes him as saying that on one of his visits to Max Gate, Emma had said it was a misfortune to be married to a writer, 'He stabs you with his pen.' One final comment from McCarthy comes from his review of *The Early Life of Thomas Hardy* 'by Florence Hardy' (London 1928) where he remembers Hardy reading his poetry 'in a curious simple sing-song, emphasising the metre, as though it was a country jig to which the words danced – not dramatically.'

Edward Clodd (1840–1930), a wealthy banker, author, and rationalist, has already been mentioned. His weekends at his country residence at Aldeburgh in Suffolk were well-known for his ability to bring together distinguished people from different cultures and different areas of human knowledge. Hardy was frequently invited and usually made at least one visit each year, often at Whitsun. He was close enough to Clodd to introduce the then Florence Dugdale to him during his early acquaintance with her and to use Clodd for furthering the 'affair' by inviting her to Aldeburgh. Florence was variously referred to as 'our friend', 'my young friend' and 'little cousin', naive terms which would not have deceived Clodd as to the affectionate regard in which Hardy held his 'cousin'. These weekends were not just pleasant short breaks, they were valuable, too, in allowing mind to meet mind, and in promoting friendship. Grant Allen (1848–99, novelist) sums it up well in some lines of verse he wrote in 1894:

> Oh, how we laughed until we cried
> In Strafford House at Whitsuntide!
> What words we spake of men and gods,
> Beneath that friendly roof of Clodd's – ...
> How late we tarried, slow and tardy,
> Yet loth to lose one tale from Hardy.

Clodd must have known Hardy very well because of these weekends spent together but was sufficiently upset by Hardy's rejection of rationalism and his inability to let go of the Christian religion completely, to be able to describe Hardy after his death as 'A great author: he was not a great man; there was no largeness of soul' (Letter to J. H. Bulloch, 14 January 1928, University of Texas). Coming from a man who did not believe in the soul this is somewhat difficult to understand.

Clodd tells of one evening in 1903 when he and Clement Shorter and Hardy 'pranced about Tussaud's by night, Hardy wearing the Waterloo cocked hat! He told me in a recent letter that he had lived so long among the characters that like George IV, he was present at the battle.' (Letter to Clement Shorter, 16 February 1908).

Another interviewer who came on the scene in 1903 was Charles James Hankinson (1866–1959) who as 'Clive Holland', journalist, wrote a whole series of articles about Hardy which appeared in magazines, occasionally during Hardy's lifetime and frequently after his death. Almost nothing he writes down can be trusted. Much of it is made up from writings of others and it is intriguing to trace in these articles the 'cannibalising' of other works and the slight changes from article to article. Hardy clearly distrusted him but had to receive him at Max Gate in July 1905 when he was one of a large party of journalists who came from London to a garden party there. Writing of a Holland article in *The Bookman*, Hardy said that 'the article was written without my connivance, and indeed, against my wish', and as late as 25 August 1923 Hardy refused yet again to grant him an interview.

The following appeared in the *Manchester Guardian*, 15 October 1904 in a series, 'Books and Bookmen'. The correspondent has not been identified:

> A correspondent who recently went to Dorchester to see Mr Thomas Hardy has sent us an account of his interview.
>
> Before long they got on to the subject of *The Dynasts*. Mr Hardy said that it did not go very well at first. People were, he thought, startled by the novelty of form and treatment, but every month has brought a greater number of readers. Eminent men, it seems, have written thanking him for the revelation the book has brought them. In America, apparently, they complain that the geography is not full enough. It is also from the United States that come the fiercest objections to the comments of the 'Spirits' or 'Phantom Intelligences'. Someone has sent him from over there a bundle of cuttings in which he is accused in bitter language of having attacked the Christian religion. He declares emphatically that he has done no such thing, and remarks that in America there is distinctly less tolerance and freedom of thought than in England, whatever the reason may be. As to the date when we may expect the other two volumes of *The Dynasts*, he said he could not give one. 'There is an immense amount

of material to compress; but I hope I shall be able to get them done – I hope so.'

Asked what he thought of the state of literature today, Mr Hardy said: 'The fatal defect of most of it is the absence of a philosophic standpoint, and what lacks that cannot be of the highest quality or enduring. Descriptions of life, however brilliant or varied, are not sufficient; some reasoned comment is essential on life as a whole, some sustained criticism – the outcome of modern knowledge – on the relations of man to the universe, both now and in the past.' He said that he was convinced that a belief in Necessitarianism is very widely adopted by the most thoughtful writers and critics today, but that they are not bold enough to express it. 'Don't suppose for a moment,' he added, 'that I am hostile to the Christian religion. I often wish that I had lived in the Middle Ages, when the Church was supreme and unquestioned.' Mr Hardy proceeded to express his profound admiration for Ibsen. 'Yes,' he said, 'Ibsen was indeed a revelation, and what an immense loss the English stage has suffered through not giving him a fair chance!' Tolstoy also was mentioned, and Mr Hardy said that he was a curious mixture, giving us new ideas disguised in old forms of language. Not many English writers were alluded to, but his visitor got the following brief comments: 'How Tennyson could write of life as he did I cannot imagine; Browning also was a mystery of contradictions, but I knew him personally and I am quite sure that he was genuine in all he wrote.'

Another friend of Edward Clodd's met by Hardy at Aldeburgh in 1905 was Evelyn Sharp, (1869–1955), journalist, author and a prominent member of the suffragette movement. She found Clodd 'a perfect host' and had no difficulty in accepting his hospitality although 'the particular type of Victorian materialism that he represented made no appeal to me'. About Hardy on that occasion she had this to say:

The chief thing I noticed about Thomas Hardy, during the Aldeburgh visit, was his modesty. In spite of Clement Shorter's typical attempts to draw him out and make him play to the gallery, he remained unobtrusively himself, speaking in his gentle refined voice when he had something to say, but never for politeness' sake or for any other conventional reason. It was a delight to watch his face, especially in repose, so wise and so sensitive, already the face of an old man, in which, for all that, shone eyes that could not grow old because they were always on the watch. I have only occasionally seen eyes like his – in Edward Carpenter, for instance – and in each case they betokened, I think, that eternal vigilance which allows no cruelty or injustice to pass unchallenged. Hardy's tendency to relate gruesome and horrible incidents he had experienced or heard of, particularly in connection with the Boer War, then fresh in people's minds, struck me as slightly morbid: it seemed as though we could not avoid the macabre in any conversation to which he contributed. He was particularly concerned over the sufferings of horses in war-time, and declared emphatically that they should never be sent to the Front. That was before the Great War had by comparison reduced the atrocities of the South African campaign almost to unimportance.

(From *Unfinished Adventure*, London, 1934, p. 96)

Henry Woodd Nevinson (1856–1941), essayist and journalist, met Hardy in 1903 at one of Edward Clodd's Whitsun weekends at Aldeburgh. On the strength of this he wrote to Hardy in August 1906 asking him if he could call at Max Gate as he was writing an article on Hardy's book. Hardy replied on 30 August 1906, agreeing to the visit and inviting him to lunch. He wrote:

> As to the article on my books that you contemplate writing, the only condition I make is that I do not personally appear in it as saying this or that: though I shall, of course, not mind giving any explanation of what may be obscure in them – that you may print it without saying how you arrived at your elucidations. (*CL* III, p. 223)

Hardy saw the article before publication under the title 'Thomas Hardy: The Son of Earth' in the *Reader* (10 November 1906), and in his reply, dated 30 September, said:

> I think the article is beautifully written, and of course there is nothing for me to object to on the score of 'interviewing'. My scruples arose from the fact that I did not foresee the possibility of that form of paper – neither an interview nor a review. (*CL* III, p. 228)

Hardy's scruples did not prevent Nevinson from making some very personal references to him in his *Changes and Chances* (London 1923), and *More Changes, More Chances* (London 1925). The first extract comes from *Changes and Chances* (pp. 307–8) and describes meeting Hardy at Aldeburgh in May 1903:

> Reached Clodd about seven, and was much welcomed. Was almost at once introduced to Thomas Hardy; . . . He was quite silent at first, sitting sadly and taking no notice of the converse. Then he began to speak a little, always with simple and quite unconscious modesty,

attempting no phrase or eloquence as Meredith does, but just stating his opinion or telling some reminiscence or story – always a little shyly, like a country cousin among rapid Londoners. He talked a good deal about General Pitt-Rivers, his wife and daughters, such as Lady Grove. But he spoke also of early days in Dorset, when life was so much fuller and more various, chiefly owing to the system of holding cottages on three lives – 'liviers' the tenants were called – which gave a permanency and personal interest to the place. Now the Cockney's idea that all country people are agricultural labourers is almost true. He himself was born only just in time to catch the relics of the old days.

As I expected, he spoke much about the hangman; also about the horrible scenes at public floggings on a waggon in the market-place, and how a cruel hangman would wait between each lash to let the flesh recover its feeling, while he squeezed blood off the thongs; and how some soldiers once saw this and forced the man to go quicker. Also how, before his time, little children used to be flogged through the streets behind a cart for stealing a penny book or toy. He had stories of magic as well; the woman who dreamt another woman sat on her chest and clawed her arm, and the other woman came next day to be healed of a terrible red mark on her arm, of which she ultimately died. He wrote a story on it for Leslie Stephen, who, however, insisted upon having a material explanation. I thought I remembered it in 'Wessex Tales', but am not sure. He spoke also of the custom still surviving that the man who kills a pig cuts out a nice little piece and eats it raw.

On 26 April 1906 Nevinson was at Terry's Theatre in London waiting to see Maxim Gorki's play *The Bezsemenoffs* when:

... Thomas Hardy came creeping into the empty pit and sat beside me. He was in his usual mood, gentle, sensible, unpretentious. He thought the books appearing on Wessex might help to advertise his own books a little! He talked much of *The Dynasts*, and mentioned the entire futility of American criticism, which always waits to see what English critics say before it dares express an opinion. He said that *Tess* had sold best of his works, and the *Madding Crowd* next best. For himself, he enjoyed concerts better than theatres, and thought Tchaikovsky's music had exactly the modern note of unrest. Best of all he liked to go to St Paul's to hear the chanting, always choosing out his favourite chant according to the day's programme. Afterwards we went to a Lyons teashop, at which he was a little alarmed, being used only to an A.B.C., and unfortunately, as we came out, he caught sight of a broadsheet, announcing, 'Family Murdered with a Penknife.' He couldn't get over that. The vision of the penknife seemed to fascinate him. But we parted most amiably, the Strand quite unconscious of his greatness – unconscious as was Dido how powerful a god lay nestling in her lap. (*More Changes, More Chances*, pp. 164–5)

Nevinson's notes on his 1906 (ibid., pp. 179–81) visit to Max Gate include the following:

Hardy came out of his study to tea, and we talked chiefly on Russia, till we set out for the old home of the Dorset poet Barnes, a beautiful cottage home, and then through Crane [Came] Park to Barnes's old church and Celtic gravestone. He told me how Louis Napoleon used to visit at the Park, and nearly married one of the girls there, which would certainly have altered European history. He talked freely about the characters in his books, how he thought people in the country were becoming more like them rather than less. The half-educated girl especially, he said, was growing like Tess or Sue (he thought *Jude* his greatest prose book, perhaps because it was his last?). Many girls of the same type wrote to him – small teachers, musicians, etc., some asking how they could get back to live in the country. He spoke a good deal about sport, how he had really induced one sportsman not to go out shooting one day; and he described the indignation of the neighbouring landowners because he had described *their* pheasant plantations in *Tess*, after which they had long refused to call on him. He showed me in the distance the monument to Nelson's Hardy, and later, in the church a tablet to a Thomas Hardy of Elizabeth's reign. The family came from Jersey, and his own grandfather used to sail to Ireland, and brought back an Irish wife.

He spoke with some bitterness of an eminent critic who had said Hardy's books would not live because they had no moral principle; and he complained that the critic had not attempted to show that there *was* such a thing as a moral principle. He thought badly of the *Oxford Book of Verse* for its love of tags and morals in the mid-Victorian manner. The poet Barnes, he thought, had the same fault, and his poems were generally better if the last verse were omitted. He pointed out the beginning of Egdon Heath, and many other places. He considered the foundation of Ruskin College in Oxford was due to *Jude*, and said the Oxford dons used to be very angry about the book, but had now got over it. People were always very stupid in taking dramatic sentences as representing his own opinions. He had ceased to care much about his prose books, and would have written nothing but verse, if he could have afforded it (which suggested to me another of the sweet uses of adversity). When a lyric was done, he said, it was something produced (which reminded me of Goethe's sneer about the dilettante poets who thought they really had accomplished something definite when they could show a verse for their pains). One is never certain about prose, he said, but you could get the whole of a novel into three pages of verse. Later on he often returned to his love of verse. He was much occupied with *The Dynasts,* and defended his way of turning Parliamentary debates into verse when the argument was high, as in one of Pitt's last speeches. He thought neither side could ever be right in those big controversies, but the English were on the whole less wrong than Napoleon. So on Home Rule he was never very enthusiastic...

Next morning we walked into Dorchester, and he showed me the shop that had been kept by the father of Treves, the great surgeon, and the house where Judge Jeffreys lived during the Bloody Assize. Also the road to the village, three miles out, where he himself was born. Then we cycled along the Weymouth road to the top of the Ridgeway, and walked out to the left to a farm beside a plantation, giving a splendid view over Weymouth and Portland, and far inland to nearly all the places mentioned in his books. The Start and St Alban's Head were both just visible. Kipling had been much pleased with the place, and wanted to build there, and when Hardy told him all his windows would be shaken by the big guns firing off Portland, he said that would especially delight him. Hardy said he liked Kipling very much as a companion, and thought he would have been a very great writer if the Imperialists had not got hold of him. He also showed me the point on the road to which the soldiers had come when they heard that the rumour of Napoleon's landing was false. In the town he showed me the railings he used to climb up as a boy to watch the hangman having his tea in a cottage room below on the evening before an execution, and how strange it seemed to him that the man could eat anything at such a time. We also went into the Roman amphitheatre just south of the station where a woman was burnt alive not very long ago [1705!] on suspicion of having poisoned her husband. She had a lover, and they waited for six months till her baby was born, and then they burnt her alive in the middle of the grassy amphitheatre. On an old plan of Dorchester, Hardy also pointed me out the hardly distinguishable spot where the gallows were marked. The subjects have for him a horrible fascination that comes of extreme sensitiveness to other people's pain. I suppose that if we all had that intensity of imagination we should never do harm to any human being or animal or bird, certainly not in cruelty.

It was probably in 1905 that James Milne met Hardy again, this time on another Aldeburgh weekend. His account of the weekend in his *The Memoirs of a Bookman* (London 1934, pp. 127–8) included the following about the journey to Aldeburgh by train.

> Thomas Hardy... sat in a corner seat, quiet as usual, even detached, except for the formalities of meetings, until we were free of London....
>
> Hardy... looked older than when I had last seen him, and in the kindly Scottish phrase he was getting 'little bookit'; that is, smaller in physique. He was balder for one thing, almost completely bald, and he happened to say that once he had a great crop of hair. He thought that perhaps the wearing of a tall hat, as the fashion was when he was a young architect in London, had been the first cause of its loss.
>
> Now he wore a soft felt hat which had once been green, but had, thanks to sun, shower, and honest service, become a medley of colours. His clothes were a heavy top-coat, of a black and white check and a tweed suit of no particular shade, though it was russet, and also of no particular cut. He had never been 'a dressy man'; everything nondescript and modest, even to his Gladstone bag of brown leather, grown darkish and tagged 'Hardy, Passenger.' A detail that, but eloquent of the novelist's simple ways and shrinkage from the eye of the world. Not for him the label which would invite the remark, 'Why that's Thomas Hardy, the great author.'
>
> At some station in our journey through East Anglia, a servant girl, good-looking and plump, jumped in among us, first asking, 'Is this first-class?' 'No,' she was assured, probably by Hardy himself, he being next the door; 'it's third.'
>
> Sure she was in the right place, and shyly recovering from her fluster, she sat down in the seat we made for her by a little extra squeezing. Presently, as if she felt she must explain herself, she said she could not read, that she was going to such and such a station, and would the train stop there.
>
> Hardy was instantly concerned with the circumstance that she could not read and asked her, sympathetically, almost earnestly, 'Why is that?' She shook her head, saying she did not know; just she had not learned and she was eighteen years old. She could, however, say the letters of the alphabet backwards; say them better thus than forward; and didn't this, her voice seemed to suggest, make up a little for her unableness to read? Here, I remember thinking, was another possible Tess or Sue, a rustic heroine, ready-made for a Wessex novel, but by then Hardy had stopped writing fiction.

Why? Perhaps there was a side-light for us on that casual remark he made about his *Jude the Obscure*. 'I have,' he said, 'seen acquaintances turn away when I met them. You get accustomed even to that, but it is not pleasant.' If he had gone on writing other novels would they have been *Judes; Jude's* more so, or less so?

Hardy did not say, but he did inferentially speak of the progress which English fiction, in its examination of human life, had made in the years following *Jude* and *Tess*. Possibly he was thinking of them as blazers of the trail which led to the emancipation of the English novel from its long Victorian shackles. His inexpressiveness about himself did not let this appear, but one learned to attach as much to his silences as to his words. Even his measured way of talking had its different significances when you got to understand them.

Jude, I had been told, was a book on which Hardy set personal store, though, when it appeared it had not nearly the popular success of *Tess* and still more criticism from the Victorian paladins of literary virtue. Remembering this, I asked him if he had a particular favourite among his novels.

He answered generally, by analogy, as he often did, that at one time an author might like one of his own books best, and at another time another of those books, a matter of mood. I suggested that perhaps a writer was apt to lay most value on the book which had cost him most mental labour, wrongly, because the perfect thing is often born, not made. He agreed, and doing so left me with the feeling that he favoured *Jude* among his stories.

How, I inquired in the course of this all-around and roundabout conversation, had the reviewing of his books affected him as a writer? Encouraged him, helped him? Or discouraged him, kept him back on his very individual Wessex road?

'Well,' he said, 'for long any praise I got was given grudgingly, and even when it became the habit to praise what I wrote, it was still grudgingly done. About *Tess*, as you know, I was abused by some papers in unmeasured terms, as if I had done something dreadful. It was, as you also know, still worse with *Jude* and the criticism of my verse has sometimes been carping, because on small points, a word or such-like.' He did not complain, or blame, and indeed was grateful for much and to many, but he just made this note on his passage through the sea of criticism and renown.

Somebody, Hardy casually told us, had wanted to summarize several of his novels for a serial work and he had not countenanced the idea. He enlarged on that refusal by saying it was an impossible idea and asking, 'What sort of thing would be the result?' He illustrated his attitude in the remark that the introduction to Scott's *Kenilworth*

– how the traveller came to his inn – set the whole tune of the story. 'One of the best pieces of writing Scott ever did,' added Hardy, 'but if there were to be a condensed edition of *Kenilworth,* I suppose it would instantly be left out.'

In 1908 Rupert Brooke (1887–1915), poet and writer, met Hardy in Cambridge at an undergraduate performance of Milton's *Comus.* He described him then in a letter to his friend, Gwen Raverat, as 'incredibly shrivelled and ordinary'. In a letter to Frances Cornford of January 1910 Brooke thought Hardy's latest book of poems, *Time's Laughingstocks* (1909) was 'very good ... His command of metre is so astounding. I met him at Comus time. He talked of the best manure for turnips, all the time. You ought to tell him, when you see him again, that a heterogeneous party of jolly people in Switzerland did nothing but read his poems, this Christmas.'

Frances Cornford (1886–1960), poet and grandchild of Charles Darwin, visited Max Gate with her husband in the middle of January 1910. Her letter to Rupert Brooke written soon after the visit contained the following:

> We went on Friday to see Thomas Hardy. He was the most touching old dear I have ever seen. We started in terror, but as soon as he entered the room we discovered that he was much more frightened of us than we of him. He wouldn't believe that anybody could possibly come to see his Dorset plays in Cambridge ... he seemed under the impression that everyone there would be shocked at his poems. I want you badly to write about *Time's Laughingstocks* in the Review. I should like to be able to send it him and show that we do, some of us, appreciate him. I know it would be a real pleasure to the old man. I never saw anyone so modest, or so needing appreciation. And in any case it's a thing that *ought* to be done. The poems are such splendid real things. They are haunting, and people don't appreciate them enough. Lines out of 'A Trampwoman's Tragedy' (*CP* 153) go round and round in my head.

Hardy may have met Lillah McCarthy (1875–1960) for the first time when she was performing the leading role in John Masefield's play, *Nan,* at the Royalty Theatre in 1908. He is described by her as bursting into her dressing-room after the performance, saying 'You must play my Tessy ... I shall send you the play I have made from my book; and you *will* play my Tessy, won't you?' She was never to play that part but did act in her husband's, Harley Granville Barker's, production of scenes from *The Dynasts* which had its first night at the Kingsway Theatre,

London, on 25 November 1914. Divorced in 1918, she subsequently became Lady Keeble on her marriage to Sir Frederick Keeble. The following passages come from her *Myself and My Friends* (London 1933, pp. 103–4):

> I saw Hardy many times after the meeting in my dressing-room. I see him still, though he is gone; slight, neatly dressed, of upright carriage, alert, with something in his eye of the retired sea-captain – direct in speech – utterly objective in speaking of his work. He went on growing all his life. And when he was very old he seemed to be still more interested in life than he was when I first met him. Until he grew old he may have nourished a grievance against life. If so, in the end he triumphed and the grievance died. His later lyrical poems show that his mind knew no pettiness; only the good and the great endure with him. 'I now tell the story of a novel in verse of twenty lines,' he said to me on the last occasion when we met, a few weeks before he died.
>
> Ah, that meeting! The happiness of it! He spoke of his life; his early days in London in an office in the Adelphi. 'Your Adelphi,' he said. He laughed to remember the fiddle which they used to play in office hours. We sat in the parlour which his presence made a palace, and only the softness of his voice told us that he was old. That and the acquiescence in life as one who says with reverence and humility, 'Thy will be done.' No elation, no despondence! 'Along the cool, sequestered vale of life he kept the even tenor of his way.' I asked whether the scene overlooking the University in *Jude the Obscure* was drawn from the sight of Oxford from Boar's Hill: a scene I often look on, and never without recalling Jude. 'No,' he said, 'it was my own hill and the lights that Jude saw were mine too.'
>
> I told him that I was staying in Lulworth Castle with Weld Blundell, and asked him if he knew it. 'No,' he said; 'they have not asked me.' I told my host when I returned and he said, 'No; I never dared to ask him.' So I made them meet. Mr and Mrs Hardy came: he very quiet, not speaking much; yet when he left, one who had never met him exclaimed: 'Why, he is even greater than his books.' So strange is it that greatness is something in itself: the high quality of personality. It needs no words in which to express itself, yet can touch the hearts of all who come within its range. Hardy was eager for me to say his poetry; wrote me letters telling me the pieces he thought best. 'They will not find me harsh when you speak my poems. They are not harsh, only inevitable.' But before we had chosen place and time – he would come, of course he would – he died.

Hardy's last letter to her was dated 18 November 1927, less than two months before he died. She had broken a leg and he expressed his sorrow at her suffering.

Hardy was fascinated by acting and while living in London in the 1860s he was a regular visitor to the theatre, a habit which continued through all the many years when he went up to London for the Season. He had tried his own hand at writing plays, an adaptation of *Far from the Madding Crowd* in 1879 and a *Tess* in 1895, but without much success. (See Keith Wilson's *Thomas Hardy on Stage*, London 1995). When in 1908 the Dorchester Amateur Dramatic Society asked him for permission to dramatise some scenes from *The Trumpet-Major* he readily agreed, and for the next sixteen years the Hardy Players, as they came to be called, produced adaptations of Hardy's novels, short stories and *The Dynasts*, or scenes from them. A leading member of the Hardy players was Edwin Stevens (1872–1948), a civil servant who described in a talk on the BBC and then in Monograph No. 61 (1969) his memories of Hardy:

> Hardy's disposition was very reserved until you got to know him well, and then he was a delightful man to talk to, especially if you were able to speak about his beloved Wessex. He objected to receiving anyone who merely wished to make his acquaintance for the purpose of exploiting him. The Americans visiting Wessex for instance never let him alone. . . .
>
> His needs were few and yet for all his philosophy he was happy. He had his work and he enjoyed a talk with an old friend, or even with a new one, if he were a man after his heart. Then his own humour would play fitfully over the surface of the conversation. He loved pottering about his garden or feeding his dog, or on his knees searching for a book on the bottom shelf in his study. His head, (like his friend Barrie's) was his most arresting feature. His handwriting (even when he was over eighty) was wonderful and it was as clear and firm as any young man's, he appeared to enjoy the actual exercise of writing.
>
> Hardy often used to attend rehearsals of our plays and some of the preliminary readings took place at his home, Max Gate. . . .
>
> We respected his confidence and kept silent about many incidents in his life which a number of people would have liked to publicise. For instance, in one of the plays we did there were some old country dances such as he'd witnessed in his childhood days. He helped us by lending us copies of the old musical scores and writing particulars of the figures. At one rehearsal he wasn't at all satisfied with our evolutions, and thereupon he asked one of the ladies to be his

partner, and notwithstanding his age he nimbly showed us the correct steps and positions. For this rehearsal we only had a violinist and as Hardy was dissatisfied with the time as well as the dancing, he took charge of the violin and played the dance for us without a note of music in front of him.

Another play we produced was from *The Return of the Native* with a Mummers' Play introduced into it. These Mummers' Plays used to be performed in Dorset villages many years ago but the custom had practically died out by the time we were doing this play. Hardy supplied the script from his collection. My colleagues and I arranged to visit Mr Hardy at his house the following Christmas and re-produce this Mumming Play just as it used to be done. Naturally it was all pre-arranged and Hardy had invited a few personal friends to be present at his house. We arrived there in costume, carrying old fashioned stable lamps, and after we'd sung one of the very old carols outside the house, I had to knock the front door, in the old traditional style, because I was taking the part of Father Christmas. Hardy answered it himself and I greeted him with the old time phrase, 'Here come I old Father Christmas, Welcome or Welcome not.' He invited us in, and we proceeded with the play in his Drawing room using the Hall as the wings of the stage and his guests being seated at one end.

Those who are intrigued about exactly what was the relationship between Hardy and Florence Dugdale, in the years of their friendship before they were able to marry in 1914, may find something of interest in Netta Syrett's account of a meeting with him in 1909. She was a novelist who died in 1943 and the passage comes from her *The Sheltering Tree* (London 1939, pp. 194–5):

It was while I had those rooms in Buckingham Palace Road that I met Thomas Hardy. His secretary introduced herself to me one day at the Lyceum Club in Piccadilly, and I remember going to dinner at her home somewhere a few miles out of London, and afterwards to some club in the neighbourhood in which her father was interested. On the strength of my acquaintance with his daughter he had written to ask if I would read one of my own short stories there, and in a rash moment I had consented. I recall a badly lighted, dreary little hall, and a very uninspiring audience. But I had been interested previously in what Hardy's secretary told me about her work with the great novelist, for whom she was anxious to find a *pied à terre* in London, and when I mentioned that I should shortly be going to Italy, she asked if I would let my rooms to him. A little later she invited me to tea at the Lyceum Club to meet him.

He was very different from the man I had pictured as the author of *Tess of the D'Urbervilles*. It was a little slight man with a fresh-coloured, rather sad face who was introduced to me – very much taken in hand and 'run', I thought, by the efficient, business-like young woman, the hostess of the occasion, and the future Mrs Thomas Hardy. His first wife was still living at the time.

We spoke of my rooms, which I said I should be more than willing to let to him, though he must, of course, first see whether he liked them, and as he was to be in town for a few days, I asked him and his secretary to Buckingham Palace Road. They came. Hardy seemed pleased with the place and said it would suit him admirably if he should find it possible to live in London for a few months. But of that he was by no means sure.

When we had finished this tentative business discussion I tried to make him talk about interesting people he had known before my day. I remember asking him about the Brownings, and trying to get him to describe them. I confess I found his replies disappointing. He seemed to have no gift for making one *see* the men and women under discussion. But I liked him. He was gentle and simple, and there was no trace in his manner of feeling himself a celebrity.

In talking of *Jude the Obscure*, I said I had always wished the last words in that harrowing story had been spoken by the sympathetic little widow and not by the coarse-grained, horrible Arabella. He replied rather animatedly, 'Well now, it's strange you should say that! I hesitated for a long time whether to give them to her, or to the widow Edlin.' He seemed interested to hear that my mother was a West-country woman, and that I recognized many of the words and phrases she used – generally in fun, but sometimes naturally – in the talk of his country folk. I asked if those words and phrases were still current in the West Country, and he regretfully shook his head. They were fast dying out, he told me. Even the pretty word *maid* for *girl* which my mother often used ('There's a good maid!' 'What's the matter with the maid?') one heard less and less frequently. The language was becoming stereotyped.

Interestingly enough in their *The Second Mrs Thomas Hardy* (London 1979) Robert Gittings and Jo Manton quote just one line from the above and it is to the effect that Netta Syrett found Hardy 'very uninspiring to talk to' (p. 46).

Arthur Compton Rickett (1869–1937), lecturer and writer, had hoped to write a life of Hardy but in a letter of late June 1912 (*CL* IV, p. 221), Hardy made it clear that 'I can lend no assistance to you in writing a book in which you say you want to deal with the more personal side of my novels and verses...' Siegfried Sassoon met Rickett at Max Gate on 27 June 1922 and described him as 'one of the mediocrities of literature'. His recollections of Hardy are published in his *I Look Back* (London 1933, pp. 176–86), and one or two of them are worth quoting:

> Being in the neighbourhood of Dorchester, and encouraged by Hardy's little note of acknowledgment, I called upon him in the summer of 1909, and from that time till the day of his death in 1928 I saw a good deal of him... I well recall the first interview. Though familiar with his photograph, I was not prepared for the Hardy who slid noiselessly into the drawing-room after I had sent in my card. I had expected a bigger man, a man of the scholar type, one whose expression reflected the austere melancholy of his portrait. And here was a little man who looked like a country solicitor, with keen, twinkling eyes and a quietly cordial manner. For a moment a look of fear flashed out. 'You don't want to talk about my books?' Of course I did, but mendaciously I assured him that I didn't. For I quickly divined that the interview would be short and unsatisfactory if I allowed my curiosity full play...
> A thrush broke out into song outside, and the smile faded from Hardy's face. 'An hour before you came,' he said vehemently, 'I saw a horrible sight – a thrush in a cage. Canaries and finches are bad enough, but a thrush! How can people do it? – the cruelty of it!' His eyes blazed with anger, and for the rest of that visit there was little else discussed except the treatment of birds and animals....
> He was obviously delighted at the attitude of the new century towards his verse, which became more laudatory as time went on. The war, which killed many poetic reputations, enhanced his. The very qualities that had disconcerted an earlier generation – the recurrent note of savage irony, the bold experimentalism in form, the questioning of current literary and moral values – these harmonized with the post-war mood. And the younger generation looked up to him as a master and leader. The Victorians laid too much stress on melody. And many of the poets of to-day in their reaction place too little stress upon it, so that what I personally feel to be the weakness of Hardy's poetry is accounted a merit by the younger school...
> Like Tennyson, he seemed hypersensitive to any criticism... And yet the impression of Hardy given by his verse and prose – that of a melancholy and unhappy man, alive for the most part only to the tragedies and ironies of life – was certainly contradicted by any intimate acquaintance with the man himself. In talking to him the humour

that flashes fitfully through his writings was uppermost. He was more often than not, when I saw him, in excellent spirits, full of amusing stories (I wish I had made notes of them), and quicker than the majority to see the humorous side of anything. He was amazingly modest, had nothing of the self-centredness of the literary artist, and if he could keep the talk off himself or his work, would do so. To speak of him as a pessimistic philosopher is absurd. I don't think he had any formulated philosophy of life. He was a highly sensitive man, and as an artist 'more vocal to tragedy than comedy.' There was a melancholy strain in his temperament, of course, as there is in every artist worth his salt; and this was the quality that he could express best in terms of art. For the rest, 'the humorous sadness' defined by Jaques in *As You Like It*, best described his temperamental reaction as a man; and I often wished he had shown more of this jollity and geniality in his work. As it is, there is only half of Hardy in his writings.

I never heard him say an unkind thing about anyone. When the faults of A or B were being discussed by others, and the faults were too obvious to be denied, he was silent. Once when C's character was under discussion and Hardy was appealed to, he merely said: 'He was very kind to me.' There you had it. Anyone who had shown him kindness was immune from personal criticism. His attitude reminded me of Lamb, who said that 'he could never hate any man whom he had once met.'

Another recollection of an Aldeburgh visit (2–5 July 1909) to Edward Clodd is that of Violet Hunt (1862–1942) novelist and journalist, who for a time lived with Ford Madox Ford. The following is from her *The Flurried Years* (London 1926, pp. 67–9):

we went to Aldeburgh to stay with Mr Edward Clodd... We travelled down with Thomas Hardy and Mrs Belloc Lowndes and a small Persian kitten in a basket... After dinner, in that library of the distinguished scientist who was also a sailor, like a ship's cabin with the telescope pointed permanently out of the window, we sat round and talked ghost-stories... Professor Gilbert Murray, not yet absolutely convinced of the survival of consciousness after death, talked philosophically and critically about apparitions. Thomas Hardy told ghost stories just as a Wiltshire peasant might, sitting in the inglenook of an old inn in Shaftesbury with a hand on each knee. He told the story of the Collingwood caul that someone, knowing his *culte* for Nelson, presented to him. It is the skinny membrane found on the heads of some babies at birth and preserved by the nurse for luck. That of Nelson's friend, so preserved, Mr Hardy put on a shelf over his bed, where he could touch it. In the night he heard it moving ... shifting ...

His zest for the macabre was not proof against traditional terrors inculcated at his mother's knee. He returned the caul to the family.

In his soft, low, yet clear, wistful tones, he related his one perennial dream.

'I am pursued, and I am rising like an angel up into heaven, out of the hands of my earthly pursuers.' With a small deprecating laugh, 'I am agitated and hampered, as I suppose an angel would not be, by – a paucity of underlinen.'

It has been impossible to date exactly the meeting mentioned in the following passage from the preface by Somerset Maugham (1874–1965) to his novel *Cakes and Ale* (1930). Lady Jeune became Lady St Helier in 1905, and Maugham had had three very successful plays produced by 1909, so 1910 seems a reasonable guess:

> When the book appeared I was attacked in various quarters because I was supposed in the character of Edward Driffield to have drawn a portrait of Thomas Hardy. This was not my intention. He was no more in my mind than George Meredith or Anatole France. As my note suggests, I had been struck by the notion that the veneration to which an author full of years and honour is exposed must be irksome and to the little alert soul within him that is alive still to the adventures of his fancy. Many odd and disconcerting ideas must cross his mind, I thought, while he maintains the dignified exterior that his admirers demand of him. I read *Tess of the D'Urbervilles* when I was eighteen with such enthusiasm that I determined to marry a milkmaid, but I had never been so much taken with Hardy's other books as were most of my contemporaries, and I did not think his English very good. I was never so much interested in him as I was at one time in George Meredith, and later in Anatole France. I knew little of Hardy's life. I know now only enough to be certain that the points in common between his and that of Edward Driffield are negligible. They consist only in both having been born in humble circumstances and both having two wives. I met Thomas Hardy but once. This was at a dinner-party at Lady St Helier's, better known in social history of the day as Lady Jeune, who liked to ask to her house (in a much more exclusive world than the world of today) everyone that in some way or another had caught the public eye. I was then a popular and fashionable playwright. It was one of those great dinner-parties that people gave before the war, with a vast number of courses, thick and clear soup, fish, a couple of entrées,

sorbet (to give you a chance to get your second wind), joint, game, sweet, ice, and savoury; and there were twenty-four people all of whom by rank, political eminence, or artistic achievement, were distinguished. When the ladies retired to the drawing-room I found myself sitting next to Thomas Hardy. I remember a little man with an earthy face. In his evening clothes, with his boiled shirt and high collar, he had still a strange look of the soil. He was amiable and mild. It struck me at the time that there was in him a curious mixture of shyness and self-assurance. I do not remember what we talked about, but I know that we talked for three-quarters of an hour. At the end of it he paid me a great compliment: he asked me (not having heard my name) what was my profession.

On 7 January 1910 an article entitled 'Some Story-Book People: Thomas Hardy' appeared on p. 18 of *T.P.'s Weekly*. It was written by Constance Smedley (d. 1941), writer, journalist, and editor, who had visited Hardy at Max Gate on 30 August 1907. Although Hardy described her at the time as 'bright and interesting', he took grave offence when more than two years later, without asking his permission, she published an account of her visit. His letter of 14 January 1910 to Clement Shorter, editor of the *Sphere*, reveals how irritated he now can become when he discovers that what was expected to be a social visit was really an 'interview':

Dear Shorter:
   When you want a theme for your literary letter could you not examine the ethics involved in obtaining admission to peoples' houses under false pretences, and then printing patronising impertinences about the inmates? This is suggested to me by an 'interview' in *T.P.s Weekly*, written by a woman who came here ostensibly to ask me to lecture; which contains lies innumerable ... (*CL* IV p. 70)

Was Constance Smedley's sin that she described him as 'born of peasant stock' and reared by his mother in a 'tiny cottage'?

Frank Hedgcock (1875–1954), literary critic and university teacher, was another 'visitor' to offend Hardy. He was first in contact with Hardy when he wrote in 1907 from the University of Paris about a thesis he was writing on the Wessex novels. A visit to Max Gate followed on 28 and 29 July 1910 when Hardy devoted two afternoons to him. At this stage all was harmony, but on receipt of a copy of Hedgcock's *Thomas Hardy: Penseur et Artiste* (Paris 1911) Hardy could not conceal his annoyance, and annotated his copy of the book with such observations as 'This is not literary criticism, but impertinent personality and untrue... All this is too personal, and in bad taste, even supposing it were true, which it is not...' Hedgcock's crime seems to have been using his visit to Max Gate as material in his book and showing how much in Hardy's novels grows out of Hardy's life. It does, of course, but Hardy did not want that area of criticism explored because of his secrecy about certain aspects of his personal life. It was a pity that Hardy's outcry to some extent hid the fact that Hedgcock's was a very intelligent piece of criticism.

Many years later Hedgcock wrote an article called 'Reminiscences of Thomas Hardy' which appeared in the *National and English Review* in October and November 1951. Memories of forty years ago must always be suspect but these read with sufficient authenticity – no implausible words put into Hardy's mouth, for example – that parts of the article earn their place here. It is possible that Hardy allowed Hedgcock to take down notes thinking that this would help him with his university work:

> On Thursday, July 28, I journeyed from London to Dorchester, put up at an hotel and, in the afternoon, walked out to the author's house, Max Gate... The site does more credit to his imagination than the house does to his architectural ability;...
>
> The drawing-room into which I was shown was furnished in Victorian style, with plenty of cushions and a full selection of photographs, scattered here and there. On the walls, if I remember rightly, there were a number of modest water-colours, probably by Mrs Hardy. My host and his wife were awaiting me and I had soon made my introduction.
>
> I was somewhat surprised at the sight of Mr Hardy; though what sort of man I was expecting to see, I cannot recall at this distance of time. Probably it was something that corresponded to the words, 'famous author'. Mr Hardy did not at a first view fill that bill. He was small, looked his age (he was seventy) and appeared to float in his loose-cut tweeds. Shy and diffident in manner, he gave his visitor one glance and turned his eyes away. But, as one observed him more, one was less disappointed. The great dome-like forehead spoke of power and his eyes, though tired, were dreamy and imaginative. His nose, which seemed slightly bent, was beak-like; and the whole face gave the impression of a bird. Above all, one could not help being struck by the simplicity and modesty of this man whose name and works were known far and wide.
>
> Mrs Hardy – I am speaking, of course, of his first wife – was more sure of herself and easier of approach... Her complexion, quite natural, was well coloured and fresh; the mouth and jaw rather heavy and

obstinate. The impression she produced is best conveyed by the word 'Victorian.' She came from what would, in those days, have been called a better social class than her husband; her father was a solicitor and one of her uncles an archdeacon. There was something in her manner which suggested that she did not forget this; one felt she was at least the equal of her celebrated husband...

I sat down and tea was served. Throughout the meal, communications were carried on almost entirely by Mrs Hardy and myself. Hardy said little; only once did he address a word to his wife. That was when he pushed his cup across the table and said, 'More tea, please.' Mrs Hardy spoke of 'our books' and asked which of them I preferred. On my giving an appropriate answer, she enquired whether I did not like some of the early ones. I said I considered *Under the Greenwood Tree* a miniature masterpiece, a naive picture of country life, worthy to hang beside *The Vicar of Wakefield*. I added that there were some beautiful scenes in *A Pair of Blue Eyes*. This pleased Mrs Hardy greatly, as the book has associations with her courtship and marriage. She pronounced it one of *their* finest works and told me she had copied much of the original rough manuscript with her own hand; 'and perhaps slipped in some little emendations' she added with an arch glance in the direction of her husband. But he made no sign...

As soon as tea was finished, Mr Hardy suggested that we should profit by the fine weather and take a stroll in the surrounding country. I said good-bye to Mrs Hardy and he and I left the house. A natural opening for conversation presented itself as we reached the high road and gazed on the extensive panorama. It must be very interesting for him, I said, to have daily before his eyes the sites of which he had made so much use in his novels... Hardy replied that the scene interested him most as a record of history. On it generations long dead had left their mark. Here were barrows, dug by primitive Celts; there an earthwork, built by Britons; near by, a Roman camp: there were the ruins of Norman castles, battlefields where Cavaliers and Roundheads had fought, market-towns which had provided quarters for William III's Dutch soldiers. On those downs by the sea the militiamen of George III had awaited the arrival of Bonaparte. In the distance was a monument to the Hardy who was Nelson's flag-captain at Trafalgar. Everywhere, in ancient churches, countless generations of Wessex folk had met for prayer and praise and had retired to take their long rest in peaceful graveyards. And, reverting to a simile used more than once in his novels, he called the land a palimpsest, on which many a record had been written only to be erased to make place for another...

Mr Hardy was glad that I had mentioned his early poems and connected them with *The Dynasts*. Poetry was his first love and, had it been possible, he would have remained faithful to her all his life; but he had to earn his living and to do that in literature meant writing novels. I asked whether he found the chosen alternative very irksome and the writing of stories very laborious. No, he answered; certainly not in his early years. *Under the Greenwood Tree* had been written in a few weeks and had come almost spontaneously; and even *Far from the Madding Crowd*, a much longer and more complicated piece of work, had not cost him much effort. The scene of the storm, when Gabriel Oak thatched the cornricks (this was in answer to a question of mine) had been written in a night – a night of thunder and lightning, like that described in the book.

But writing a serial was no joke; in order to sustain the interest each instalment had to contain some striking incident; and editors often insisted on alterations to suit the taste or to avoid shocking the susceptibilities of their readers – subscriptions could not be lightly cast away. To be ready with the necessary portion of manuscript at the proper date was often a trial and, when one was ill, a nightmare. He always recalled with a shudder the writing of *A Laodicean*. Critics had said it was one of his weakest works; it was a miracle it was ever completed. Yes, he always made a scheme before he started but left it fluid, so as to be able to insert any developments which suggested themselves. A novel written exactly to plan would be too stiff. He felt that some of his books, e.g. *The Mayor of Casterbridge* and *Tess* were well constructed; but from that point of view the best examples were in his short stories. . . .

I next enquired whether, among the many offspring of his brain, there were any he would call his favourites. He replied that his interests were wholly in poetry now and he looked on his novels almost as belonging to another existence. Moreover, people perhaps hardly realised how glad an author was to have finished a work on which he had toiled for months and be released from bondage to it. He found nothing so boring as re-reading an early edition of a book in order to establish the definitive text. Still, after a lapse of years, one returned, at least in thought, to some early creations with pleasure, birth-pangs having been forgotten. The novel for which he had most affection was *The Return of the Native*; it had a suggestive atmosphere and he thought Clym an interesting and loveable figure, though he had no personal connection with himself. He liked *The Woodlanders* too, more for its trees than its human actors. *The Mayor* moved on with something of the inevitability of fate; he sometimes recalled its scenes in the streets of Dorchester. There was a bustling cheerfulness about *The Trumpet-Major*. Those were the books he preferred. *Tess?* He thought that public opinion was probably right in regarding it as his best novel; but he had put too much feeling into it to recall it with pleasure.

Did he read the novels of his contemporaries? He tried to keep in touch with what was being produced; but, after a certain age, novel-reading was an unsatisfactory business. The saying goes that every man over forty is either a fool or a physician; it might as well have run a fool or a novelist. If one did not know by then how most life-stories would develop, one had not learnt much. H. G. Wells's imaginative tales and dreams of the future always amused him. It was a pity he did not write better. Of real novels he had written only one good one; and though, it seems, it annoyed him to be called the author of *Kipps*, that would probably be his best claim to literary fame.

Meredith? Well, said Mr Hardy, with some hesitation, Meredith was, of course, a fine writer. Some of his stories, *Evan Harrington, Beauchamp's Career*, were well told; though the hero's end in the latter novel was as cruel as anything *he* had done to Tess. In the former, Meredith had made considerable use of his family and the circumstances of his youth; though later he had been extremely reticent about such matters. (Rather an amusing remark, coming from Hardy!) In general, the sequence of the story was confused by the disquisitions and comments of the author. Meredith was a writer to be admired rather than loved. He was more at home in the world of ideas than in that of living men and women. Some of his characters – Sir Willoughby Patterne, for instance – were over-developed, too much explained, to the point of boredom; and his coruscating style dazzled more than it enlightened. He could not help it; that *was* Meredith.

Knowing that Mr Hardy had been very friendly with his fellow-author and had been accustomed to pay him a visit once a year, I asked whether Meredith's conversation was as witty as some of his writing. Mr Hardy smiled and replied that he was always greeted with a display of fireworks, due possibly to the excitement of receiving an old friend, plus some mental preparation for his arrival. But this display died down after an hour or so, after which communications proceeded on a less lofty level. 'No one can be witty for twenty-four hours in the day,' he concluded.

I agreed, but instanced Sydney Smith and Oscar Wilde as talkers who could keep their friends in a state of hilarious excitement for long spells. Mr Hardy accepted the examples as good. Sydney Smith must have been an entertainment in himself, not only for the things he said but for the verve with which he acted scenes and represented persons. As to Oscar Wilde, while admitting that his conversation must have had an extraordinary fascination, he declared that much of his wit was contrived to a formula, the contradictory formula. He would take some well-known saying or an opinion expressed in straight-forward fashion and distort it, to provide the shock of the surprise. Thus the proverb says, 'Never put off till to-morrow what you can do to-day.' Wilde would change this to, 'Always put off till to-morrow what you don't want to do to-day'; or, 'Never put off till to-morrow what you can do the day after.' The unexpected turn delighted the listeners, who would repeat the phrase, possibly incorrectly, to their friends. That formula accounted for half Wilde's aphorisms and, indeed, became a mania with him . . .

I mentioned the name of Henry James. Yes, he read him with pleasure, in spite of the over-subtlety of his psychological analysis and the dryness of his style. It was striking that this man, who had no poetry, no fancy, little humour and certainly nothing spontaneous nor inspired in his writing, could yet produce attractive books. 'I probably like him,' said Mr Hardy, 'because he is the antithesis of myself.' He preferred the shorter novels, those of James's early and middle periods, and instanced *Washington Square*, 'the tragedy of a broken heart.' Here the action was confined practically to four characters, whom we learnt to know from the dialogue, for there was little description. The book was perfectly constructed and moved on smoothly to its inevitable end. *What Maisie Knew* was a clever if somewhat unpleasant study. In the later books the writing was unduly elaborate. James became too fastidious in the choice of words; he thought it inartistic to call a spade a spade or even an agricultural implement. That was probably the influence of his French models, Flaubert, Daudet and others. Had not someone said of France, 'Art is too artful here'? But he (Hardy) preferred the spontaneous irregularities of Shakespeare to the dry precision of Racine.

He did not care for Stevenson and thought him overrated. His stories were often well-written; though there again the admiration for his style – which R. L. S. fully shared – was exaggerated. In any case, the tales, of which *The Master of Ballantrae* was the best, remained tales. Stevenson had not enough experience of life to write for men and women. His books would remain favourites with children, but he did not believe they would be read by adults.

I asked him what he thought of the women-novelists. Hardy thought they were too numerous and had too great a share of public attention, to say nothing of the monetary rewards. Miss Braddon, Mrs Humphry Ward, Ouida, Sarah Grand, Marie Corelli had all written best-sellers. He had forgotten how many thousand copies of Mrs Henry Wood's

East Lynne had been sold, but it was something prodigious. And the book had been refused by George Meredith for Chapman and Hall; and quite rightly; but probably the publishers had been disappointed when they saw its subsequent success. It only showed that a man of Meredith's intelligence and refinement was not the best of readers when it was a question of judging a popular work. The only woman writer for whom he (Hardy) had any respect was Mrs Craigie (John Oliver Hobbes), who was both wise and witty.

All the same he thought that some of these women authors – Rhoda Broughton, for example – had more courage than the men when dealing with the relations between the sexes. If the present movement for the emancipation of women succeeded – and he hoped it would – he fancied the female novelists would go farther still. Sexual relations were very important to them and they would insist on treating them frankly. The conventional prudery of the English on this point had always hampered him; and when, in *Tess* and *Jude,* he had handled them with more freedom than in his other books, what howls of protest had been raised by the reviewers and the public! In *Jude* there were two tragedies; that of Jude, whose attempts to rise to a higher and more intellectual life were frustrated by the sensuality of Arabella; and that of Sue, who attempted to stifle her love for Jude by giving herself to the respectable Phillotson, only to find that the physical contact of marriage with a man she did not love was more than she could face. These two misfits then tried to retrieve their failure by coming together; but conventional morality was too strong for them. Their brave effort ended in disaster. That surely was a tragic theme of modern life, worthy of consideration. His only feeling was that, in adapting his story to the requirements of serial publication, and then trying to restore it to its full statement for volume form, he had blurred the outlines and achieved less than he had hoped. He could have done it better in France! And even in England, especially if the equality of men and women were accepted, the relations between the sexes – the most important of human relations – would have to be treated with greater candour. But, thank goodness, he would not be the one to do it!

On the second day of his visit Hedgcock visited Hardy's Cottage at Higher Bockhampton and mentioned this on arriving at Max Gate in the afternoon:

> The effect of this simple remark on my host was astonishing. He half rose from his chair, supporting himself on its two arms, and, in a state of high nervous tension, stammered out: 'But ... you prom-

ised you would not go into any private matters... and that you would not publish anything... ' He stopped as if unable to express himself further.

I was for the moment taken aback; but, quickly realising that this was only an exhibition of his curious apprehension as regards any curiosity about his origin, I said: 'My visit to Higher Bockhampton was certainly not undertaken with any desire of prying into private matters; and I have no intention of publishing an account of my visit to you. It was only natural that I should wish to see the birthplace of an author to whose work and thought I have given so much time.'...

My opening gambit was *The Dynasts*, for which, I supposed, he had had to undertake very extensive reading. 'Yes,' he replied, 'though you must remember that the subject has been in my mind for many years. I have talked with survivors from Waterloo, both at Chelsea Hospital and in Dorset, and have heard many stories and traditions handed down in country families. I have also visited the battlefield itself. But, when I finally took the subject in hand, there was still much to be done; and not comfortable armchair-reading either, but work at the desk with notebook and pen ready, much like preparing a thesis.'...

For enjoyment, he continued, he nearly always turned now to the Greek classics. He never wearied of Aeschylus and Sophocles. He found the Greeks stimulating and suggestive. They put their thoughts in a way that kindled thought in others. He often laid the book down and pondered what he had just read and, perhaps, linked it to some experience of his own. Sometimes these reflections led to his taking pencil and paper and jotting down suggestions for a poem or even a few lines of verse, to be worked up later. It was a pleasant and fruitful way of passing a morning. Perhaps people did not always realise that, just as a singer would rather sing than listen to a concert or an actor rather act than see a performance by others, so a writer gets more satisfaction from personal creation than from much reading.

Modern poetry? Yes, he saw most of what appeared in the literary reviews and magazines and, if he liked what he read, would procure the collected work of a poet. Since the loss of the great Victorians Tennyson, Browning, Matthew Arnold, Swinburne – poetry had been passing through a dull phase. A revival was overdue, and there were signs of it in the writings of some of the younger men – Walter de la Mare, Laurence Binyon, Wilfrid Gibson, Edward Thomas. He thought some of John Masefield's sea ballads were delightful. There was the tang of the brine in them and the romance of the Spanish Main behind them.

Of contemporary poets, his favourite was A. E. Housman. *A Shropshire Lad* was full of striking things. He quoted, I think, these lines:

> He stood, and heard the steeple
>   Sprinkle the quarters on the morning town,
> One, two, three, four, to market-place and people
>   It tossed them down.
>
> Strapped, noosed, nighing his hour,
>   He stood and counted them and cursed his luck;
> And then the clock collected in the tower
>   Its strength and struck.

In any case, the poem reminded him of an incident in his own youth when, through a telescope from a hillock near his home, he had watched the public execution of a criminal on the roof of Dorchester Gaol, three miles away. It was eight o'clock on a fine summer morning and the sun lit up the front of the prison, the gallows and the doomed man, dressed in white. He had just succeeded in getting the scene focused in his glass when the white figure dropped and disappeared. In that instant a flame of life had been extinguished.

Hardy's interest in the Hardy Players' productions of adaptations of his works is made clear from several recollections of those years. About 1910 Evelyn Evans, daughter of the Players' producer, Alfred Evans, describes how as one of a group of children they met Hardy looking out over the wicket gate at the fields opposite Max Gate. 'He did not even notice us; the slight, erect figure remained motionless at the gate, the blue-grey eyes in the pale wrinkled face focused on the distant scene.' She goes on, 'The Hardys dearly wanted children. The first Mrs Hardy, as I remember her, with mauve satin ribbons waving from her bonnet, used to dismount from her bicycle ... to inspect the Evans perambulator, sighing enviously over each new baby ...' (Monograph No. 17, 1964).

On 2 June 1912, two poets, W. B. Yeats (1865–1939) and Henry Newbolt (1862–1938) called at Max Gate to make a presentation of a gold medal to Hardy on behalf of the Royal Society of Literature. Newbolt preserved that occasion for ever in *The Later Life and Letters of Sir Henry Newbolt* (London 1942, pp. 166–8):

> In the earlier months of 1912 the public became generally aware that a great poet and novelist, who was still among us, would attain his 72nd birthday in June, and the Academic Committee [of the Royal

Society of Literature] perceived that they had an opportunity before them which should not be missed. They had the power, not of offering, but of recommending that the Council should offer to Thomas Hardy a gold medal in recognition of distinguished work on the grand scale. The qualification was a rare one, and the recipients of the gold medal had hitherto been few – I can only think of the names of two – Walter Scott and George Meredith. The Council accepted the Committee's recommendation on April 17th, and sent a formal offer to which Hardy replied that he was surprised to hear of the proposed honour and would accept it with pleasure. On May 8th, when I returned from Italy, it seems to have been decided that the duty of making the actual presentation should be performed by W. B. Yeats and myself at Max Gate, in order to ensure the privacy which Hardy desired...

The date of the birthday being Sunday, June 2nd, he seemed likely to have his wish in this matter: and in fact when Yeats and I reached Dorchester on the appointed day we found a deserted platform and a town without any sign of public interest in the matter we had in hand. At the house we were received by our host and hostess, who told us to our surprise that they had asked no other guests to meet us – our ceremony was to be without witnesses...

The dinner lives in my memory beyond all others unusual and anxious. Mr and Mrs Hardy faced one another the longer way of the table: Yeats and I sat rather too well spaced at the two sides: we could hold no private communication with each other. I had the feeling that I was about to play a card game which I did not know. Hardy, an exquisitely remote figure, with the air of a nervous stranger, asked me a hundred questions about my impressions of the architecture of Rome and Venice, from which cities I had just returned. Through this conversation I could hear and see Mrs Hardy giving Yeats much curious information about two very fine cats, who sat to right and left of her plate on the table itself. In this situation Yeats looked like an Eastern Magician overpowered by a Northern Witch – and I too felt myself spellbound by the famous pair of Blue Eyes, which surpassed all that I had ever seen. We were no longer in the world of our waking lives, and I wondered whether my three companions perceived the fact as I did.

At last Hardy rose from his seat and looked towards his wife: she made no movement, and he walked to the door. She was still silent and unmoved: he invited her to leave us for a few minutes, for a ceremony which in accordance with his wish was to be performed without witnesses. She at once remonstrated, and Yeats and I begged that she should not be asked to leave us. But Hardy insisted and she made no further appeal but gathered up her cats and her train with perfect simplicity and left the room.

Hardy sat down again and asked us to open the business upon which we had been good enough to come. His manner was courteous but not easy – he seemed to have some anxious perplexity upon his mind: as if he too was playing a game and was doubtful of the rules. I was not surprised that he listened uneasily to my little lecture On the Novels of Thomas Hardy – but when I ended and Yeats began his much longer and more remarkable oration, the shadow on his face deepened unmistakably. On and on went Yeats – in his happiest and most serious manner: but the look on Hardy's face was one of apprehension – the ceremony was all but over and he was still dreading the worst.

Yeats ended, drew out the medal and presented it. He did it well and I thought all fear of awkwardness was past: but Hardy sat with the trophy in his hand and dismay still on his face. Then he put his other hand into the tail pocket of his coat and drew out a roll of paper, which he began to smooth out before him. 'I thank you', he said, 'for your kindness: and this is my reply.' We were moved to protest – we genuinely felt that we had caused him nervousness enough already. But he explained that he had a particular reason – he was bound to give us his speech aloud – we were offering to read it later to ourselves – because he had already given a copy of it to the reporters from London. The world would read next morning that he had addressed the Deputation in such and such words and phrases – he could not allow himself to make the falsehood theirs instead of his.

Hardy's speech was recorded in the *Nation* of 20 June 1912 thus:

In accepting it, Mr Hardy remarked that he was rather an old boy to get a medal, and that, unfortunately, he had no boy of his own to whom to pass it on. He added that the distinction was one which he could not fail to value, but he had been led to wonder 'whether prizes of some kind could not be offered to makers of literature earlier in life to urge them to further efforts.'

The sort of efforts Mr Hardy had in mind he proceeded to indicate by dwelling on the need of keeping alive a taste for 'real literature'. In the very spread of the reading habit he saw a growing danger that such a task might be lost. Millions are learning to read but few are acquiring the power to discriminate in their reading. Mr Hardy did not refer so much to the substance of books as to their form. He perceives a marked deterioration in style. As he looks over the field of current publishing he sees 'an appalling increase every day in slipshod writing that would not have been tolerated for one moment a hundred years ago.'

It must have been on the occasion of the Gold Medal presentation that the incident described here by Yeats and extracted from *James, Seumas and Jacques: Unpublished Writings of James Stephens* (pp. 69–70) appears:

> One day – this was in Paris – I asked him what he did about books that were sent to him for signature. He became quite thoughtful about this, and then he became very happy. And then he told me this story:
> He was dining once with Thomas Hardy, and as they were finishing their coffee he asked Hardy the very same question: 'What do you do, Hardy, about books that are sent to you for signature?'
> 'Yeats,' said Hardy, 'come with me, there is something upstairs I want to show you.' At the top of the house Hardy opened a door, and the two poets entered a larger room. This room was covered from the floor to the ceiling with books. Hardy waved his hand at the odd-thousand volumes that filled the room – 'Yeats,' said he, 'these are the books that were sent to me for signature.' [Some exaggeration surely! Ed.]

The following is extracted from an anonymous article in the *English Illustrated Magazine* of June 1912, pp. 276–80, said to have been written by a cyclist:

> The picture he presented was, for the moment at least, all-satisfying; there was more than nervousness in the strangely harassed-looking face, with the most sensitive features that I had ever seen. The deep-set eyes were troubled, but there was no mistaking their fearless courage. I knew that I was looking at a man whose soul was more ravaged than ever his careworn features were with the riddle of life and the tragedy of it, and yet a soul utterly self-reliant, for all the shyness of the outward man.
> I attempted no compliments, and asked him instead why he was so pessimistic a writer, why he wrote at once the most beautiful and the most dreadful of stories, and why he had not shown us far more often than he has done a picture of requited love, or of requited love that was not victimised at once by some pitiless act of fate.
> Mr Hardy had not sat down himself, but had stood by the fireplace, with his white hands holding the lapels of his old-fashioned tweed coat.

We were on better terms in a moment, as Mr Hardy replied, his voice curiously halting, but not as if he was in any doubt of his sentiments. It seemed a mixture of irony and diffidence.

'You are a young man,' he said. 'The cruelty of fate becomes apparent to people as they grow older. At first one may perhaps escape contact with it, but if one lives long enough one realises that happiness is very ephemeral.'

'But is not optimism a useful and sane philosophy?' I asked him.

'There's too much sham optimism, humbugging and even cruel optimism!' Mr Hardy retorted. 'Sham optimism is really a more heartless doctrine to preach than even an exaggerated pessimism – the latter leaves one at least on the safe side. There is too much sentiment in most fiction. It is necessary for somebody to write a little mercilessly, although, of course, it's painful to have to do it.'. . .

Here was one of the most successful of all men, and at a ripe old age still hale and even vigorous. In all his works there is no note of morbidness – only that stinging reminder of fate's cruelty – and it was painful to have to do it. It is this courage that is always demanded of those who dare to write tragedy. And the price he had paid for his courage is written on his brow.

I knew the tenderness of his nature best, perhaps, when he spoke of the passion that we call 'love'. 'Love is tragic,' he said, 'but it is very beautiful.' And few writers have ever made it seem a thing more beautiful than he has. [Hardy has written 'partly faked' against this article in his scrapbook.]

An article entitled 'Tale of a Chimney Pot' written by Leonard Patten (1867– c. 1945) was published in the *Dorset Year Book* 1940–1 (pp. 78–83). On 9 October 1912 he was sitting in the garden of Hardy's Cottage at Higher Bockhampton working on a pencil drawing when Hardy cycled along the lane and came and stood by his side. Patten tells us:

When he stood at my side, I gladly granted a polite request that he might see what I was doing. It gave me great pleasure when this unlooked for visitor said 'I think you have caught the spirit of the old place capitally, but I want to see a slight alteration, or addition, I should say to your sketch, and that is the placing of another chimney pot on the middle stack. The second one at the back has only lately been taken down.' I made the suggested addition of course at once. 'Now that looks more like home to me. Thank you,' the speaker said. I replied 'and that is by special request of Mr Thomas Hardy I am sure.' . . .

Knowing my name... Mr Hardy then asked me if I was related to the manager of the Dorsetshire Bank who was at Portland years ago. I said that he was my father who opened the branch at Fortune's Well in the 'Isle of Slingers', and then Mr Hardy kindly enquired in those well-known words – and I thought how finely they came from him:–

'Is your father well....' 'Is he still alive?'

I replied that both my father and mother were in good health and living in Bournemouth. They often speak of you I added, and my father has told me that he had the unique privilege, and at your special request of being the first admittedly unprofessional reader of your first novel, which was I understood *The Poor Man and the Lady*. Mr Hardy said this was indeed true, and he well remembered it, but naively remarked that the doubtful 'privilege' could have given little satisfaction he feared, and, playing with the criticism of the MS by a subsequent well-known publisher's reader, he quite agreed that 'it was indeed a very curious performance' and had more *'Stuff* than purpose in it.' We had quite a long talk, and though 'easier to know man in general than men in particular' – I almost wrote perticler – I recalled that it was not a first meeting. Mr Hardy was amused when I told him that years ago when a very small boy – 'you must have been,' said T. H. – I remember you at a wedding of Miss Dora Cosens – I believe you were best man – and you had a dark beard. I disliked beards very much – then so fashionable – but this facial growth conjured up dark deeds, Blue Beard and Co! in my infant mind, and though this was somewhat relieved by the possibility of a share in the cake before me – I was a bit afraid of you! 'You are not afraid *now* I hope?' said Mr Hardy with a smile. Well, I am not sure about that I replied – for you are *famous*.

Douglas Goldring (1887–1960), lecturer, writer and novelist has this interesting story to tell about Hardy at one of Ford Madox Ford's parties:

... I remember seeing a little, quiet, grey old man wearing a red tie, who turned out to be Thomas Hardy. I was standing next to Hugh Walpole at the back of the room, when he was pointed out to me. The conversation among the lion cubs in our neighbourhood was no doubt very brilliant and very 'literary' but suddenly there came the usual inexplicable hush. It was broken by Hardy who, turning to an elderly lady by his side, remarked, with shattering effect, 'And how is Johnny's whooping-cough?'

(From *South Lodge*, London 1943, p. 33)

This is an amusing example of Hardy's ability to undercut pomposity and to laugh silently at the pretentious pseuds who surrounded him on that occasion, and presumably on many other occasions during his visits to London.

Hardy's sister, Mary (1841–1915), was born only a year after Hardy and they were very close to each other. She probably understood him as much as anyone. The following letter to 'Cousin Gus', (Augustus Hardy (1839–1916), son of James, Hardy's father's older brother) says something about Mary's insight into Hardy's character:

> My dear Cousin Gus,
> I enclose you a copy of the inscription which Tom has put up in Stinsford Church to the memory of our Grandfather, your Father and our Father. I thought you would like to have it as your Father's name is mentioned and as you know the Church and the road they took to go to it every Sunday, after having worked very hard all the week. People in those days used to work harder than they do now, don't you think so? The inscription on the brass is simply in Latin. The English words underneath which I send to you are that you may see exactly how it stands. I would rather it had been an English inscription and no Latin and I dare say you would also, but you know how fond Tom is of books and languages and I think he could not feel satisfied unless there was some show of learning in this. He said it was not necessary for every stranger to be able to read it.
> (Letter dated March 1912)

Mary's translation of the wording on the memorial brass in Stinsford church reads:

> A sacred monument to the memory of Thomas Hardy the father, of James and Thomas the sons, who formerly in this church for forty years (from 1802 to 1841) performed the office of violinist. Thomas, Henry, Mary, Katharine, the sons and daughters of the junior Thomas, caused (this) to be placed (here) 1903.

Arthur Christopher Benson (1862–1925) was a man of letters who introduced himself to Hardy by sending him in 1892 a copy of a book of verse he had written. He became a Fellow of Magdalene College, Cambridge, and from 1915 until his death he was the College Master. He was conceited, a snob, did not like women, defective in literary judgement, and kept a diary which eventually totalled four million words. Your editor has not read them all. Cambridge University conferred an Honorary Degree of Doctor of Letters on Hardy in 1913 and he was made an Honorary Fellow of Magdalene College later that year. There is an interesting account in his diary of a visit with Edmund Gosse to Max Gate on 5 September 1912 and some extracts follow. For this reading of Benson's very difficult handwriting I am indebted to Ann Thwaite:

> We made our way out among the neat villas and suburbs – at the very end of the town where it melts with the country, there appeared a little hedged and walled plantation – Max Gate – with a red house dimly visible, bordered by turnip-fields. We descended at the gate and made our way by a winding little drive to a small gravel sweep, all ill-kept, at the door of the house. It is a structure at once mean and pretentious, with no grace of design or detail, and with two hideous low flanking turrets with pointed roofs of blue slate. In the vestibule a frightful ornament of alabaster, three foliated basins tiara-like with doves drinking and a little notice appended in firm writing that it is to be 'Dusted not touched.' There was a smell of cooking all about. A tiny maid took us into a rather nice drawing-room with a bow window, with many pictures and ornaments and a large portrait of Hardy. Here was a small, pretty, rather mincing elderly lady with hair curiously puffed and padded rather fantastically dressed. Gosse took her by both hands and talked to her in a stream of exaggerated gallantry which was deeply appreciated. A solid plebian over-dressed niece was presented. Then Hardy came in – very small and lean and faintly browned. His features are curiously worn and blurred and ruinous. He has a big rather long head, bald, with thin longish hair at the back, fine expressive brows and rather lustreless dark eyes. One would take him for a retired half-pay officer, from a not very smart regiment. He greeted Gosse very warmly and me cordially, and enquired sedulously after our health complimenting us on our looks, as if discharging a natural courtesy. Presently we went into lunch. It was hard to talk to Mrs H. who rambled along in a very inconsequent way, with a bird-like sort of wit, looking sideways and treating one's remarks as amiable interruptions.
> Lunch was long and plentiful – rather coarse fare ... Hardy offered claret and rose on each occasion to pour it in my glass. ... Two wholly unsatisfactory portraits of Hardy, one a Herkomer – giving him a solid almost sleek air, whereas really he looks very frail, worn and thin. He was carefully dressed, with a tie curiously chosen to carry on the line and pattern of his coat.
> Mrs H. produced cigarettes – Hardy said he never smoked, but Gosse playfully insisted that Mrs H. should have one. She said she had never smoked, but lit a cigarette and coughed cruelly at intervals, every now and then laying it down and saying 'There that will be

enough' but always resuming it, till I feared disaster. Hardy looked at her so fiercely and scornfully that I made haste to say that I had persuaded my mother to smoke. ...

After lunch we went out into the garden, ... Hardy sat on a little bench in the sun and talked freely and amiably. He told me how Cockerell of the Fitzwilliam had asked him for a MS, and when he suggested that C. should choose, C. contrived to carry away *all* the MSS, and to give them to various museums & c. These MS were not drafts, however. Hardy said he wrote his first drafts on scraps of paper, altered them and then copied them fair for the printers destroying the first draft and corrected the proofs a good deal – 'I hope they won't lay hands on the corrected proofs' he said. What vexed him was that it had been announced in the papers that Mr Hardy was presenting his MSS to various museums. 'What a conceited attitude to take up!' he said. He mentioned the same thing to Gosse afterwards and said that he didn't regard the *value* of the MSS. He had no children and enough money for his wants...

It was intensely interesting, but it gave me rather a melancholy impression; the poor house, uncomfortable and rather pretentious, in its close plantation, airless and dark, like a house wrapped up and put away in a box, the crazy and fantastic wife, the stolid niece didn't seem the right background for the old rhapsodist, in the evening of his days. It gave me a sense of something intolerable the thought of his having to live day and night with the absurd, inconsequent, huffy, rambling old lady. They don't get on together at all. She confided to Gosse once that they were always squabbling. 'I beat him!' she said. Gosse said that it was very improper, so she added, 'only with the *Times* rolled up.' Today she told Gosse that he was more difficult to live with than ever, so inflated with his greatness that he wouldn't let her have a motor, and would accept no honours except what he could keep to himself. This referred to the O.M. and the fact that he had refused a knighthood. The marriage was thought a misalliance for her, when he was poor and undistinguished, and she continues to resent it.

He is not agreeable to her either, but his patience must be incredibly tried. She is so queer, and yet has to be treated as rational, while she is full, I imagine, of suspicions and jealousies and affronts which must be half insane. She must be a singular partner for a man interested in a feminine temperament; and they neither of them seemed at all content, and he waiting stolidly for destiny to declare itself – the thought which lies behind all his books. One would like to have seen him in some little stone-built manor at the foot of the downs, in a happy circle, with children about him. He seems a kindly and courteous old man, with a mild rusticity not very far from the surface, interested in life in a remote way, and with little power of expressing sympathy or of saying what is really in his mind. That is a rustic trait, too. The suspiciousness of the rustic, the idea that he must guard himself, not give himself away – like his own Wessex labourers who, as Gosse said Hardy had told him, would see you pass and greet you with respect and make fun of you when you had gone. There is something secret and inscrutable about him, I think.

But their kindness and courtesy today was great. Gosse is a very old friend, and they gave me a very cordial welcome for his sake and entertained us very gladly.

It is a pity that demands of space will not permit the printing in full of both Benson's and Gosse's account of that visit to Max Gate on 5 September 1912. It would provide evidence, if any evidence were needed, of how some interviews tell us almost as much about the interviewer as the interviewee. Gosse for all his weaknesses was so much nicer a man than Benson, and *he* liked Hardy. I am indebted to Ann Thwaite's *Edmund Gosse: A Literary Landscape* (London 1984) for the information that their friendship began when they met for the first time in the winter of 1874. It was a friendship that lasted, with just an occasional hiccup, for fifty-three years until Hardy's death in January 1928, to be followed only four months later by that of Gosse. Hardy had a genuine affection for Gosse, and Gosse had a great admiration for Hardy and never doubted his greatness even if, when reviewing *Jude*, he posed the question, 'What has Providence done to Mr Hardy that he should rise up in the arable land of Wessex and shake his fist at his Creator?' (*Cosmopolis*, January 1896, pp. 60–9). Although Gosse is critical in the following extracts from his account of the visit with Benson, there is a warmth and objectivity which Benson lacks:

Today, I took Arthur Benson in his motor to visit Thomas Hardy. A dark cold morning, with a shrewd wind that reddened our faces. . . .
We flew through Cerne Abbas, and the Chalk Man, strongly drawn on the hillside, naked, unabashed, the Man that Caesar saw as we see him leaned above us in his colossal nudity, symbol of the fertile earth, of dim inconceivable horrors of primal worship. Through Dorchester we race, Dorchester with its prettiness, its dapper air, thrown like a modern dress over the ancient force of its members. As we approach Max Gate, all semblance of age ceases; here is the twentieth century unashamed, its railway lines, its mean useful buildings, its painful vision of the new Benthamism, cheap and tame and commonplace. . . .

We are received, as though unexpected, by a bewildered maid. In the drawing-room, a pleasant, slovenly place crowded with incongruous objects, Emma Hardy greets us with effusion, absurdly dressed, as a country lady without friends might dress herself on a vague recollection of some nymph in a picture by Botticelli. So long we waited, that I remonstrated, 'But Tom expects us?' 'Oh yes, he has been talking about your visit all the morning.' At last the great man appears, grown, it seems to me, very small, very dry, very white. He greets me with a tempered affection, Benson with a reserved graciousness. His eyes are smaller than ever, drawn with fatigue down deeper between the thin pencilled eyelids. The hair has almost wholly worn away from the forehead, the moustache, once yellowish red, has faded into pallor, it is like the sparse whiskers of some ancient rodent, a worn-out squirrel for instance. The almond shape of the head, rapidly arching above, and as rapidly arching to the small, almost pointed chin, is more pronounced than ever. The thin lips tremble a little, not from age so much as from an excess of introspection. One would say that under that cover of extensive leafage, he had grown pallid and bloodless. The eyes wake up, and seem to peer out into space. Very gently, with a soft, toneless voice, he talks, at first uneasily, then fluently, with an exquisite simplicity, with no parade or self-assertion, without curiosity, of things at hand.

Benson, who had only seen him in company, expected once more to find him distrait and silent. On the contrary, he talked with instant effusion, mainly about Wessex, about places and houses, without the least affectation, of his own associations, and with reference to his own books...

The texture of his own old novels occupies him still. He spoke to me of having just been re-reading *Desperate Remedies;* he spoke as if it were some book written a long time ago, by someone who was no longer of much importance. 'A melodrama, of course,' he said; 'but better as a story than one would think. Have you read it lately? Don't you think, just as a story it is rather good? Of course, I put all that in just in obedience to George Meredith. He said there must be a story. I did not care. The first book of all had no story at all. There was just the Woman interest. It is amusing to me that I thought I knew so much about women. I was so confident about it, knew exactly what they felt and what they wanted. That was what struck Meredith, with the Woman interest in the book. But he said it would never do, so I tore it all up. The other day I found I had kept three or four pages of it; I think they must have been the worst, they were dreadfully bad. But about Women; I wonder how I came to write like that. Now I know them better, I should write just the same. I think I must be right – the women always hate it so. But I have said it all best in the poems, I suppose. I don't know; it is all so far away.'

And *he* seemed far away. We stayed two hours and a half. He was much brightened up by our visit, one could see that. His eyes were now wide open, a little red on his cheeks, the skin less puckered and parchment-like, as he waved farewell to us from the doorstep. He had been, for him, quite affectionate to me when we two were sitting alone in the garden; he talked then of our protracted friendship, of little incidents of more than thirty years ago. But one needs to have known him long to perceive that he is moved at all. He is so hushed, so irresponsive, so gently immobile. Old age has not, however, made him feeble; he seemed brisk and well, without any species of malady or incommodity. But it has accentuated his inwardness, his incapacity for any expression that is not quite superficial and unexcited. He remains, what he has always been, a sphinx-like little man, unrelated, unrevealed, displaying nothing that the most affectionate solicitude can make use of to explain the mystery of his magnificent genius.

(reprinted from Ann Thwaite's
Portraits from Life, London 1991)

Stewart M. Ellis (d. 1933) was a writer of literary and historical articles and books. The following is taken from an article in the *Fortnightly Review* (March 1928, pp. 393–405):

I first met Thomas Hardy in 1913, when I was living at Southwold, in Suffolk. A near neighbour there at that time was Mrs Arthur Henniker, the daughter of Monckton Milnes (Lord Houghton), herself a writer, and a very valued friend of Hardy, who addressed to her a long series of letters wherein, I understand, he gave free vent to the whimsical humour which was one of his characteristics, a trait quite unknown to the world outside his intimate circle, the world which, quite wrongly, believed him to be a melancholy pessimist. In April, 1913, then, Hardy, accompanied by Miss Florence Dugdale (who became his wife ten months later), paid a visit of a week or so to Florence Henniker at Southwold House. My mother and I were invited to meet them at luncheon. There were no other guests, as Mrs Henniker most kindly desired that I, as a young writer with then but one book to his name, should have the opportunity for a prolonged conversation with Mr Hardy. I remember it was a very long lunch, lasting from two until four o'clock, based on the generous profusion of a vanished Victorian menu. Which reminds me that Hardy was indifferent to food, and quite unaware of what kind of wine he might be drinking. In later years Mrs Hardy told me how on one occasion when her husband was ill a friend sent a case of fine champagne, and in jest she asked: 'How do you like this brand of cyder?' To which he replied: 'It's very nice, but rather drier than what we usually have.'

At the conclusion of Mrs Henniker's luncheon I, no doubt rather presumptuously, invited Mr Hardy to come over and see me on the following morning. He accepted, duly arrived, and stayed for over two hours. My old home, Hill House, possessed something which interested him very much. It was a house built and added on to at various dates, one wing having been the ancient Custom House of Southwold; and here, in the cellars, were two small prison cells which had been used in the late eighteenth century for the detention of smugglers after arrest, pending their removal to the gaols of Yarmouth or Ipswich. This little link with the period ever nearest to Hardy's heart, the years of England's great conflict with Napoleon, to the episodes of which he had given such magnificent expression in *The Dynasts* a few years earlier, led him to speak much of the dramatic picturesqueness of life in our grandfathers' era as seen from our retrospective angle of vision – for I doubt if either the incarcerated Suffolk smugglers or the soldiers of the Peninsular War had any conception that they were formative figures of romance: rather did they only curse at their ill-luck and hardships. Our conversation naturally passed on to historical romance in the form of fiction, and I was delighted to find that he had a great admiration for that best of historical romancers, William Harrison Ainsworth, whose biography was the one and only book I had at that date written. Mr Hardy said that Ainsworth was the most powerful literary influence of his boyhood, and *Old St Paul's* his favourite romance, so much so that when he paid his first visit to London as a boy of nine, in 1849, he procured a map of the City, marked out all the streets, lanes, and purlieus described by Ainsworth, and then made a personal tour, first going to Wood Street, thence following the movements of Leonard Holt as depicted in the story. In later years Hardy liked Ainsworth's *Windsor Castle* very much, and he said the unexplained mystery of Herne the Hunter was most artistically treated. . . . .

Rather curiously, in view of his liking for the romances of Ainsworth and G. P. R. James, Hardy did not much care for those of Walter Scott and R. L. Stevenson. In fact, for the latter he had no inclination at all. He considered Stevenson overrated, and could no more finish a story of his than he could *The Egoist* of George Meredith. *Old Mortality* was also a story he found it difficult to get through, and he thought Scott was at his best in the novels with English settings, such as *Kenilworth* and *Peveril of the Peak*. It cannot be that Hardy disliked Scotch romances, for he had greatly enjoyed in his youth the now almost forgotten James Grant, particularly *The Scottish Cavalier*, with its artistic presentation of the sadly fickle Annie Laurie. Mr Hardy said this was also one of the books which had influenced his imagination in boyhood; and when I told him that James Grant was living at No 25 Tavistock Road, Westbourne Park, at the time he himself was near by at Porchester Road in 1872 and 1874, Mr Hardy said he wished he had known, so that he might have seen Grant and expressed his admiration in person. . . .

Some of Mr Hardy's later opinions concerning contemporary writers that I remember include his intense admiration for A. E. Housman's *Shropshire Lad*, and his dislike for Mr Garnett's *Lady into Fox*, which he thought stupid. The works of Miss Sheila Kaye-Smith – described by some of her admirers as 'The Hardy of Sussex' – he considered clever, and her descriptions of peasant life imaginative, but not based on personal acquaintance with the subject. He laughed about one of her farmers dressed in a smock. He said such a thing hardly was to be seen even in his own youth: labourers, of course, wore smocks, but not their master-farmers.

On one occasion I asked him what kind of wife he imagined Fancy Day, in *Under the Greenwood Tree*, would turn out in the future. He replied: 'I don't quite know. We had better draw a veil over her; and yet I have known women of her type turn out all right, some of those early examples of independent schoolmistresses included.' I also asked him about the old superstition of the Key and the Bible mentioned in *Far from the Madding Crowd*, and he said the girl's garter was tied about the key, and both were placed hard against the text chosen; and if impress from the Bible type was made upon the light garter it was presumed to be an omen that the suitor was the right man and that he should be accepted . . .

I look back to a very memorable visit to Max Gate on Michaelmas Day, 1922, a lovely autumnal day. On leaving, Mr and Mrs Hardy walked with me by the field route to Dorchester station, not forgetting 'Wessex' [his dog], who provided vocal noise. The distance must be quite a mile, but Hardy, though then eighty-two years of age, walked along as quickly and actively as a boy, talking humorously the while. On reaching a bridge over the railway line, I said goodbye and proceeded to the station some distance away. My train left quite a quarter of an hour later and passed under the same bridge I have mentioned. By a fortunate inspiration I looked out of the carriage window, and there was Mr Hardy still waiting on the bridge and waving a final adieu. It was an incident that touched me greatly, and I am glad to say Mrs Hardy wrote to me later: 'My husband saw your final wave to him out of the carriage window. I was amazed you could see him on the bridge as the train passed beneath.'

Hardy would have enjoyed meeting Ellen Glasgow (1874–1945) the American novelist, regarded as one of her country's greatest regional writers. She visited Hardy in June 1914:

> Early in June I spent some unforgettable hours with Thomas Hardy and his fine young wife, to whom he owed the subdued tranquillity of his later years. My friend Louise Collier Willcox was with me, and, in response to an invitation from Mrs Hardy, we drove out from Dorchester to tea at Max Gate. The afternoon was brilliant with one of those rare English days in which heaven appears to touch the earth. Our reception was charming, and I had no difficulty in hearing Hardy's voice. Somewhat to my surprise, for I had heard that he could not be made to speak of his work, Hardy talked to me, freely and frankly, about his books. His poetry would outlive his novels, he believed, and he gave the impression of caring little for the Wessex Tales, which had brought him fame. He did not hesitate to say that he considered *The Dynasts* his greatest work (he may have said 'best') and he was pleased when he found that I had read it all, and was able to repeat from the 'Semichorus of the Years':
>
>> O Immanence, that reasonest not
>> In putting forth all things begot,
>> Thou build'st Thy house in space – for what?
>
> Hardy smiled. 'Not many have read that.' His reticence was attractive to me, for it made whatever he said well worth the saying. He was small in stature, and, unlike so many other old men, especially old men of letters, he was immaculately neat in his appearance. His face was small and worn to sharpness, but the skin was singularly clear, with a tinge of red of the cheekbones; and in both his expression and his manner there was the quality of wistfulness, as if he wished to be kind, but was not quite sure he was going about it in the right way.
> I told him I thought 'A Blinded Bird' the most beautiful of his shorter poems. He replied that he liked it, too, and that it was written to a real bird...Of all the human beings I have known, none could have been more natural or less pretentious. From the beginning, it was easy to reach an understanding. In our philosophy of life we soon touched a sympathetic chord; for he told me that he also had suffered all his life over the inarticulate agony of the animal world. 'I

have often wondered,' he added, with that wistful smile, 'whether I'd choose the lot of a wild or of a domestic animal; and I think, all things considered, I'd choose the lot of the wild.'

His wire-haired terrier Wessex, afterwards famous in literary biography, never left his side, except to jump up in a chair at the table when tea was brought in. He was a very attractive little dog, not yet a year old, and as his master remarked, affectionately, 'always ready for his tea.' As we drove away from the house, in the late afternoon, I looked back and saw Hardy standing in the doorway with Wessex in his arms.

(from *The Impenetrable Wall*)

These were the years of the First Great War and Hardy's sympathy with those who were called upon to serve in the forces manifested itself in his readiness to grant hospitality to any who found themselves stationed near Dorchester and wished to call on him. A Private Reginald L. Ball of the RAMC left notes of his visit to Max Gate on 16 September 1915. Hardy soon made him feel at ease, 'he was quiet and interested so that my diffidence vanished', and on his departure presented him with a signed copy of *The Trumpet-Major*. The most informative of these accounts of visits to Max Gate are those of Elliott Felkin, an officer on the staff of the Prisoners of War Camp at Dorchester. He had been to Cambridge, was, according to Florence Hardy, brilliant and pleasant, and was such a good conversationalist that he was invited to come again. Felkin recorded in a contemporary journal at least six visits to Max Gate in the year 1918–19. He went on to serve as an international civil servant with the League of Nations and the United Nations and died in 1968. The following passages are extracted from an article in *Encounter*, April 1962:

October 21st, 1918
Tea with the Hardys – Mrs Hardy and a man called McDougall and his wife, the author of a book just published on 'Realism', and myself. Thomas Hardy in better spirits than last time and amazingly lively, interested and interesting. A long discussion arising out of McDougall's book on whether there could be such a thing as scientific treatment in a novel. Hardy said that all imaginative work was events seen through a temperament. That unconscious or conscious selection by the personality of the author must colour the work. I instanced Flaubert as a man who attempted to get at the events in themselves but who so definitely had a point of view – and McDougall, who has apparently made a study of Flaubert in his book, agreed. Hardy said he found from experience that one could suppress one's feelings deliberately,

but even so one knew that one was still exaggerating personality in the selection of what was significant, in fact that what was to anyone significant was a kind of projection of personality. McDougall said he supposed that the difference between Art and Life was that in Art one always was selecting, while in Life one had to take what came along.

June 25th, 1919

Hardy on Sunday said that he liked owls; they were such philosophical birds; fell into chimneys and forgot where they were and so did not get away before a fire was lit and they were burned.

June 30th, 1919

Max Gate yesterday. —— was not there and we had as usual a delightful tea with Hardy and Mrs Hardy alone.... He said of George Eliot that she was not a story-teller, and he would range her with Goethe and Kant rather than with Shakespeare or Sophocles. (I'd quoted Acton's opinion.) He said she was such a neglected writer.

I asked him what the big house standing back on the road was, and he said it was Henchard's house in *The Mayor of Casterbridge.* At the time there was a hot-headed town clerk in Dorchester called Giles, and he nearly called Henchard Giles, and then it struck him how awful it would be and everyone would think he intended the town clerk, so he changed it to Henchard. Mrs Hardy said Henchard suited better.

Hardy said that at one time he had as a youth all sorts of writings and then he got a clear handwriting by making as few strokes as possible in order to make each letter recognisable...

He said that great ladies, *e.g.* Lady Portsmouth, had so often told him that they longed to get out of the racket of a London society whirl to a quiet and simple life. But he supposed they perhaps only said it to please him.

Of Browning he said that he used to come in to Mrs Procter and talk social backchat and gossip in an ordinary way 'as if he did not at all know what life was really like, like the butcher's son.' He hazarded the theory that Browning wrote *Easter Eve,* etc., in order to make his book sell.

He takes a delightful view of Meredith. 'He goes on all right and then just when he might put in a touch of pathos he doesn't do it. I wonder he didn't know better.' And on another occasion – 'Meredith's characters are like flowers in a garden. But when you come to look at them closely you see that they are all made of jewels; *they never fade.'*

One day Goldie and [E. M.] Forster and I went up to tea and we discussed Arthur Waley's poems. Hardy thought they lost so much in not being rhymed and compared them to another book of translations that he had been reading, which Mrs Hardy brought at once, as usual.

He said that day, too, I remember, how words got hold of people and coteries and circulated like microbes and then disappeared again. . . .

When I went Hardy came out for a little walk with the dog. We turned our money at the sight of the new moon 'in case,' and then talked about poetry. Hardy was in a very cheerful mood and ran along the road a little way to make 'Wess' run.

Hardy rolled about on the sort of 'umpty' with gestures and vivacity of a young man. I have never seen an aged face which becomes so animated and in which the eyes are so bright and piercing. —— seemed by his side so old and sedate and settled and with the 'Young man, I have had the experience and made a fairish success of my life, believe me' kind of attitude – so absolutely lacking in Hardy, who has the capacity . . . of treating young people not as if you were pretending to make yourself young out of politeness, nor as if you were instructing or guiding by the wisdom of experience, but as if you really felt that age and youth had something to give each other. In that way age and youth don't sympathise with each other, if they do anything they envy each other. The point is that there is mutuality, no superiority implied or felt on account of years and maturity or on account of youth and vigour. I should like to be like that when I am old.

July 21st, 1919

To Max Gate yesterday to tea. Hardy in very good spirits, lively and excited. We talked a good deal about Browning, as I had been reading the privately printed letter about Mrs Browning's death. He said he often used to meet Browning at Mrs Procter's but he never saw him alone and never heard him talk anything but small talk. He likes best of his poems 'The Statue and the Bust' because it has the characteristic of all great poetry – the general perfectly reduced in the particular. 'Procrastination, that's what it is, and there's nothing to be said about procrastination that is not in that poem.'. . .

Talking about time, he said that he always saw it stretch away in a long blue line like a railway line on the left (the past) and disappearing just round the crossing on his right. 'It's like a railway line covered with a blue haze, and it goes uphill till 1900 and then it goes over the hill and disappears till it rises again up to about 1800, and then it disappears altogether.'

He went on to talk about days of the week and colours and associations. Monday was colourless, and Tuesday a little less colourless, and Wednesday was blue – 'this sort of blue' pointing to an imitation Sèvres plate – and Thursday is darker blue, and Friday is dark blue, and Saturday is yellow, and Sunday is always red...

August 10th, 1919

On Friday I went up to Max Gate... I thought we might (Hardy and I) have gone over to see the little temple at the Hanburys, but it was hot and he was tired, so we sat and had tea. Hardy *was* tired and not in very good spirits at first. He talked a lot about Swinburne; said he was such a gentle, unselfish, naive and charming creature. Mrs Hardy had put the question whether great men were not perhaps quite different from the general estimate, *e.g.* Meredith, not worldly and socially ambitious.

Hardy talked about Shelley; said he was the only man whose steps he had ever cared to trace, and suggested I should go and see Millicents, Bread Street, where P. B. S. and Mary were married. It was in exactly the same state now as then. He agreed what a delightful person Shelley must have been. He showed me the first edition of Godwin's *Political Virtue*, and we wondered whether some pencilled notes in it could have been by Shelley, and compared it with some MSS....

Mrs Hardy said the funniest letter they had ever had was addressed 'To the Poet Laureate, England', and on the envelope was written 'Try Mr Thomas Hardy'. We laughed to think of the number of names that had got on to it like that before Bridges received it. We talked about Poet Laureates and how Tennyson kow-towed, and did receive 'laurels greener from the brows of him who uttered nothing base,' and Hardy said it would be hampering to be Poet Laureate, and that 'one's works would sell less on account of the prejudice.'

August 13th, 1919

Up to tea with Hardy. We talked over tea about publishers. He spoke more than ever before about himself and his work probably because we were alone together. He said he did not know which of his stories he liked best. He did not give up architecture until he was certain of a living from writing. His first two books were anonymous, and no one knew who had written them. Architecture, though a good profession, did not tax the brain as writing did. He used to give little literary lectures as all the apprentices did at Sir Arthur Bloomfield's [*sic*], instead of doing their work, and he said in one of them that he would not have the reputation of Dickens for anything. He did not in the least care about novelists. He had always thought he ought to be a poet. He had always meant to write poems, and he found later that, as a poet, one was much freer, one did not have to write a story for some particular magazine and then adapt one's story to the readers of the paper. He showed me a little book of twenty-three new poems. Then he wondered whether he should state that one of the poems in his collected works was in sapphics. He said he often wrote verse in sapphics, but intentionally not quite correct – a bad thing to do, he said, because then people thought he did not know what sapphics were. We looked at Swinburne's poem in the first volume of *Poems and Ballads*, which Hardy said he had imitated from Omar, only it was a pity that he had rhymed the unrhymed lines in one quatrain with the unrhymed line in the next quatrain. He said all the old French story at the beginning was entirely invented by Swinburne. Everyone thought it came from an old MS!

Then we walked over to Stinsford together... He showed me the old path boundary and the double hedge, both of which must be hundreds of years old. Then he took me into the churchyard, and showed me the tombs of his family and of his first wife, and asked me about the pediment and inscription which he had altered. As he talked about it and her his voice became quavery, and there were tears in his eyes, and all the time we were round the spot he lost the thread of what he was saying...

Then we went into the church and he pointed out the old Norman pieces and the good arches, and where the old choir loft joined into the arch, and exactly where Lady Susan lies buried, the tablets having been mixed up when the church was restored. It is really just under the tablet to the right. Then he showed me the monument of Laura Pitt; and exactly where he used to sit, on the inside next to the wall, being a little boy, and just under the carved skeleton; and said how, as the afternoon service went on and there were only the two candles in the pulpit, he used to get so frightened, looking up into its jaw.

Then we looked at the tablet he had put up to his grandfather and his uncles who had 'fiddled in this church forty years' – '*Fidicicis munere sunt perfuncti per annos quadraginta.*' He said he had not put it in Latin out of affectation but because he did not like the idea of trippers and strangers whom he did not wish to know the meaning of it, to come there during his lifetime and put it in the papers. Didn't I think that a good reason?

Then we walked back very slowly, and he seemed so tired and exhausted and tottering that I wondered how he would get back. But he talked all the time about the town and his life.

Hardy said of course in writing one had to keep up the immense illusion. In one's heart of hearts one did not of course *really* think one's heroine was as good and pure as all that, but then one was making out a case for her before the world.

He said he found that writing verse helped one to write prose, and that paradoxically, verse was the best prose, and it was a test of good verse that if you tried to translate it into prose you always produced an inferior thing, and quoted Gray's 'Where ignorance is bliss 'tis folly to be wise' as an example of this.

One of the extraordinary things about him is the rapidity of his change of moods. He seemed quite broken up round the graves, then on the way home physically tired but mentally alert, then at the garden gate he hopped on to the bank like a young man, to put his hand over the wall and find the key.

From 1915 onwards there were several thousand Australian soldiers stationed at Weymouth and one of them, whose name is unknown, contributed the following to a magazine called *The Australian at Weymouth* in March 1919:

Be it said that Mr Hardy is a sealed lock to interviewers, and has over and over again refused to be interviewed – in fact he dislikes publicity. However... Mr Hardy readily consented to have a chat with the Australian visitor, and had a lot of very nice things to say about Australians and their doings... "I have often longed to go to Australia... but I fear now that cannot be at my age, for even we in Dorset get old." (Incidentally Mr Hardy looks hale, well and hearty, despite his years...)

Asked as to Australian Literature, Mr Hardy replied. "Well, in the history of peoples that is the last which comes to it. First people go for what is practicable and useful, then comes Education, followed by Arts and Sciences and last comes Literature. All other things are necessary to the making of literary characteristics in a race. But it will come. The nature of Australia and of the Australians all makes for this.

"I have met a large number of Australians, and had the pleasure of spending two afternoons at the Australian Camp at Weymouth some time ago. Now that the Australians are going back home and will soon be leaving us, would you please tell them that I wish them a safe return and very good luck wherever they may go."

The novelist and playwright, Eden Phillpotts (1862–1960) was in correspondence with Hardy as early as 1897. In 1915 he dedicated his novel *Old Delabole* to Hardy. It described the large slate quarries at Delabole in Northern Cornwall which Hardy had seen at the time of his first visit to Cornwall in 1870. 'We visited each other annually' in the following extract is not borne out by the evidence available, but on 10 June 1915 Hardy and Florence were driven by car to Torquay where they visited the Phillpotts and there was another visit in October 1917. The Max Gate Visitors' Book for the period 1922–7 – not by any means a *complete* record – is signed by Phillpotts only on 12 August 1925. The following passage is from Phillpotts's *From the Angle of 88* (London 1951):

It was a profound privilege to know Thomas Hardy upon my pilgrimage. We visited each other annually during his later years and, while a man little disposed at any time to talk about himself, implicitly one might gather his attitude to life in general and his mental reactions to circumstance between vanished youth and present old age. From existing conditions, as they obtained during the first World War, he turned for relief to the past and memory of other, earlier times. His sense of irony was always mitigated by a deep and dominant pity awakened before the predicament that confronted all mankind, and sometimes he declared emotions akin to despair at the continued failure of human intellect to compose human differences without the destruction of rising generations. Repeatedly he expressed his commiseration and abiding sympathy before the griefs of the world, but never uttered any cynical comment on its eternal torments and self-created confusions. He would always speak on any subject that interested his companions of the moment, yet proved most animated when concerned with the past and never ceased to regret so much that was gracious and beautiful in vanished time, even to myths and legends that had still possessed a measure of reality when he was young, for his memory treasured traditions once hallowed, now forgotten...

When he was staying with me I once took him to a little limestone bluff situate not a mile from my home – an uplifted spot surmounting a woodland region lifted above Torbay and reserved as a public pleasure-ground. On the summit a small plateau spread and here still stood the stout, roofless walls of a ruined building that dated from ancient days. It had given a name to the spot, which is known as Chapel Hill. Hardy enjoyed the fine sweep of the Bay extending between Torquay and Berry Head, and was interested in the sturdy little ruin surmounting it. He inspected this and learned what I could tell him concerning its history. Then some connecting links, furnished by the sea and the dismantled place of worship on the hill, awakened recollection and turned his thoughts to another church and another sea that still shone for him through the murk of intervening years. He spoke of Cornwall and the days when, as a young architect, he had gone to work at the fane of St Juliot nigh Boscastle, to supervise its restoration and enter upon the supreme adventure of his own young life. There he had met his fate and lost his heart; and now, half a century later, those days of bygone happiness could still warm his soul and bring a glimmer of contentment through the grey ambience of old age. Not seldom those gleams of recollection are to be found in his later poems, when memories of a girl he loved and won seem to twinkle, like a steadfast lighthouse beam, over the storm-foundered nights that were destined to follow.

Broadcasting was not as yet the addition to existence it would become, but Hardy valued music, and at Max Gate he liked to listen to the gramophone and best, I think, he enjoyed Beethoven. He was a generous host and jealous for the pleasure of those he entertained. He did not smoke himself but rather enjoyed the aroma of tobacco and always found a good cigar for those who liked them. I recollect a box he bought for the Duke of Windsor, on an occasion when that Prince lunched at Max Gate. His workroom was austere, withdrawn and secluded, upon an upper floor with a window through which appeared the crowns of trees that he had planted long ago and were now grown as tall as the house and could look in upon him at his desk. He cared not much for flowers but valued the trees extending in a belt round about his pleasure garden. He felt an uncommon regard for animals and revealed strange understanding of his pets, for his imagination enabled him to see life from their point of view and, more or less, to understand what was passing in their little minds. He was never sentimental about them, but always sympathetic and concerned to read their emotions. Cruelty to animals awakened his sharpest indignation and he held that the average farmer's treatment of sheepdogs was much to be deplored and lacking in either gratitude or humanity...

Another experience gave him much entertainment among the jests he treasured. When *Tess* was filmed, in the silent days of cinematography, they sent the picture for him to see. Detail abounded in the lavish American manner, and he told how they illustrated the kine for milking, and how cows and cows and yet more cows streamed in a prodigious herd from all sides until an insoluble problem arose in the mind of the spectator. 'How did they imagine that poor Tess was going to milk them?' asked Hardy.

The Life and Letters of John Galsworthy (London 1935, p. 416) records a visit (*c.* 28 September 1915) by Galsworthy to Max Gate and Galsworthy's summing up: 'Nice, alert old fellow; liked him.' Arnold Bennett (1867–1931) was, like Galsworthy, an acquaintance rather than a friend, and his judgement of Hardy's books was somewhat erratic – he thought that Stevenson's *Weir of Hermiston* was 'far beyond anything that Hardy could compass'. The visit to Barrie's flat mentioned below was probably on 25 July 1917 when there was a raid on London by German Zeppelins:

> ...went to dine at Barrie's with Thomas Hardy and his wife. Barrie has an ugly little manservant, and the finest view of London I ever saw. Mrs Hardy a very nice woman, with a vibrating attractive voice. Hardy was very lively; talked like anything. Apropos of Chekov he started a theory that some of Chekov's tales were not justifiable because they told nothing unusual. He said a tale must be unusual and the people interesting. Of course he soon got involved in the meshes of application and instances, but he kept his head and showed elasticity and common sense, and came out on the whole well. He has all his faculties, unimpaired. Quite modest and without the slightest pose. They both had very good and accurate appraisements of such different people as Shorter and Phillpotts.
>
> Later in the evening Barrie brought along both Shaw and the Wellses by 'phone. ... At dusk we viewed the view and the searchlights. Hardy, standing outside one of the windows, had to put a handkerchief on his head. ... Soon after Shaw and the Wellses came Hardy seemed to curl up. He had travelled to town that day and was evidently fatigued. He became quite silent. I then departed and told Barrie that Hardy ought to go to bed. He agreed. The spectacle of Wells and G. B. S. talking firmly and strongly about the war, in their comparative youth, in front of this aged, fatigued and silent man – incomparably their superior as a creative artist – was very striking.
> (*The Journals of Arnold Bennett*, London 1932, II p. 202)

Leonard Woolf (1880–1969), writer and publisher, visited Max Gate for tea with his wife, Virginia, on 23 July 1926. (see p. 222) This led to a note about Hardy and that air raid in the *Nation* (21 January 1928, p. 598):

> This impression of simplicity and of something which is almost the opposite of simplicity was the strongest impression which I got from Hardy personally. At first sight, and when he began to talk to you, you might have thought that he was merely one of many men born in English villages. But he is one of the few people who have left upon me the personal impression of greatness. I saw him last spring

in the house which he had built for himself at Dorchester, and which, with its sombre growth of trees, seemed to have been created by him as if it were one of his poems translated into brick, furniture, and vegetation. He talked about his poems, and London as he had known it in his youth, and about his dog 'Wessex', all with great charm and extraordinary simplicity. He was a human being, not 'the great man.' And then he told a story which left me with that curious feeling which I so often get from his writing, of the mixture of simplicity and complexity, of doubt as to the degree of consciousness which he had of the implication of what he was saying. He was telling me how he had been up to London during the war and one evening there was an air raid. He had been dining with (I think) Sir James Barrie, Mr Shaw, Mr Wells, and Mr Galsworthy. 'A bomb might have fallen on the room,' he said. 'Just think! Well, all the chief English writers were there – there wouldn't have been much left of English literature. Just think of it!' It was said with extraordinary simplicity, without the slightest implication that he was himself to be included among the chief English writers in that room, indeed somehow with the implication that he was not to be included. And yet, unless I was entirely mistaken, there was at the same time a tiny, charming twinkle in his eye.

It was probably at the end of 1918 that Harold J. Massingham (1888–1952), writer on natural history and the countryside, and Head of the Anti-Plumage Trade Group for which he solicited Hardy's support, visited Max Gate with his father. Henry Massingham (1860–1921). He had been Editor of both the *Nation* and the *Daily Chronicle* and had earned Hardy's gratitude for his support of *Tess* and *Jude* in the battle against Mrs Grundy. Massingham describes Hardy, as others have done, as having a 'head slightly cocked on one side, like a bird's', and with looking like a 'country doctor, old style, with humour in the mouth and tragedy in the eyes'. (*Remembrance: An Autobiography,* London 1942, p. 45)

Another active member of the Dorchester amateur dramatic and debating society, later to become the Hardy Players, was E. J. Stevens (see p. 84) and the next memories are those of his daughter, Vera, who on her marriage in 1926 became Vera Mardon. They are in one of the most valuable of the Monographs, No. 15 (1964). She had first met Hardy in November 1910 when she was aged eleven, and was present at a rehearsal of *The Mellstock Choir.* At another rehearsal in 1918 she describes how Hardy, dissatisfied 'with the evolutions of the dancers in the dance, "The Triumph"...took a lady as his partner and then, despite his age (77) he nimbly demonstrated to the assembled company the correct steps and positions.' Here are some more of her recollections:

Soon after I returned from my musical studies in London Mrs Hardy wrote to me and said Mr Hardy would like to see me. She suggested a date and I replied, accepting the invitation. On my visiting Max Gate Mr Hardy explained that he would like me to accompany him on the piano while he played old dance tunes on his fiddle. This I agreed to do, and it was the first of many such interludes. They gave him great pleasure. He never sang and only on one occasion did I hear him hum and that was the tune of 'O Jan, O Jan, O Jan'. There was nothing noticeably attractive about his intonation; actually it was rather difficult to follow...

I arrived about 4.45 and had tea. This consisted of home-made cakes and very small dainty sandwiches. Afterwards I accompanied Hardy for about an hour and then I told him I thought I ought to return home. He agreed and I left on my cycle. Tea had been more of a ritual than a meal and at that time I looked on it as an afternoon custom of the middle-class, not for the purpose of nourishment but to provide a suitable background for a social chat. At the age I then was I had an appetite which the dainty fare could not satisfy.

As I had only recently, as I have already said, returned from London and my studies, and Hardy knew this, he questioned me about a student's life in London during the War of 1914–18. Some of his questions I remember were: How many hours a day did I practise? How many hours was I supposed to practise? What were the subjects in the curriculum? How was the time apportioned between them? How had I fared in the Zeppelin raids? Other questions concerned food, accommodation and boy friends. He was keenly interested in all the happenings of a student's life in London and I felt he was taking a more than ordinary interest in what I had to tell him...

For several years I frequently visited Max Gate to play piano accompaniment for Hardy's musical evenings.

It was on one of these evenings that he told me something of his life in London when, as a young student of architecture, he had seen, hanging in a shop window, an old violin which took his fancy. The price he found was more than he could pay, so he started saving for it. During the period of saving over several months he would often visit the shop to gaze in the window at his hoped-for prize. When he had accumulated the required amount of money he purchased it, and this was the same violin that he had been playing earlier in the evening...

Hardy wanted the old traditional Dorset song and dance 'O Jan! O Jan! O Jan!' produced and played to the public and in 1923 he asked me to tea to discuss the project. On this occasion we had tea on a circular table situated in a corner of the sitting-room. As usual Mr Hardy sat at my left, and on my right, on his own chair, sat Wessex and then Mrs Hardy.

After tea Hardy led me to the piano and hummed the Wessex folk tune of 'Nancy's Fancy' to which the dances of 'O Jan!' could be performed, and then, almost apologetically, asked me if I would be so kind as to write down the tune. . . .

I still have the words and music I wrote down, and that was the way in which this old folk tune, which Hardy called a recension, was rescued from oblivion. Hardy had remembered the words and music he had heard played at his father's house, Upper Bockhampton, when he was a boy. It was an amazing feat of memory – a prodigious feat. . . .

Hardy never enthused or got excited and yet I know from at least two personal experiences, which I prefer not to relate, that he could get very irate and show it by his facial expression, angry words and sarcasm; but even in anger he did not raise his voice. . . .

He had a strong aversion to meeting anyone who, he imagined, might only want to exploit the acquaintanceship, but he greatly enjoyed visits from a few accepted friends. He made few demands of life and was not a self-indulgent man.

He did not speak the Dorset dialect, but could understand it and enjoyed the simple conversations in their native dialect of the Dorset peasants.

His garden was another of his sources of joy and he once told me that he had helped in the planting of the Beech, Elm, and Sycamore trees which still form the back-drop of the Max Gate garden . . .

In 1923 shortly after the Prince's visit, Mrs Hardy told my father with whom she was very friendly, an amusing story about the Prince of Wales when he visited Max Gate to see Mr Hardy and to lunch with him in that year. He had been touring his Duchy of Cornwall estates. Previous to the visit, Mrs Hardy had been informed that a private room was to be made available to the Prince for his personal use, and a bedroom was prepared for him. The day of his visit was uncomfortably hot and soon after entering Max Gate, the Prince retired to the bedroom with his valet, while his secretary remained standing on the landing outside the bedroom door. Mrs Hardy waited nervously at the foot of the stairs. The minutes passed, but the Prince did not put in an appearance and the sound of voices could be heard in the bedroom. At last the bedroom door opened and Mrs Hardy felt relieved and made ready to greet him, but the Prince did not emerge; instead, Mrs Hardy saw a waistcoat fly out of the bedroom door and land on the secretary's head, while at the same moment she heard an angry Prince exclaim, 'It's too damned hot! You wear the bloody thing yourself!' Soon after this episode the Prince descended without his waistcoat, and in the subsequent photographs of him that day it is noticeable he is not wearing a waistcoat.

PART II   THE POST-WAR YEARS 1918–1928

With the end of the Great War in 1918 the number of visitors to Max Gate increased and among them were many of the younger writers whose aim now was to meet the Grand Old Man of English Literature, and, very probably, write about him. H. G. Wells (1866–1946) and Rebecca West (1892–1983) were in Weymouth at the end of January 1919 and Wells wrote to Hardy and asked for permission to visit. Hardy replied in his usual generous way, 'Certainly come and see us, and bring the lady who is as yet only a floating nebulous bright intellectuality to me.' He regretted that he had not read Rebecca West's latest novel but was sure that she was 'one of that excellent sort (which I flatter myself I am, and I am sure you are), who don't care a d— whether friends have read their last book or not, or any of their books.' (CL V, p. 293) The visit took place on 29 January, and resulted in a cartoon by Wells of Hardy talking about Max Gate being built 'entirely on skelingtons'. Later Wells told Virginia Woolf that Hardy was a very simple, subtle old peasant man much impressed by clever people who write!

Siegfried Sassoon (1886–1967), poet and prose writer, was such an admirer of Hardy's verse that he dedicated his early book of poems, *The Old Huntsman and Other Poems* (London 1917), to Hardy and the dedication was acknowledged on 4 February 1917 (CL V. p. 201). This led to a visit to Max Gate by Sassoon on 7 November 1918 which was followed by at least another ten visits before Hardy's death. The two poets got on so well together that sometimes Sassoon stayed for two or three days as guest of the Hardys, and he was clearly a favourite of both Hardy and his wife.

These visits were recorded in considerable detail in Sassoon's diaries and other writings – there was even an article by Sassoon entitled 'Hardy as I knew Him' in *John O'London's Weekly* as late as 7 June 1940 – and an editor is confronted with an embarrassment of riches. Sadly, the same riches are not available to pay copyright charges, and this makes any selection a peculiarly difficult task. The opening recollections are of his first visit in November 1918:

... I travelled towards Dorchester in bright frosty weather. Naturally, my mind was full of speculations as to how far the Mr Hardy of Max Gate would harmonize with the writer whose works I had absorbed so fruitfully. ...

For in spite of his letters to me I still looked on him as such an eminent and almost legendary figure that it was puzzling to imagine oneself with him in any ordinary human relationship. He was seventy-eight, too, and I could only approach him agape with veneration. I had a notion that he was a modest sort of man; and Mr Gosse had told me that, of all the famous writers he had known, Hardy was the least likely to say anything which one remembered afterwards. The nearest I had got to picturing him 'in real life' was through an anecdote of Robbie's. [Robert Ross 1869–1918, writer and close friend of S.S.] He had described how – more than twenty years before – he had spent a rather dull evening with the Hardys at a flat they had taken in Kensington. He had been discussing with Mr Hardy the methods by which authors coped with the laborious process of writing their books. Mr Hardy having remarked that he had written one of his early novels on his knees, Robbie wittily replied, 'We *read* it on our knees.' Whereupon the late Mrs Hardy had exclaimed in reproving tones, 'Don't flatter Mr Hardy in that foolish way!' ...

November 7th. arrived 6.45 in darkness. Horse cab rumbled up to a porch of small house among trees. Found little old gentleman in front of fire in candle-lit room; small wife with back turned doing something to a bookcase. Both seemed shy, and I felt large and hearty. First impression of T. H. was that his voice is worn and slightly discordant, but that was only while he was nervous. Afterwards it was unstrained, gently vivacious, and – when he spoke with feeling – finely resonant. Frail and rather wizard-like in the candleshine and dim room, with his large round head, immense brow, and beaky nose, he was not unlike the 'Max' caricature, but more bird-like. He knelt by the log fire for a bit, still rather shy. They both gained confidence, and then there was a charming little scene of 'which room is he in, dear?' 'The west room, my dear,' though of course he must have known. He lit me up the narrow staircase with a silver candlestick, quite nimble and not at all like a man of almost eighty. ...

Meanwhile I was learning a lesson which has leavened my imperfections ever since. He was giving me a demonstration of the simplicity of true greatness. By this I do not mean that he was simple, when viewed apart from his writings, though his modesty sometimes misled superficial observers into thinking so. This modesty was instinctive and quite unaffected. For example, he once remarked to me – with one of his wistful little sighs – that he didn't suppose he'd have bothered to write *The Dynasts* if he could have foreseen the Great War. The comment may have been only half serious; yet no one but he could have made it. It was impossible to imagine him talking for effect, and he was adroit at declining to be drawn out by visitors angling for oracular utterances. J. M. Barrie had a story of him at the Savile Club, where the secret of style was being discussed by a group of writers. When all the others had set forth their views, Hardy was unable to produce any explanation except by some quite trivial remark. He was interested in cleverness but not attracted by it. The homely strength and ripe integrity of his nature were somehow apparent in his avoidance of the brilliant and unusual. When he did say something profound he contrived to make it seem quite ordinary. He was, in fact, a wise and unworldly man who had discarded intellectual and personal vanity. He has described himself as 'a private man', which merely meant that he liked to live quietly, shunning active competition with his contemporaries. He regarded authorship as an unobtrusive occupation rather than a struggle to attract attention. He had written his novels to earn a livelihood. He wrote poetry to please himself, and even in 1918 was not fully aware of the admiration for his verse prevalent among other poets, both old and young. Anyhow, what I carried away from Max Gate, both then and thereafter, was an impressive awareness that Hardy – who was, as I remarked to myself, 'the nearest thing to Shakespeare I should ever go for a walk with' – had no vestige of vanity, and wore his illustrious laurels with no more concern about them than if they had been his hat. The pessimism which has often been imputed to him was – in his own words – merely 'the sad science of renunciation.' In spite of what Meredith called his 'twilight view of life', he was not a melancholy man. He had a normal sense of humour and could be charmingly gay. The bitterness in his writings was meditative and impersonal. He was disappointed rather than disillusioned in his attitude to life. Instinctively compassionate, he had suffered deeply through the apparently fortuitous victimization and injustice in many human happenings. I was often astonished by an octogenarian agility and quickness which matched his alertness of mind, and can remember how – at eighty-four – when discussing some variant reading in Shakespeare, he went up to his study to fetch his facsimile edition of the First Folio. As he re-entered the room with it under his arm I realized that he must have run both ways – had at any rate performed his errand at a lively trot! His movements were brisk, purposeful, and compact. He always chose a straight-backed chair to sit in, and carried himself with an almost military erectness. Seen in a strong light he looked all his age – a bird-like ancient whose monumental head might well have belonged to some ex-Mayor of Dorchester, some local worthy – though obviously derived from the fine stock of a naturally noble ancestry. Hob-nobbing with him of an evening I could almost forget that he was anything more than a dear and delightful old country gentleman. But I have watched him when he was in shadow and repose, and have held my breath in contemplation of what seemed the wisdom of the ages in human form. For that time-trenched face in the flicker of firelight was genius made visible, superhuman in its mystery and magnificence. . . . He was sitting with one arm around his old friend 'Wessex' – that unruly and vociferous sheep-dog whom he has enshrined in a poem. But when he gazed down at 'Wessie' he ceased to be Merlin. The face of the wizard became suffused with gentle compassion for all living creatures whom he longed to defend against the chanceful injustice and calamity of earthly existence.

(From *Siegfried's Journey 1916–20*, pp. 89–93 and 147–50)

February 22, [1921] T. H. very gay. At 4 walked across the field-path toward Winterbourne Came, with him. He walked slowly; not so well as last time, but the path was uneven. I tried to draw him out about eye (visual) and ear (non-visual) music; but he seemed a bit hazy, and thought I meant rhyme-endings done by spelling instead of sound (lion and carrion idea). People confuse 'poetry' with 'verse', he said (re polyphonists and imagists etc.).

Mentioned 'The Last Signal' (*CP* 412), pointing out William Barnes's rectory among the trees.

Writing to order. He was asked to do *Titanic* (*CP* 248) and Armistice Day (1920 *CP* 545) poems: but did not feel that he was forced to, and wrote them with feeling of spontaneity.

Referred to old words (Dorset etc.) 'orts', 'huffle', said how the old words of his childhood moved him still, and seemed a base to his work. (This was when talking of Conrad, who knew no English till sixteen years old, and missed that feeling in words.)

Hours of work. Found he wrote best between tea and dinner. In early days he had a meal at 5, and then worked till midnight. Afterwards he 'became theatrical', and went to plays four nights a week.

I asked him about Donne. He said he didn't greatly care for it, as poetry. Made him feel all the time that D. was being too clever, intellectual agility instead of emotion of poetry.

I mentioned Tupper and R. Montgomery, whose books I'd bought for two shillings in Weymouth. He said he'd looked at R.M.'s hoping to find them good so as to be able to have a dig at Macaulay whom he hates. But found M. no good at all.

He remembered in 1860 asking a London bookseller whether Shelley was selling, and the bookseller said, 'No; he's almost dead. Soon he'll be quite finished with!' And tried to sell T. H. a Tupper...

September 18 (Sunday)   T. H. fumbling 'morning hymn' on the worn-out piano before breakfast. Looking at *Baedeker* (Rome) after breakfast. Talking about his projected new volume of verse.

6.30–7.45 walked with T. H. to Dorchester. Listening outside churches for 'evening hymn'. Looking at war memorial (only one Hardy on it). Talking about Palestine and Mespot on way home. After dinner I playing hymn-tunes, 'New Sabbath and Mount Ephraim', T. H. humming, and very pleased, imitating how they used to fiddle in Mellstock gallery.

I suppose T. H. has aged since I was here in February. He seems to live more 'in the past' than he did, although his interest in contemporary affairs is quite remarkable...

June 25 [1922]   After yet another happily-spent afternoon with T. H. and F. H., I feel an unwillingness to try and reconstruct the hours. I don't want to record trivialities. It seems too much like what T. H. calls 'betraying the cloven hoof of the interviewer'.

'T. H. has never seemed more loveable than this afternoon,' I thought, as I was walking back to the King's Arms before dinner. And to a Hardy-worshipper it *was* a wonderful afternoon. Probably it is sentimentality on my part, but it did seem rather poignant to be playing 'She wore a Wreath of Roses' while T. H. sang the words with the most naive simplicity. (Clutton-Brock in his *Times Lit. Sup.* review compared a poem 'The Old Gown' to this early-Victorian ballad, and T. H. fetched down a yellowed old copy which belonged to his wife Emma *and her mother*.) This music-making on the old 'heavily-haunted' piano began after lunch when I tried over some settings of H.'s poems by Gustav Holst and Armstrong Gibbs.

Somehow the episode of his singing that old ballad seems infinitely precious. Ridiculous words by the author of 'The Mistletoe Bough'! Yet he sang them with tenderness, as though he were handling some relic of youth long-cherished and hallowed by memory. And he does these things with the same half-humorous seriousness and simplicity that pervade his poems. This quality is the key-note to his greatness. It is his strength and his sweetness. It makes me feel a grateful worm....

People complain that he is over-sensitive to criticism; but the old wounds still rankle; he certainly does worry too much about the small pin-pricks of reviewers. And he has his little vanities about his work; dislikes criticism except when favourable. But, as I've said again and again, he is fundamentally humble. He has given me spontaneous and unconscious proof of this ever so many times.

Speaking of 'An Ancient to Ancients'(*CP* 660) he said: 'I didn't print it in any magazine because I thought it was too much like *putting myself forward*. I was even doubtful about printing it at all. So I *buried it at the end of my book*, where no-one will notice it.' He was genuinely surprised that the poem has attracted attentive admiration.

I can't help comparing this sort of thing with the arrogance and conceit of many of the younger poets today (including self, I suppose). . . .

June 26 [1922] Very interesting talk with T. H. after lunch. He spoke very freely about his methods of writing stories. I asked why he hadn't written any long tales in verse. 'Like Crabbe's, you mean?' he replied quickly, and went on to say that he liked *condensed* tales in verse and urged me to try my hand at some. He mentioned Browning's 'Statue and the Bust' – a favourite of his.

His talk has decided me *against* trying any long tales in verse. There *must* be a reaction against the diffuseness of present-day writers. Why shouldn't I develop the style of poem which T. H. has invented (the *condensed plot* kind)? Strolling in the green-shaded garden-alley before tea-time I felt that T. H. had helped me greatly – kindled a spark perhaps. . . .

Labour. 'They want to learn that half a loaf is better than no bread.' 'Why don't they read History, and realise that a Revolution always ends in a Dictatorship?' T. H. doesn't realize the Industrial problem. He looks at Trade Unionism from the farmer's point of view. He has been a discreet Liberal all his life, I imagine. . . .

June 28 [1922] F. H. (at lunch) speaking of A. C. Benson. 'He is very fond of young men, and gets on extraordinarily well with them. But he takes *no interest in women*. Even refuses to lecture at the women's colleges.' The remark startled me. I realized once again how remote my secret affairs are from even the Hardys who are so fond of me. T. H. speaks of 'that man Oscar Wilde'. It isn't likely that T. H. would be unfair or prejudiced. It is merely that he doesn't recognise the existence of the problem. F. H. would be horrified, I'm afraid. . . .

I have arranged for Blunden to come to see T. H. (a thing I intensely desired to bring about). . . .

(From *Siegfried Sassoon's Diaries 1920–1922*, pp. 42–5 and 83–5)

Several women claim to have had the last dance with Hardy but the winner must surely be Ellen Vincent, who was a nanny with the wealthy Hanbury family who lived in Kingston Maurward House. After the war, she remembered a village war-memorial being opened in Bockhampton by Hardy. It took the form of a club-room, and she writes, ' . . . T. Hardy opened it and I had the honour of leading off the first dance with Thomas Hardy, which was the Sir Roger de Coverley' (Letter to Mrs R. Skilling, 8 August 1984).

Another personal tale which seems to bear examination is that of a Mr Harold Porter who as a scout went from Bolton where he lived to a camp near Lulworth Cove in the summer of 1919. Their Scoutmaster, a Mr A. H. Hope, had some connection with Hardy and took all his forty scouts along to Max Gate to meet him. Although unprepared, Hardy came out, 'looking very small', welcomed them, and told them not to 'bother about my novels; read the poems.' (Information supplied by Trevor Johnson).

But not all visitors were so welcome, and Hardy could be cutting to those who came to exploit him. Samuel G. Blythe called at Max Gate with the intention of writing an article on Hardy for the *Saturday Evening Post*. He recorded the following conversation:

'Mr Hardy, I have travelled three thousand miles to see you.' This reverently.

'Really?' This politely, but with a certain disinterestedness that was depressing.

'Yes, I have travelled three thousand miles to see you.' This with less reverence and more emphasis.

'Really?' This with an intonation that expressed, with sufficient clarity, the thought: 'Well, you've seen me; what else do you want?'

Imagine an earnest pilgrim at a literary shrine able to dig out but two cold and clammy 'Reallys' as a starter! The situation was precarious, and needed the tonic of instant diversion into other channels.

'You have a lot of crows on your place.' This with an appropriate sweep of the arm that included an immense flock of black and busy birds on the lawn.

'My word! Those are not crows; those are rooks!' And the author of *Under the Greenwood Tree* and *Far from the Madding Crowd* proceeded along the terrace by himself.

(*Saturday Evening Post*, 17 April 1920, pp. 18–19)

Among those who called on Hardy at Max Gate in August 1920 were the poet Robert Graves (1895–1986) and his wife, and the Swedish writer R. E. Zachrisson. An intelligent critic of Hardy's work, Zachrisson nominated him unsuccessfully for the Nobel Prize in 1921. The only reason he could find for the repeated failure to award the prize to Hardy was 'that the adverse criticism which was bestowed on Hardy in the eighteen-nineties, especially from clerical quarters, and which even now has a few spokesmen among English men of letters, had prevented the majority of the Academy with its susceptibilities to traditional influences, from acknowledging Thomas Hardy's greatness, in spite of the many protests which were raised by practically a unanimous Swedish press, every time his claim was disregarded. (*Thomas Hardy as Man, Writer and Philosopher*, Stockholm 1928, p. 23)

In the summer of 1920 I was staying at Weymouth in Dorset to study the dialect and to see Hardy's country. . . .

An introduction from a mutual friend, Professor W. Morgan, resulted in an invitation to have tea with Mr and Mrs Hardy. One sunny afternoon in August I betook myself to Max Gate, Mr Hardy's house near Dorchester, which was built in 1885 to his own design, and where he has lived ever since. I was received by Mrs Hardy, who asked me if I was a newspaper reporter, for in that case Mr Hardy could not possibly see me. He was not fond of publicity, and some newspaper reporters had recently made some very tactless comments on Mr Hardy's personal appearance and dress. I said I was a Swedish scholar who had no connection whatever with any newspapers, and had simply come to pay my homage to Mr Hardy as a great literary man in whose works I was particularly interested. I was then invited into the drawing-room, whose walls were hung with a wealth of beautiful pictures, and with numerous pen-and-ink sketches of the great author himself. Hardy had a great predilection for illustrating various situations in his books with references to pictures. To take one instance, when Angel and 'Liza Lou had witnessed Tess's tragic death, they leave the place hand in hand 'the drooping of their heads being that of Giotto's Two Apostles'.

After a few minutes Mr Hardy entered the room, accompanied by his pet-dog, which had been given the very appropriate name of Wessex. Mr Hardy was of medium height and figure, his features were regular, his face furrowed with thought, his expression placid rather than sad. He wore a blue suit and a white waistcoat with black stripes. When Mr H. Wells first set eyes on his great fellow-writer, he is supposed to have exclaimed 'What! is this little grey man Hardy?' That is a very good description, but the greyness was lighted up by a pair of wonderful light blue eyes which seemed to look far into the past. They recalled to me one of his poems, which begins with the words: – 'Attentive eyes' (*CP* 336). Nothing escaped his keen observation, for as Mr Squire says (*Observer* Jan. 15, '28) 'he had the roving eye as well as the musing eye'.

There was nothing whatever of a pessimist in Mr Hardy's manner. He had all the qualities which we appreciate in an English gentleman, kindness, courtesy, humour, and modesty, a rare but becoming quality in a great author. I quite agree with what Mr A. Bennett, who had met him in London a few months earlier, says about him in this respect: 'He had authority but did not show it. This man is all right. No nonsense about him. No pose. No secret but apparent preoccupation with the fact that he was the biggest living thing in English literature'. Mr Hardy was not sparing with words. His conversation was easy and natural, passing from grave to gay subjects.

I told my host I had been visiting many of the famous places in his novels, 'Talbothays Farm', where Tess met Angel, and found solace in work after her little child had died, the curious stone pillar on which Alec made Tess place her hand and swear never to tempt him, 'Wellbridge House', where Angel left Tess after she had made her confession the day after their marriage and many others. Mr Hardy then pointed out that these places only formed the background and setting of his stories, and that he had not aimed at correctness in all details, as he had had no idea those localities would be analysed so minutely (*cf.* the second preface to *Tess*) . . .

Some time ago Mr Hardy had helped a pupil of Professor Brandl's (Berlin) to take gramophone records of the dialect, but they were not quite reliable, because the speaker had been a man of education, who used to give recitations in the Dorset dialect. The genuine dialect speakers were shy birds, who were no good at this business. The dialect was dying out rapidly. It was best preserved in the northern districts, *e.g.* near Sturminster Newton.

Mr Hardy also told me that there still lived a member of the D'Urberville family in Dorchester, a poor artisan whose name had been corrupted into Tollerville (with a vernacular *o* for *u*, as in *cob* for *cub* etc.), and who had no idea of his noble descent. Some months before, Mr Hardy had visited 'Wellbridge House', an old seat of the D'Urbervilles, where above the doors there are still the mural portraits of two noble ladies of the family, who look very haughty and vicious, and are supposed to bring bad luck to those who view them too intently. (*Ibid.* pp. 5–9)

Robert Graves made good use of his August 1920 visit to Hardy. It appeared in its first form in the *Sphere* (28 January 1928, p. 129 *et seq.*) and then in his autobiography, *Goodbye to All That* (London 1929). These extracts are from the text which appeared in the *Sphere*:

> The first time that I met Hardy was at Oxford shortly after the War, when he had just been given his honorary doctorate at the University. He was staying with Sir Walter Raleigh. But there was little talk, for I had been warned that he was tired out by the journey from Dorset! and by the excitement of the occasion. It is not difficult to read in Hardy's *Jude the Obscure* the parable of his own thwarted

ambitions to graduate at Oxford; and the honour, awarded in spite of the opposition of a few elder members of the University who thought that *Jude* was an unforgivable insult to Oxford, clearly gave him the keenest pleasure. I was present at the degree ceremony, and the Sheldonian Theatre has seldom seen such enthusiasm as when Hardy came forward to be presented to the Vice-Chancellor, and was introduced in Latin as 'easily the greatest of living English novelists, nay, indeed, of English poets too,' and was invested in his gown of cardinal red. But perhaps he was even more pleased with the performance of his *Dynasts* by the Oxford University Dramatic Society that same day, and the reception that followed.

Hardy was very simple-minded where his reputation was concerned, and was always apparently surprised and encouraged if anyone had read his work and spoke well of it. It was characteristic of him that even when he had reached a point of fame when any journal would have been glad to print anything whatever that had his signature to it, he still diffidently kept the habits of his early years and enclosed a stamped addressed envelope for the return of his manuscript if rejected. He was without ambition in the vulgar sense, though old-fashioned enough not to be superior about accepting proffered distinctions. His Order of Merit, I think, meant a lot to him.

My next meeting with Hardy was in August 1920. . . . We found Hardy looking ten years younger than he had seemed at Oxford. He was active and gay, with none of the aphasia and wandering of attention that we had noticed. He took in everything that was said, letting nothing pass. He seemed to regard us as representatives of the post-War generation, and was humbly anxious to know how we looked at things, and ready, if necessary to revise his opinions. He lived such a quiet life at Dorchester, he said, that he feared he was quite behind the times. He wanted, for instance, to know whether we had any sympathy with the Bolshevik regime, and whether he could trust the Conservative newspaper that he took in its accounts of the Red Terror. Then he was interested in Nancy Nicholson's hair, which she wore short, in advance of the fashion, and in her keeping her name unaltered after marriage. His comment on the name question was, 'Why, you are old-fashioned. I knew an old couple here sixty years ago that did the same. The woman was called Nanny Priddle (descendant of an ancient family, the Paradelles, long decayed into peasantry), and she would never change her name either.' Then he wanted to know why I no longer used my army rank of captain; I said that it was because I was no longer a soldier. 'But you have a right to it; I would certainly keep my rank if I had one. I should be very proud to be called Captain Hardy.' And he meant it.

He told us that he was engaged at the time in restoring a Norman font in a church nearby. He only had the bowl to work upon, but enjoyed doing a bit of his old work again. Nancy Nicholson then mentioned that we had not baptised our two children. He was interested, but not scandalised, remarking that his old mother had always said of baptism that at any rate there was no harm in it, and that she would not like her children to blame her in after-life for leaving any duty to them undone. 'I have always found that what my old mother said was right.' He said that he found the new generation of clergymen very much better men than the last... Though he now only went to church three times a year – one visit to each of the three neighbouring churches – he could not forget that the church was in the old days the centre, for good or bad, of all the musical, literary, and artistic education in the country village. He talked then about the old string orchestras in Wessex churches, in one of which his father, grandfather, and he himself had taken part, and regretted their disappearance.

After tea we went into the garden, and Hardy asked to see some of my recent poems. I showed him one, and he asked if he might make some suggestions. He objected to the phrase the 'smell of thyme,' which he said was one of the clichés which poets of his generation studied to avoid. I replied that they had avoided it so well that it could be used again now without offence, and he withdrew the objection. He asked whether I wrote easily, and I said that this poem was in its sixth draft and would probably be finished in two more. 'Why!' he said, 'I have never in my life taken more than three, or perhaps four, drafts of a poem. I am afraid of it losing its freshness.' He said that he had been able to sit down and write novels by time-table, but that poetry was always accidental, and perhaps it was for that reason he prized it more highly. ...

At dinner that night he grew enthusiastic in praise of cider, which he had drunk since a boy and thought one of the finest medicines he knew. ...

He began complaining of autograph-hunters and their persistence. He disliked leaving letters unanswered, particularly as if he did not write, these people pestered him the more; he had been rather upset that morning by a letter from an autograph-fiend which began – 'Dear Mr Hardy, I am interested to know why the devil you don't reply to my request'... He asked me for my advice, and was grateful for the suggestion that a mythical secretary should reply offering his autograph at one or two guineas, the amount to be sent to a hospital ('Swanage Children's Hospital', put in Hardy), which would forward a receipt.

Talk of autograph-hunters led round to professional critics. He regarded them as parasites no less noxious than autograph-hunters, and wished the world rid of them. He also wished that he had not listened to them when he was a young man; on their advice he had cut out dialect-words from his early poems where they had no exact synonyms. And still the critics plagued him. One of them recently complained of a poem of his where he had written 'his shape *smalled* in the distance.' Now what in the world else could he have written? Hardy laughed a little, and said that once or twice recently he had looked up a word in the dictionary for fear of being again accused of coining, and had found it right enough – only to read on and find that the sole authority quoted was himself in a half-forgotten novel! . . .

We went off the next day, but there was some more talk at breakfast before we went. Hardy was at the critics again. He was complaining that they accused him of pessimism. One man had recently singled out as a single example of gloom a poem he had written about a woman whose house was burned down on her wedding night. (*CP* 48) 'Of course it is a humorous piece,' said Hardy, 'and the man must have been thick-witted not to see that. When I read his criticism I went through my last collection of poems with a pencil, marking then S, N, and C, according as they were sad, neutral, or cheerful. I found them as nearly as possible in equal proportions, which nobody could call pessimism.' In his opinion *Vers Libre* could come to nothing in England. 'All we can do is to write on the old themes in the old styles, but try to do a little better than those who went before us.' About his own poems he said that once they were written he cared very little what happened to them.

He told us of his work during the War, and said that he was glad to have been chairman of the Anti-Profiteering Committee, and to have succeeded in bringing a number of rascally Dorchester tradesmen to book. 'It made me unpopular, of course,' he said, 'but it was a hundred times better than sitting on a military tribunal and sending young men to the War who did not want to go.'

On 9 April 1920 Vere H. Collins, a publisher responsible for educational books at the Oxford University Press who had been in correspondence with Hardy, paid the first of several visits to Max Gate. In 1928, very shortly after Hardy's death he published in various journals a number of talks with Hardy presented in dramatic form. These were collected together later in the year in a book with the title *Talks with Thomas Hardy at Max Gate 1920–1922*. It is a book that contains so much original material that it cannot be ignored, but the reader is left wondering how the 'exact' words of Hardy can be quoted with such authority when it is extremely doubtful whether Hardy at this stage of his life would have allowed any note-taking. Vere Collins had already upset Hardy when in 1922 he had proposed doing a translation of that 'offensive' book by Hedgcock. On 24 June 1922 Florence had written to Collins (almost certainly at Hardy's dictation) saying that Hardy disapproved of the book because of 'the dissection of his supposed personality... and the advancing it as fact, is of a particularly pointed and even prying kind, not at all in good taste when the subject of the assumed dissection, or vivisection, is still alive' (CL VI, p. 139). Well Hardy was now dead and Collins could publish. In his introduction he said:

> When I met Hardy he was an old man of eighty. I hesitate at the word 'old', so opposed is it in its ordinary associations to the vigour of intellect and the liveliness of sentiment which marked his conversation; the quickness of his thought; the versatility of his interests; the alertness in his voice, his gestures, his walk; his keenness of sight; the extraordinary clearness and steadiness of his hand-writing – all outward signs of that vitality which produced between the ages of seventy and eighty-five four volumes of verse, throughout which, whether we regard the intellectual or emotional force or the technique, it is impossible to detect the slightest mark of any falling-off from his earliest work.
> In his manner Hardy was quiet – though genial – and unassuming. He was very ready to respond to any question, and to follow up any subject that was introduced. (I noticed that he seemed to prefer that the thread of conversation should be directed by me.) The expression of his thought flowed easily and informally – often as of a person thinking aloud; sometimes in a half-questioning tone as if inviting rather than demanding assent. Literature was our chief topic of conversation, but he showed very little disposition to enter into literary theories and principles. The references he made to his own work were always modest, and very practical – the attitude of a craftsman towards a trade, with no tendency to regard the writing of books as an elevated pursuit superior to that of the common man – though, having chosen the career of letters, he made no pretence of not being concerned by the fortunes that befell his work. His references to contemporary writers were generously free from any note of jealousy or malice, he was specially interested in the work of the younger poets...

And here are extracts from the book:

9 April 1920. *The drawing-room at Max Gate, Dorchester, into which C has just been shown.*

Mrs H. (*after shaking hands with him*): I will go and tell my husband you are here. I don't think he heard the bell ring. (*She leaves the room.*)

C looks round. On the left of the fireplace he notices below a photograph of Mrs H. a photograph of Galsworthy, with an autograph quotation from one of the latter's stories, giving a definition of Optimism and Pessimism. While he is reading this Mrs H. re-enters, with her husband. H and C shake hands.

H. is about five feet five in height. He is dressed in an old, yellowish brown tweed suit. Aged 79, he might easily be taken for not older than about 65. His carriage is erect; utterance clear and strong; hearing perfect. He inclines to spareness, but for an old man of that habit he is noticeably not very thin. His complexion is healthy, and neither ruddy nor pale. He has a quiet, easy manner: composed, unassertive, but alert. His face is deeply lined, but the expression is not melancholy.

H: Do you often go to Oxford?

C: Fairly often. I was sorry I was not able to get there for the performance of *The Dynasts*. I saw it when it was done some years ago in London. May I know which of the two performances you preferred?

H: Of course neither was complete. There were only about thirty scenes out of 150. It was really a misnomer to call it *The Dynasts*. I suppose, however, they had to. On the whole I preferred the Oxford performance, because it was done by young men. Moreover, in London the effect was too much as if the whole thing occurred indoors. Even the battles looked as if they were under the architraves. I wrote to the people at Oxford about this, and it was altered. I thought the Nelson scene was rather too noisy. . . .

C: I have been collating your *Collected Poems*, Mr Hardy, with the original editions, and have been very much interested to see what a large number of alterations you have made.

H: I made the corrections as I went along. There are a considerable number of misprints in the Collected Edition. Macmillan has issued an errata slip. Had your copy one?

C: No, but I bought the book when it first came out.

H: I will get a copy of the slip for you. (*He leaves the room*)

H: (*returning with an errata slip which he hands to C*): That will save you having to buy a revised edition. I cannot understand how mistakes occur in a printed book when a proof has been corrected properly.

C: Sometimes a word or line drops out when the formes are being moved and the printer resets carelessly without referring to the proof.

H: I remember Tennyson being very much annoyed because one

of his poems was printed with 'hairy does' instead of 'aery does'. On another occasion 'mad phases' became 'mud phrases.' . . .

[27 December 1920]

H: You do not publish novels, do you?

C: No, except reprints of the classics in series like the 'World's Classics.'

H: Oh yes, of course, you took over the 'World's Classics' from Grant Richards. . . . Some people talk of novels as if they were the only books. . . . Do you publish any of Trollope's novels?

C: Yes: we are issuing him in the 'World's Classics'.

H: I like Trollope. You know, at one time it was thought he was going to be recognized as the greatest of the early Victorian novelists. Dickens was said to be too much of a caricaturist; Thackeray too much of a satirist. Trollope was put forward as the happy mean. . . .

Mrs H: I like Mrs Garnett's translations. I have been reading some of Chekov's stories translated by her. They are very good.

H: Is that the wife of Edward Garnett?

C: Yes.

H: The son of Richard Garnett?

C: Yes.

H: I had some correspondence with him once. He did not believe in Art. His theory was that to write a novel all one had to do was to go to a farmhouse and just describe what happened there during the day. I pointed out to him that if one wanted to make people read a book one must have something special to interest them with. I don't know if I ended by convincing him. Some of the younger men applied Garnett's idea to poetry: Siegfried Sassoon, for example. Some of his poems are quite good, though. . . .

C: Mr Hardy, you remember I wrote to tell you that I was classifying your poems. I have now finished the classification. I don't know if it seems to you rather ridiculous to apply arithmetical tables to poetry. . . .

H: Let me see what headings you group them under.

C produces his tables and lists, and explains briefly the principles of the classification.

H (*looking at the table of general classification*): I see there are most poems on 'Love and Marriage.' More than on 'Death' – which I am told I am always bringing in. . . . (*C turns over the pages to the table sub-classifying the Love poems.*) Which comes first here? Oh – 'Ill-mating and Disharmony'! (*Amused*). . . . Ah, the 'Unclassified' poems!

C: But there are not many – only twenty-two out of 510.

H: That is the total number, is it?

C (*turning over to the sub-classification of the 'Philosophical Poems'*): 'Philosophical' is rather a vague word, but I could not think of a better term under which to bring a number of poems on metaphysical and abstract themes which did not fall into the other categories.

H: Yes.

C: There are a few poems – very few: only about a dozen in all the five volumes – in which there are allusions that are obscure to me. I wonder if you would be so good as to let me ask you about them.

H: Certainly. I am very anxious not to be obscure. It is not fair to one's readers. After all, Spencer was right in saying that the energy devoted to finding out the meaning of what one reads is spent at the cost of what might have been given to appreciating it. Some of the younger poets are too obscure.

C: And some of the Victorian writers too – Meredith for example.

H: Yes, that is why his poetry has never been read much. ...

H: ... (*turning over the pages of* Collected Poems, *and pointing to* 'Near Lanivet' [CP 366]) This is a poem which is often neglected. (*Turning over some more pages, and pointing to* 'At the Word Farewell' [CP 360]): This is quite a good poem too. But of course there are plenty of love poems to choose from. ... Do you think the price of books is likely to go down?

C: I fear not for some time, and probably never back to the old prices.

H: It's a great pity. It is to the interest of authors that a large number of copies should be sold at a low price, and often of the publisher that a comparatively small number should be sold at a higher price. That seems to be the only point on which the interests of publishers and authors clash. ...

C: Was the title of *The Dynasts* settled from the beginning when you first started writing it?

H: I forget when I chose it. It must have been at a fairly early stage, for as you know it was published in three consecutive parts.

C: Do you pronounce the 'y' long or short?

H: I think I got it from the 'Magnificat' – the Greek version. The Greek 'u' is short. ... I have thought of reprinting the lyrics from it – say in small type at the end of *Collected Poems*. Two or three of them for example 'Trafalgar' and 'My Love's Gone a-fighting' – are as good as anything in the *Collected Poems*.

[29 October 1921. 4.30 p.m.]

C (*to Mrs H, handing her a book which he has brought with him from London*): I thought you would like to see this *Book of Women's Verse* by J. C. Squire, which the Oxford Press have just published.

Mrs H: I see he has not given anything by Miss Mew.

H: Nothing by Miss Mew! Perhaps he doesn't include any living writers.

Mrs H: Yes, he has Frances Cornford and Mrs Woods.

C: And Mrs Meynell and others.

H: Miss Mew is far and away the best living woman poet – who will be read when others are forgotten. . . .

H: Do you think anthologies injure the sale of an author's books?

C: I should say that they tend to stimulate the sale.

H: I suppose so. I often get letters from people who have seen an extract from my work, telling me they are now starting to read me up.

Mrs H: That was how I first got to know my husband's work.

H: From a book in a series called 'Half Hours with Living Writers.' I think afterwards it was called 'Gleanings from Living Writers.' In one of the volumes there was a selection from A *Pair of Blue Eyes*. They chose an extremely sensational passage – where Knight falls over the cliff. . . .

C: Used you to make many corrections in the MSS of your novels?

H: It depended. If there was a passage of straightforward narrative there would not be many. There is no rule. . . . They tell us that Shakespeare never made any corrections. I don't believe that. Ben Jonson, who said it, probably only saw a revised copy.

C: Did you prepare scenarios of the novels?

H: If I did I fear I did not follow them very closely. It was a hand-to-mouth matter – writing serials. I don't remember very well what I did. You see it is twenty-seven years since I wrote a novel. People write and ask me what I mean in a passage. Do they expect me to remember now what I meant over a quarter of a century ago? . . .

C looks at his watch.

H: Where are you stopping?

C: I am returning to London to-night by the 7 o'clock train.

Mrs H: Won't that be very tiring? I have done it once or twice. and been exhausted.

H: One ought not to be really. If one takes things easily a day or two beforehand it makes a lot of difference. The Masefields were here the other day: they left London in the morning; stopped here very late; and went on in the evening to Galsworthy on Dartmoor.

Mrs H (*to H*): You remember how tired your sister Mary used to be.

H: She used to go up to London in the morning, visit the Royal Academy, and return in the evening. She did not like sleeping in London, but she loved to see the pictures.

Mrs H (*to H*): The last time she did this she nearly collapsed at the station when she got back. But then she was over seventy. (*To C*)

However, if you think so little of coming down here and going back the same day it makes me feel I really ought to go up. I should enjoy a week in London very much.

H: I should too – when once I was there. But perhaps it is hardly worth while...

C: Mr Hardy, I know you must be often bothered for autographs, but I should be very grateful if you would put your name to this copy of the first edition of *Satires of Circumstance*. Would you write it on the half-title of 'Poems of 1912–13', which is the section I love most of all your work? (*C hands him the book open at that part of the volume.*)

H: I had better write at the beginning of the book.

C: My own name is already written there. (*He offers H a fountain pen.*).

H: .... I think I had better sign where I generally do. (*He turns back to the general half-title, and underneath 'Satires of Circumstance' writes 'Thomas Hardy.' The writing is clear and steady.*)

C: Thank you very much. I fear it's a very bad nib. Do you use a fountain-pen?

H: I press so heavily on my pen that I should ruin one. I suppose they hold quite a lot of ink? It does not dry up?

C: I should think there's enough ink in this to write about twenty quarto sheets.

H: Really!

19 August 1922. Scene as at the last interview...

H: Oh – Mr Collins!.... I am very glad to see you.

C: Mrs Hardy has been showing me this Japanese fan.... She tells me that *Tess* has been translated into Japanese.

H: *Tess of the d'Urbervilles*? Yes.

C: But only half of it, I hear. That is strange.

Mrs H: The professor from Tokio explained that the latter portion of the book would not appeal to the Japanese. It would be outside their comprehension. In Japan it is thought a virtuous thing for a girl to sell herself to obtain money for the help of her family. There would not seem to them to be any tragedy in Tess living with Alec d'Urberville.

H: The whole book would be rather long for the Japanese. They like literary works to be very short, they realize that short poems live the longer.

C: What about the great epics?

H: Even of them it is only passages that are remembered.

C: Chaucer?

H: Chaucer too. Shakespeare's songs are the best known and most commonly repeated parts of his plays. Or take Ben Jonson – 'Drink to me only with thine eyes.'

C: What a pity it is that so many poets apparently allow everything they write to be published.

H: An author cannot always tell what people will like most. Posterity alone can decide. So I generally publish everything. When I have been in doubt (as I was, for example, with my last volume) about two or three poems, I afterwards found that those were often what some people liked best; and poems I have been on the point of discarding have sometimes been used in anthologies.

H: (*taking up Mr Hedgcock's book*) Would you like to take this away with you? I have marked in the margins the errors in the biographical chapter. I have not re-read all the rest of the book. You might like to go through my annotations at your leisure.

C: Thank you very much. May I show them to Mr Hedgcock?

H: Certainly. I should be quite glad to see a translation published if he would make the alterations I have indicated.

C: How do you like Blanche's portraits, which are reproduced in it? Mr Hedgcock told me that you had refused to accept the original of one of them.

H: It was never offered to me. But perhaps now I think of it, what I said would have given the impression that I did not care for it. The finished portrait is a much better one than the study. (*Opening the book at the latter*) Now can you see me in that? It was done fifteen years ago, and it makes me look about ninety.

Mrs H: It's very much nicer in the original.

C: Where is the original?

Mrs H: In the Tate Gallery. It was presented by Mr Debenham.

C: Is the finished portrait there too?

H: I think Mr Debenham must have that in his house. He bought both...

H *and* C *rejoin* Mrs H *in the hall. All three leave the house, walk down the drive and out through the gate, and crossing the road go along a footpath across some fields.* H *walks briskly.*

H (*pointing to a field on the left*): They have nearly got in all the corn to-day, and are working overtime. They ought to work on Sunday to finish. Before the repeal of the Corn Laws they used always to work on Sundays at harvest time. It will be raining within twenty-four hours. Look at the clouds over the Monument. . . .

C: Has the cottage been repaired?

H: It has been thatched. In the old days thatching was done with freshly cut corn. The heads were cut off, and the reeds were used as they were. In that condition they were very straight and strong. But now on account of shortage the corn has to be threshed first, and so one gets only straw, which is not so strong...

They part. H and Mrs H turn in their homeward direction. When a few yards off C looks back to catch a last sight of them. They have reached the middle of the bridge. C sees them stop. They remain standing there, facing towards the station.

The next recollections are those of a Marjorie Lilly who wrote an article called 'The Hardy I Knew' for the *Thomas Hardy Society Review 1978* (Vol. I. No. 4, pp. 100–3). On the evidence of articles like this it is again difficult to understand Florence Hardy's constant complaints of how lonely Max Gate was:

It was the summer of 1920 that my first meeting came about, almost casually, with Mr Hardy. I was visiting Dorchester to be near a brother who was stationed there at his regimental depot, when one day I heard him say to a friend 'See you at the Hardys' on Sunday.' 'Do you mean the Mr Hardy?' I asked. 'Yes, the novelist.' I regarded them with awe. Do you think I might come too?' I ventured. 'Oh, do; they like seeing people. I'll tell Mrs Hardy we are bringing you.' It all seemed to be taken very much for granted, but I could hardly believe my good fortune...

The front door was ajar and, on entering the hall, I caught sight of a trough of water labelled 'Wessex' in large black letters which indicated that the Hardys kept a dog. My bodyguard seemed to know their way about, and we all marched into the chintzy, comfortable room where Mrs Hardy was presiding over the tea table. Our hostess was small and slender, with large melancholy brown eyes and a gentle manner;...

In the midst of the talk and laughter, the door knob slowly turned... A few lines from a half-forgotten poem stole across my mind: 'An aged thrush, frail, gaunt, and small, / In blast-beruffled plume'. When he wrote that, he described himself.

He had entered so quietly that the guests did not notice his arrival. As he stood surveying us, there was plenty of time to take him in. At a glance, his appearance was not striking; no stately port, no Jove-like front, no steely eye; merely, a spare little figure in a sober suit, even his voice quiet, level, precisely modulated. It soon became apparent that there was more to it than that: the extra element was already making itself felt, and one could hardly fail to notice his air of complete unselfconsciousness. But I was unprepared for his placidity. Like most people, I had regarded him as the professional prophet of doom, and if he had come among us with bowed head and stricken mien it would have seemed more in keeping with what he ought to be; but no, he looked alert, serene, in fact incorrigibly cheerful. . . .

After the war, young intellectuals who had lost their way flocked to Max Gate with their problems, confident that they would find in him their leading spokesman and soul-mate. . . . In his old age the disciples arrived at Max Gate in ever increasing numbers, and it was embarrassing to find himself regarded as a second Tolstoy. There was little that he could say to help them; if he tried to cheer them up, they could always quote his own words to confute him. But the constant role of priest and confessor was rather strenuous for a man in his eighties, and the robust outlook of the Dorset regiment provided him, in his turn, with relief from too much earnestness.

It will be clear by this time that the Hardys had a lucky hand with young people. I set forth on my next visit to Max Gate full of confidence . . . On this second occasion we had tea in the dining-room, and I was disconcerted to see a lavish spread before me, including some very thick sandwiches. Mrs Hardy explained that her husband had suggested the sandwiches; he thought I should be hungry after my journey. 'Young people have hearty appetites,' he remarked, beaming complacently at the display of food. But I was not so young as all that, and it was hard work battling with this mountain of bread and jam while I wanted to give all my attention to my host. He was doing just what I longed for him to do, talking about his work.

We started off with *Tess*. This was his favourite novel, simply (I think) because Tess was his favourite heroine; 'my Tess' he called her. When the book was dramatised and played in Dorchester, a local girl took the part of Tess; on the good nights, he told me, she gave an excellent performance. I saw Gwen Ffrangcon-Davies as Tess some years later in London. She was a sensitive and moving Tess but her approach was, perhaps inevitably, too intellectual, and her physique was wrong for Mr Hardy's young goddess, tall, deep-bosomed, all largeness and warmth, a daughter of the soil. Gwen Ffrangcon-Davies was small, slight, sophisticated. One could never really believe in her, especially in the big scenes. The difficulty of reconciling the emotional and physical qualities of Tess in one actress was almost impossible in his opinion, and he lost interest in the play accordingly . . .

One afternoon, during tea, there was a sudden tumult in the hall. A large party of tourists from goodness knows where had invaded the garden and burst into the house, filling it with their clamour. 'Oh, for God's sake, Florence! Get rid of them!' groaned Mr Hardy. Mrs Hardy got up, hastened into the hall, and faced the intruders single-handed; there were no servants about, and even Wessex had disappeared. Within the shelter of the dining-room Mr Hardy and I cowered among the teacups, speaking in whispers lest we should be overheard, expecting to be attacked at any moment. Our visitors showed fight but, after violent protests, loud arguments, and general commotion, they did at last retreat, finally disarmed by her gentle determined pleading. I would prophesy that they departed convinced that if had not been for her unwarranted interference they would have attained their object and 'scen Shelley plain'. As it was, baffled of their prey, they expressed their disapproval by hacking off large portions of his front gate, brandishing their souvenirs as they went.

Wives of prominent men are seldom popular, but I have never known any of them so maligned as Florence Hardy. Not only noisy tourists but serious admirers felt they had been kept away from him. Long after his death one read barbed comments from Hardy fans about her lack of co-operation with importunate callers. It did not occur to his aggrieved followers that he was tired, and that there were so many of them. Their souvenir-hunting annoyed him, and with good reason: if any of them got into the hall at Max Gate, a stick, a hat, a coat, or any article was likely to be taken: the Americans were better, taking only chips and slivers from his front gate.

And there can be no doubt that Florence deserved this praise for her protection of her husband.

Another perceptive comment on the Thomas–Florence relationship was made in a letter written by Katharine Adams (1862–1952) to Sydney Cockerell on 4 August 1920. She hadn't seen Hardy for thirty years and she thought he had changed from a 'rough-looking man' into a 'gentle little gentleman... a gentle and smooth voice and polished manners'! Mrs Hardy, she thought, was the 'most melancholy person I have ever seen... she longed to go to America – "but I never shall", she said with a deep sigh, and with a still deeper sigh she said "this place is too depressing for words in the winter, when the dead leaves stick on the window-pane and the wind moans and the sky is grey and you can't even see as far as the high road." Does she think too late, think you, that youth and age cannot be mated?' (*The Best of Friends*, London 1956, pp. 24–5)

William M. Parker (1891–?) was a writer and literary critic who claimed to have been in charge of the first bookshop at sea, where he met Conrad. He was co-editor of *The Letters of Sir Walter Scott* and wrote *On the Track of the Wessex Novels*. The following extracts are from Monograph No. 24 (1966). Parts of it had previously appeared in the *Cornhill* (February 1929, pp. 149–57). The visit was in September 1920:

A rap of the knocker on the door brought the housemaid. Mr Hardy was at home. I was ushered into the drawing-room. As I passed in, Mrs Hardy, who was alone in the room, rose from a chair at one side of a tea-table. She came forward and greeted me.

After general remarks, she told me not to ask Mr Hardy for his autograph; he was so pestered by autograph hunters. It was an unnecessary warning, as I had no idea of such an objective, and, in any case, would not have utilised this privileged visit as a means of obtaining a specimen of his handwriting, however greatly that would have been cherished. . . .

Perhaps the first aspect of Hardy's appearance to strike the observer was his high-domed head; in the majority of cases a sure sign of great imagination. Sparse hair, accentuating the bald cranium, grew to comparative thickness behind the ears. From back to front it was a decidedly long-shaped head; and I could not rid me of the impression how much it resembled Wagner's, as depicted in profile photographs of the great musician. It sat upon a thinnish neck which connected with sloping shoulders and a small body. The chief feature of his wonderful face was the remarkably aquiline shape of nose, drawn up tight at the top of the bridge and broadening towards the nostrils. But the object of surpassing interest was the face itself. Sad, intensely sad, and deeply wrinkled, it possessed a certain likeness to a large withered walnut. . . .

He possessed a soft-cadenced voice with just a faint suggestion of rough rustic flavour in it – an English voice, but not of the mincing, or high-pitched order. His speech came clear and liquid, and his conversation was free and easy. When humour became uppermost (and I discovered that Hardy the man appeared a much happier entity than Hardy the creator as revealed in his works), he gave way to subdued laughter accompanied by a merry twinkle in the eyes.

Though I had determined not to speak too much about his own work, thinking he might be sensitive on the point, and was prepared to steer an adroit course if, by chance, I should make allusion to it, of his own accord, and greatly to my delight, he brought the theme into conversation.

At that time, and indeed from the last years of the nineteenth century onwards, Hardy's interest had almost entirely deserted fiction and centred on poetry. He told me he had never anticipated his novels would become so popular as they eventually turned out to be. To learn style, he thought the reading and writing of poetry were more serviceable than the reading and writing of prose. Poetry was a more concentrated form of art. You could gain more from reading one or two lines of poetry than from several pages of fiction. Before the

Great War, when certain persons imagined the public had stopped taking any interest in poetry, that poetry, indeed, was a dead thing, the creator of *The Dynasts* had declared it was not dead, but would flourish. . . .

When Hardy was a young man, Morley advised him on no account to go in for journalism – it was apt to land a writer in a rut. 'But,' he said, turning to me with a twinkle in his eyes, 'Morley himself stuck to journalism for a long time, and was very far into it indeed.' He viewed with disfavour the conscience of a publisher's reader, as that personage had constantly to be on the look-out for what would be a commercial success, and often had to turn down really good literary matter. He cited the case of James Payn, reader for Smith, Elder, who turned down Shorthouse's *John Inglesant*. Then Macmillan, who had first refused it, took it up after Mr Gladstone's eulogistic review, and the novel became a gigantic success. But Hardy could not understand this, as he had always considered *John Inglesant* very dull – 'like,' he added, with a merrier twinkle, 'so many "goody" books.' . . .

After a brief pause, Hardy threw back his head. 'All this talk about my pessimism!' he exclaimed, in a rather disgusted tone. 'What does it matter what an author's view of life is? If he finally succeeds in conveying a completely satisfying artistic expression, that is what counts.' . . .

With reference to revision of literary work after it has been published, Hardy held decided views on a man of letters tampering too much with his creations. He was of the opinion that they lost their freshness and spontaneity in the process. He instanced the fastidious retouching in which Meredith and Henry James habitually indulged. He became particularly entertaining when speaking of James's fondness for emendation. Hardy had asked him if he ever saw his work finished, completed. No, James had replied, it was never finished because he was never satisfied with it, and he believed in constant revision. Hardy looked upon that as a sort of 'eternal proof reading'. When it had been necessary for the Wessex novelist to go over his works for new editions, he had corrected obvious errors. and had retouched very little indeed.

The new methods of novel writing and the so-called realism of the younger generation made very little appeal to Hardy. In discussing realism, he recounted that a friend had told him how much he had enjoyed Richard Jefferies' *Amaryllis at the Fair*, because everything happened in that novel just as it happens at a farm. Hardy, be it remembered, was born and bred among rustics. He had not only understood the English peasant through and through, but had given to the world's imaginative literature the most artistic and living representations of rustic character ever created. When, therefore, he pronounced the opinion that he had never heard farm folk talk in the manner they were made to do in Jefferies's book, he spoke with the voice of authority.

His chief points of criticism against the younger novelists of the period were with reference to their want of plot and lack of romance. Romance must always be an essential element, no matter how many other qualities it contain, in a novel addressed to a wide novel-reading public. He felt out of sympathy with these methods of the younger men, methods which, he thought, they owed largely to Mr Arnold Bennett. The kind of fiction being read at that time by the public was, to him, appalling.

From fiction our talk drifted to criticism. He did not think we had a great critic in this country, and certainly there were none in America. There was lacking a great critic who, instead of following the lead, would think for himself. Saintsbury had read too much, and he did not possess sufficient insight.

Another of the Hardy Players who described a visit to Max Gate was Henry A. Martin (1869–1949). He was a valuer and auctioneer with the long-established firm of Henry Duke. The visit was in November 1920 at the time when the Players were producing *The Return of the Native*. During the visit Hardy said that to him the last great English orator was John Bright and that he had often visited Drury Lane when a young man in London. Hardy recalled an amusing incident during a visit from G. B. Shaw and his wife. They had been at Max Gate on 28 April 1916 and this could have been the occasion. Shaw had hoped for a quiet chat with Hardy but 'he found a countrywoman of his there, who', said Shaw, 'fell upon and rent and trampled me in a flow of talk on our unhappy country, leaving me hardly any time for a word with Hardy.' The other guests on that occasion were the great classical historian, John Bury (1861–1927), whose wife was Irish. Mr Martin's article appeared in the *Dorset County Chronicle* (6 June 1940, p. 8).

It is difficult to know just how much credence can be given to the memories of anyone when they are written down forty or more years later. Of the two Max Gate maids who did respond to enquiries about the past the only one worth giving space to is Ellen Titterington (*c*. 1899–1977), who was in service at Max Gate from 1921 to 1928. According to her last employer 'Nelly' developed an 'even better' memory for the old days as she grew older, and, invited to return to Max Gate not long before she died, she 'had her revenge' by pouring out the 'real truth' of life fifty years before for her at Max Gate to 'a string of

American scholars'. 'Her voice throbbed,' the employer wrote, 'with the knowledge of old wrongs revenged.' Well, your editor happened to be there at the time, has no memory of any voice throbbing, and of the fifteen or so people in the room listening only a very few were American. Nor could anything she said of her life at Max Gate be regarded as a 'wrong'. It is difficult not to see an advanced case of jaundice here, but she does have straightforward information to give about life in the twenties:

> I was engaged by Mrs Hardy as a parlour-maid in 1921, and I stayed in the employ of the Hardy family at Max Gate, Dorchester, until shortly after Mr Hardy's death in 1928 ... The household consisted of Mr and Mrs Hardy, a housemaid, a parlour-maid (myself) and a cook. There was a full-time gardener, who lived out. We others all lived in. There was no motor-car or chauffeur until Mr Hardy passed away. ...
>
> Mrs Hardy, although difficult to work for, was devoted to her husband's comfort. She was relatively young and night after night she would dutifully read to him for two or three hours. She was like a nursemaid caring for her charge. I think she was proud of being married to a man as famous as Mr Hardy. She had, before their marriage, acted as his secretary.
>
> Mr Hardy did not like meeting the public, and before he went out for his daily walk he would always ask a member of the staff if there was any one about, so that he could miss him or her. He was a man who sought solitude. He used a little green side-door that led into the lane to Syward Lodge. Sometimes his walk would take him up the hill leading to West Stafford, at other times he would go down the path to Came Wood, but on that walk he often had to dodge the public. Usually the walks were taken alone, but sometimes he was accompanied by Mrs Hardy and always by Wessex, his beloved terrier. ...
>
> Mr Hardy's special pet, slept in his bedroom ... Wessex was a terror. No guest could pick up a spoon or anything dropped without the probability of a nasty nip on the hand by Wessex. Mr Hardy was passionately fond of 'Wessie' (his pet name for Wessex) and he could do anything with the dog without any danger, while if the dog was in a good mood, Mrs Hardy could sometimes pick up a dropped object safely. Col. Lawrence, a great friend of Mr Hardy and a frequent visitor, was the only other person who could safely deal with Wessex: he could pick up anything without any ill humour on its part. Wessex was very fond of Col. Lawrence, who would pat him and speak to him and had a wonderful power over him. To

understand what a remarkable influence Lawrence had on this dog it must be remembered that no one, with, as I say, the sole exception of Mr Hardy himself, could or would dare touch, or go near him without the probability of a snap or a bite: he was a fierce, ugly-tempered beast. ... One evening a gentleman, who had an appointment to see Mr Hardy, knocked at the door. Wessex, in his usual aggressive manner, rushed to the door barking and snarling, as he always did whenever any one came to the door ... as soon as the door opened and the dog saw the visitor he stopped snarling, and with its coat bristling, whined, then retreated into the house with every appearance of fear. The man did not speak to the dog and there was nothing about his appearance or conduct to cause such behaviour. ... Next day we had an early morning telephone message to say that the man had died during the night. Shortly after this queer incident Col. Lawrence called and I told him of the remarkable happening. Lawrence said 'I am not surprised. There is an Arab proverb that says: "The dog sees the Angel of Death first", and that is what he saw.' ...

Breakfast was at 9 a.m. and there was a choice of tea or coffee. Toast and marmalade were served and usually bacon and eggs, but sometimes kippers, boiled eggs or kedgeree took its place, but on Sunday mornings sausages were the rule. Mr Hardy drank tea and Mrs Hardy coffee. A favourite dish of Mr Hardy for lunch was lamb and caper sauce. Often in the season he would receive a brace of pheasants as a present, and both beef and chicken also appeared on the household menu and were enjoyed by him. At the end of his lunch every day he had a baked custard pudding.

Tea at 4 p.m. was a very small meal. I used to think that if a visitor was hungry what was served wouldn't be very satisfying. When I was first instructed in my duties at the Hardys I was taught to cut the bread wafer-thin and in small squares. This I did to the hidden despair of more than one guest. Bread and butter, tea and small home-made cakes were invariable fare at this meal, for which we often had guests. Dinner was at 7.30 p.m. Then Mr Hardy would most enjoy a cup of soup in a white cup followed by two boiled eggs, but during the last couple of years of his life he had only one egg. Mrs Hardy liked omelettes. A favourite drink of Mr Hardy was burgundy. This was served at lunch and dinner. ... After the dinner-table was cleared it was Mrs Hardy's duty to sit and read to her husband until 10 or later and it was my duty at 10 p.m. to leave a jug of hot water outside the dining-room door for Mrs Hardy to collect and prepare her husband's nightcap. I don't know if he had whisky or what he had with the hot water. ...

His conversations were often about the Dorset countryside and birds: he was a great nature lover and we maids had to feed the birds daily. He spoke quietly and softly and I never saw him angry. He never smoked indoors or out. Games were never played by him, either in or out of the house: neither chess, draughts, cards, dominoes nor any other games had any place in his life during my stay at Max Gate.

His pleasure was sitting in his study, with his fawn crocheted shawl over his shoulders, writing all day. He rarely came downstairs unless called for a meal. If one excepts walking and meditating, to my knowledge he had no hobbies: he did not collect coins or stamps or anything else, as some men do. I think his pleasures were wholly in his mind and quite apart from his surroundings. He would often have a far-off look, as he gazed down at his hands resting on his lap. He was an intensely introspective man and always seemed to live within himself. Until the end of his days he walked quickly, with his long overcoat flapping open. He had a favourite walking stick which he always used.

He also enjoyed motor trips and an occasional picnic in the Dorset and Somerset countryside in a hired chauffeur-driven car.

In good weather he would often go out to the garden and stand contemplating on the lawn in his favourite corner under an apple tree, near the shrubbery. In springtime this tree was surrounded by daffodils that grew amidst the grass. . . .

He was a thinker, not a man of action. I never heard him tell a funny story all the years I was there. He would sometimes give us maids quiet little smiles as he met us on the stairs, but although he never passed the time of day, he did regularly comment on the weather, which he studied every morning before breakfast, as I have already said. He was very reserved in the house, very drawn in upon himself. You always thought he wasn't really living in the present, although nothing escaped his notice. One had the feeling he was living in the past or the future. On one occasion I remember the gardener, who had been digging near the house, leaning over his spade. Hardy had noticed it too. He turned to me and said, 'He must be tired' and he smiled his wan little smile. That was all. . . .

Unless a person was a member of the small circle of his intimate friends, it was necessary to have an appointment to see him, and very few entered the house otherwise. One of these exceptions was made when a foreign warship visited Portland and three officer admirers of Mr Hardy called at Max Gate and bowed and scraped their way in by winning over Mrs Hardy, after which Mr Hardy agreed to see them. He left his study and came downstairs and met them in the drawing-room; but this was very unusual. Weekly during the winter two or three persons with no appointments would unsuccessfully try to see him, but during the summer the number of callers rose higher.

To persistent callers, who would not accept our explanation that an appointment was necessary, we exhibited a specially prepared card on which was written a message to the effect that 'Unless you have an appointment, you cannot see Mr Hardy. You should write and make an appointment'. The majority of callers were reasonable, but to those that were rudely persistent we showed the card and then firmly closed the door.

Sir James Barrie had a great liking for Hardy and he often stayed with us at Max Gate. When Hardy was ill Barrie made a special journey from London to see him and unobtrusively called at the kitchen door instead of going to the front door, so as not to make any fuss. Barrie was a likeable man and was a great favourite of mine. I also liked Lawrence, and although he looked ordinary and unassuming, I could sense he was no ordinary being, but a man of great strength of character. He had a wonderful sense of humour, at least that is how he looked to me, and I always saw and chatted with him when he came and I opened the door. When he called I always asked, as a joke, 'Is it Col. Lawrence, Mr Shaw or Mr Ross today'; he would smile and say, 'Mr Shaw today.' He never failed to ask if there was any one with T. H. If he didn't want to see Mr Hardy's visitor, he would leave at once without seeing Mr Hardy. In front of us maids Mr Hardy always referred to Lawrence as Mr Shaw, and Lawrence always called Mr Hardy T. H. when speaking to us or in front of Mr Hardy. Lawrence would come over from Bovington several times a month to talk to him. Indeed he would never pass through Dorchester without a call and a chat. He gave Mr Hardy a copy of his privately printed *Seven Pillars of Wisdom*. I asked if I could borrow it to read. Mr Hardy agreed, and I read and enjoyed it. . . .

Mr Hardy's last meal before he died was kettle-broth, of which he was very fond. He always asked for it when out-of-sorts. Kettle-broth was made from finely chopped parsley, onions and bread cooked in hot water. He had specially asked me for this on the morning of his death-day. He preferred my preparation, as I chopped the ingredients smaller than cook. He also asked for a rasher of bacon to be cooked in front of him in the flame of his bedroom coal-fire. While I cooked the bacon he quietly watched from his bed. He drank the broth, but could not eat the rasher. He only picked at that.

At the time of Hardy's illness Miss Eva Dugdale (Mrs Hardy's sister) was staying in the house with us. When Mrs Hardy or Miss Dugdale had to leave Mr Hardy's bedroom to go downstairs for any reason I was called to sit in the dressing-room and watch Mr Hardy through the half-opened door. On the evening of his death as I was sitting in the dressing-room I heard Mr Hardy call to Miss Dugdale 'Eva! Eva! what is this?' Those were the last words I heard him utter. Miss Dugdale called to me to fetch quickly hot water bottles, eiderdowns, and ring up Dr Mann. The doctor soon arrived, dropped his coat and scarf on the hall floor and hurried up the stairs. Dr Mann had brought a nurse earlier in the day to help, but Hardy did not like strangers and the nurse never saw Mr Hardy alive.

(Monograph No. 4, 1963)

The memories of the other maid, Dolly Gale (b. 1897) were written down in 1972, sixty years after she had spent just twelve months as Emma Hardy's maid when she was fourteen, in 1911–12. Her parents were not keen on her working at Max Gate because 'Mr Hardy's morals were not of the best.' Her anxiety to pretend to be knowledgeable was such that she claimed to have seen T. E. Lawrence riding his motorcycle through the Dorset lanes several years before he came to Dorset. She is not a witness to be trusted.

But one who can be trusted is John Middleton Murry (1889–1957) a critic and author, husband of Katherine Mansfield, who as Editor of the *Athenaeum* and later of the *New Adelphi* was frequently asking Hardy for 'a poem'. He stayed at Max Gate on 26–27 May 1921 and the following extracts describing his visit are taken from his *Katherine Mansfield and Other Literary Portraits* (London 1949, pp. 215–29):

I first met Thomas Hardy at Dorchester in May 1921. I had long desired to meet him; but when the volume of his collected Poems appeared in the winter of 1919 the desire became almost a monomania. Certainly I had never longed to meet a living writer so much.

Hardy had sent me some very kindly letters, and in particular one concerning a review of the 'Collected Poems' which I had written for *The Athenaeum*. In that letter he was generous enough to say that the history of English poetry ought to be re-written in accordance with the principles I had tried to establish in regard to his own. . . .

At that time Hardy was, in truth, for me a being set apart. It was not merely that I was convinced that he was the only great English writer living in the world. There was also a peculiar quality in his greatness which made an intimate and almost painful appeal. In Hardy it seemed honesty was made absolute. He had purged out of himself the last trace of the lie in the soul. He was the only man in whom I believed. And to give this belief something of the passion of despair there was the precise point of time. It was at the end of the year of complete disillusion which followed the Armistice of 1918. We had hoped against hope that the peace would be so glorious and generous that it would somehow justify the sacrifice made to gain it. It was quite a different peace, and as the news of its shameful terms gradually became known the sense of the hideous waste and the utter futility of the whole monstrous war became steadily deeper and deeper. One felt that England, the true England, had ceased to exist. . . .

Hardy seemed very small. As he sat there sideways turned away from the light of the window, he seemed not so much old as shrunken. That old brown suit, so well worn, must have fitted him well once; it hung loosely on him now. . . .

It was a room without personality, full of gilt framed pictures, cretonne, mahogany and silver. Afterwards, when I looked more closely, I found that everyone of the pictures had some personal or local justification; but few of them combined with this the beauty of a work of art. The one obvious exception was the portrait of Hardy between fifty and sixty painted by William Strang, I think, in 1893. Hardy told me that Strang had been sent down by John Lane to make a drawing of him for some edition of his work. The drawing finished, Strang took out a panel and painted it swiftly, within an hour. Some twenty years afterwards, Strang had returned to make another drawing (perhaps for the Mellstock edition) and Hardy had produced the old panel. Strang had quite forgotten it. 'I painted well in those days,' he said. He signed and dated it and had it framed for Hardy. It is a portrait of Hardy in full maturity, and it deserves the praise the artist gave it. Yet all I remember of it is the old-fashioned low collar, the big tie, and the generous moustache.

The rest of the pictures were watercolours, many by amateur hands, of places in Wessex; there was a sketch from imagination of Egdon Heath, sent Hardy by a lady. 'The curious thing,' he said, 'is that it is very like what I meant.' Another represented 'Eustachia's Barrow,' according to the written legend beneath. I pointed out that Eustachia was wrongly spelt. 'I never noticed that before,' said Hardy, 'it was done by my wife.' I was annoyed with myself for my clumsiness, although I could not have known. But when he told me, the misspelling of the name reminded me of his poem –

It was your way, my dear. . . . (CP 282)

Personality in this intricate and detailed sense there was in the room; but none in the larger. No touch of fastidious arrangement, nothing to one's immediate sense inviolable, nothing from which one might have guessed at Hardy. It might have been the drawing-room of a country vicar who combined a passionate admiration for Hardy's work with antiquarian tastes: for there was a glass case filled with Roman bowls. They had been discovered when the foundations of Max Gate were being built. Three skeletons were also found in shallow oval holes scooped out of the chalk. Hardy said that he had kept it from his wife, that she might not be frightened; but he too had felt that the omen was evil. Still, nothing had happened.

'I never have cared for possessions,' he said. 'What is in this house has come together by chance. The things I have bought, I bought as I needed them, and for the use I needed them for. Those chairs, for instance, I paid thirteen shillings for at a sale. Now I'm told they're Chippendale. I remember my mother selling a dozen, much better than those, to the cheap-jack at two shillings apiece, so that she could get some new-fashioned ones for her drawing-room. The cottagers bought them of him for half-a-crown. But I've never troubled about these things. A good table to write at and a solid chair to sit in.' . . .

'We won't change for dinner – we call it supper, here – if you don't mind,' he said. When I came back to the drawing-room, I found Mrs Hardy there. 'An awful thing has happened. I'm afraid it's one of the things that can't be believed. But I've lost the key of the wine cellar. But there's whisky and cider.'

I said that it did not matter in the least: I wasn't a regular wine drinker.

Hardy came in again. He had changed his brown tweed for a dark suit.

'You have heard of the disaster? You're sure you don't mind?'

In the dining-room, Mrs Hardy asked me: did I mind sitting to face the light? Hardy's eyes were weak. I sat opposite him. Mrs Hardy was at the head of the table. We ate soup and mutton chops and trifle.

I poured myself some whisky. Hardy watched me.

'I think I'll have a little of that.'

'Do you think you ought to?' said Mrs Hardy.

'I'll have a little.' He poured himself out a finger and a half.

We talked – about mead, and firmity; about modern writers – as a whole they seemed to Hardy 'to have lost grip' – he felt very often that they did not know what they wanted to say; he said how he had enjoyed Katherine Mansfield's story 'The Daughters of the late Colonel,' how he had laughed when his wife had read it to him. 'She has got right into her characters. But she mustn't stop there. She must follow their lives right through to the end. You must tell her that from me.' What a lot of verse was being written now! He felt he must be getting out of touch; there was very little of it that he could appreciate...

I was glad when dinner was over. For a moment I was alone with Mrs Hardy in the drawing-room.

'I hope I'm not tiring him.' And I felt a sudden sense of acute shame that I should be talking of Hardy behind his back, as though he were a child.

'No, I'm very glad you were able to come. You've taken him out of himself. He has been worrying over some business arrangement for the last two days. He has quite forgotten it now. He *will* do his business himself.'

'But why doesn't he use an agent? The biggest agent in London would think it an honour to do his business – for nothing; I should imagine so, anyhow.' I rushed into the opening I had made to escape from my sense of guilt. 'And why aren't his poems sold simultaneously in America? I understand that he may not care. But it's almost a question of principle. Why should the Americans have the best poetry that England produces for nothing, while any common or garden English author takes care (quite rightly) that the American copyright remains his own?'

'You must tell him that when he comes in. We're comfortably off; but still a little extra money would be useful nowadays.'

When he returned, Mrs Hardy began: 'Mr Middleton Murry was saying that you ought to have an agent to sell your poems in America.'

He thought for a moment. 'I don't think it's worth while, now. And besides poems are such very personal things. I can't get quite used to being paid for them at all. I don't think I can make a change now. I'll see.'...

I urged the question of principle. 'Yes, there's that way of looking at it. I had forgotten. But the difficulty is that they're written almost as people ask for them. Not written to order, of course. But there's always someone who has been asking me.'...

'I have always been on such good terms with my publishers. They do a great deal for me. And I've known them so long....' Again he turned away with relief. 'There's one thing I would like to have your advice upon. A man [Vere H. Collins] who works for the Clarendon Press was here the other day; and he urged me to have a thin India-paper edition of my poems printed. He said that when the Oxford Book of English Verse was printed on India-paper, the sale suddenly trebled. What do you think?'

'It's an excellent idea,' I said. 'Your *Collected Poems* make rather a heavy volume – heavier than the thick Oxford Book of English Verse.

People like books of poetry they can carry about easily. They read them on their holidays. As it is, they can only take the little Golden Treasury book of selections.'

'I'm glad you agree. Do you hear that, Florence?' He turned to Mrs Hardy. 'Mr Middleton Murry thinks that it would be an excellent thing to print the poems on India-paper. Now *that's*' – he turned back to me – 'the kind of suggestion that M—'s [Macmillan] like. They're very good about practical things like that.'

I had a fairly clear conception of the kind of suggestion that M—'s didn't like. . . .

It was ten o'clock; time to let him go to bed. I said good-night. There was the same impersonality in my bedroom. Everything was exquisitely clean and polished, but without centre or focus. The furniture refused all attempts at alliance. . . .

I woke early in the morning and sat on the turf in the sun outside the door. . . . The surrounding trees isolated the house completely from the surrounding country. Hardy came out, and we began to walk on the path that runs through the trees, making a square alleyway round the house. 'It's never one moment the same,' he said, pointing to the trees. 'They change continually. When you know them, they are different every morning. I planted them; and now the waste wood from them is more than enough to keep us in firing for the year. One doesn't realise how fast they grow.'

At breakfast he sat with a pile of letters. One was opened. It was from a remote cousin, enclosing an essay by his son, aged sixteen, and a photograph of the boy. His masters at school said he showed great ability. Would Hardy give his opinion of the essay, and advise whether the boy should adopt literature as a profession? 'I've never seen either of them: I suppose I shall have to reply.' His correspondents were so persistent. For a time he had tried to answer them all; but now he had given up. They were always asking for specimens of his handwriting. He was sorry, but it was impossible; if he replied, his whole day would be occupied. But one thing had grieved him. A young man, who had been a friend of Rupert Brooke's, had asked for a fragment of his handwriting. He had not given it. And now he had learned that the man was suddenly dead. . . .

Middleton Murry married again after the death of Katherine Mansfield and had a daughter in 1925 by his second wife. Sometime after this the Murrys were at Max Gate and the following occurred. It was described by Middleton Murry in a broadcast on the BBC on 19 February 1955:

I was staggered to receive an invitation to stay with him for a weekend, I think because I happened particularly to admire a poem about which he had a strong personal feeling. I went... He talked about his mother and his grandmother, and got me talking about my great grandfather who was a shipwright in the royal dockyard, anything but literature – anything but his own work. I remember he told me how Sir Francis and Lady Jeune took him off suddenly after dinner one night [11 April 1892] to see Lottie Collins sing "Ta-ra-ra-boomdee-ay", and the whole theatre went mad, and he found himself shouting at the top of his voice "Ta-ra-ra-boomdee-ay". That sort of talk – and Hardy was full of it – suited me beautifully...

Hardy generally sported a very big handkerchief of the pattern of red – an old fashioned farmer's handkerchief. One day when he had the little girl on his knee, he drew out this handkerchief and said "I'm going to make you a rabbit." She, being barely nine months old of course didn't understand a word, but she stared at the big handkerchief, which he spread on his other knee. Then he put her on the floor facing him and said "I wonder if I've forgotten how, I haven't made a rabbit for. . . ." he paused to count ". . . . seventy-five years – at the very least 75 – and I haven't seen one made either," he chuffed. I thought to myself "he can't possibly remember". Nevertheless, he began and worked on slowly and steadily, with just one long pause for recollection, but without a single mistake, and there was a really magnificent red rabbit! He was delighted with it and so was my daughter. That, I think, is the most astonishing feat of memory, at any rate of corporeal and instinctive memory, that I have ever witnessed. It struck me then, and strikes me now, as almost miraculous, and in some way I can't define it has always seemed to me of a piece with Hardy's peculiar genius.

James Barrie (1860–1937), dramatist and novelist, was in correspondence with Hardy in the 1880s, and by 1893 Barrie had become 'My dear Barrie', and Hardy, in London for three months that year, hoped that Barrie would call on him (*CL* II, p. 6). They became sufficiently friendly for Barrie to visit Max Gate and for the Hardys to stay with Barrie in his flat in the Adelphi in the centre of London. (see p. 121) Writing to Florence on 29 December 1916 Barrie said, 'I often think of my happy visit to you. It was a singularly happy one to me, Hardy's fireside is a very cheerful place.' Another visit took place on 11–12 May 1921 and on this occasion Barrie was accompanied by his secretary, Lady Cynthia Asquith (1887–1960), described in the *D.N.B.* as a writer who 'cultivated friendships with writers and artists'. Her account of that visit appeared first in *Portrait of Barrie* (London 1954, pp. 105–10) and the passages below are extracted from that. A slightly different version was published in *The Listener*, 7 June 1956, pp. 753–4.

I had heard it said that Hardy – 'that quietest figure in literature,' as Barrie described him – looked like a shrewd country solicitor or the provincial architect and surveyor he had, in fact, been. But at first sight he struck me as far more like a wary, weather-wise farmer. I could picture him in leather gaiters at an Agricultural Show, either leading round, by the ring in its nose, a red-rosetted prize bull, or delivering in the luncheon tent a quiet, sagacious, pithy speech. Superficially there was certainly little in Hardy's appearance to remind one of the popular conception of a poet. One could scarcely imagine those steady eyes 'in a fine frenzy rolling'; nor would one have expected their calm gaze either to conjure up the beauty of Tess, or to see into the mind of Napoleon. Yet in the very inconspicuousness of Hardy's appearance there was something unobtrusively impressive, and as you watched him this impression deepened. The high, broad forehead was very fine, the resigned eyes – they looked as if nothing could ever surprise them again – unforgettable. . . .

While Thomas Hardy was staying at the flat he attended the rehearsals of *Mary Rose*. I sat beside him in the empty stalls and watched his alert interest in everything, particularly in certain technicalities of production. Like so many others who have excelled in one branch of literature, he, who had excelled in two, had set his heart on writing a successful play, an ambition never realised, for though, mercifully, he was never, like Charles Lamb, given the opportunity – that opportunity so gamely seized – to join in the hissing of his own play, all his dramatisations of his own books proved disappointments. He spoke with wistful respect of that mysterious 'sixth sense' of Barrie's – the sense of the stage which he said he was sure he did not himself possess . . .

To my great delight, Thomas Hardy, not long after his London visit, invited me to come with Barrie to stay at Max Gate, his house near Dorchester. On our long journey down to Dorsetshire, Barrie talked much of Hardy. There was about him he maintained, 'something more attractive than in almost any other man'. 'He has,' he said, 'a simplicity that merits the word 'divine'; I could conceive some of the disciples having been like him.'

Next, he spoke of Hardy's perception. 'That man,' he declared through a particularly long drawn-out tussle with pipe and cough, 'that man couldn't look out of a window without seeing something that had never been seen before.' . . .

Entering the house through a gloomy little porch, we arrived at about four o'clock and were given very strong tea in the small, dark, rather overcrowded 'parlour', of which my memory holds only a jumbled impression of blue Bristol glassware, bowls of potpourri and – sole characteristic item – a collection of large hour-glasses. If I remember rightly, a door out of this room opened into a curiously dismal little conservatory...

After tea at half-past four we sat talking till seven without being shown our rooms. Barrie began to look as pale and wan as I felt....

At times Hardy was quietly caustic, particularly about a certain, what he called, 'Well-known Society Lady', who, though he has never met her, has just sent him a complete set of his works with the request that he should inscribe each volume 'To So-and-so from her friend Thomas Hardy!'

The question was asked which, if any, living author would be known in five hundred years from now; 'Someone whose name we have never heard,' quickly answered Hardy.

While Hardy and Barrie sat on in the dining-room, I had some talk with Mrs Hardy. 'Florence' is no prettier than the house, but extremely nice. She obviously adores her husband, and seems very good at what can't be – she looks very strained – an easy job...

Later in the evening Hardy read us some poems by Charlotte Mew – heart-rending name for a poet! – for whom he has a great admiration... We sat up till close on midnight – a delightful evening...

Next morning Hardy came down very spry – positively garrulous – to breakfast, after which he took us upstairs to see the small 'study' where he writes. This, bare, simple, workmanlike and pleasantly shabby, was the only room in the house that had any character at all. I can't remember many details. The well-faded walls were distempered an unusual shade of coral-pink. Several tin deed-boxes, piled one on top of the other, stood under the very plain, exceedingly neat writing-table in the middle of the room; a framed 'wage-sheet' – Hardy's father's or grandfather's, I forget which – on the shelf over the fireplace. I can't remember a single photograph, nor I think were there any pictures, but Hardy's old violin hung on the wall above the bookshelves which faced the window.

Soon after breakfast, Hardy took Barrie and me for a long walk. At over eighty he still had the stride and figure of a young man – we could scarcely keep up with him – and when he came to a hill he quickened his pace. We went to see the churchyard where the Dorsetshire poet Barnes is buried, and then to Hardy's native village, Higher Bockhampton. He pointed out the cottage in which he had been born, a genuine cottage, but compared with that, with 'but and ben' [a two-roomed house], in which Barrie was born twenty years after, a commodious dwelling. The cottage was locked. This led to an incident for ever graven on my mind. Barrie, refusing to be thwarted in his intention to enter the hallowed precincts, made me hold together two decayed ladders while, treading on my fingers, he precariously clambered up to the window and contrived to open it. He scrambled through, and shortly afterwards, with a bow, opened the door to Hardy, who, returning the bow, re-entered the home in which, eighty-one years ago, he had first cried because – to quote words so much after his own heart he had 'come to this great stage of fools.' . . .

On 14 March 1985 Lord David Cecil, who knew so many of the writers whose names appear in these pages, wrote to me. It is worth quoting from his letter: 'Internal evidence should have shown that a writer cannot describe noble characters like Diggory Venn and Gabriel Oak so convincingly unless he was drawing from his own perceptions and moral feelings. But apart from all this, Hardy made an impressive moral impression on the people who met him whom I knew. These were a distinguished lot: Max Beerbohm, J. M. Barrie, Siegfried Sassoon . . . All these felt him to be an outstanding nature – not a brilliant talker or anything of that kind, but remarkable for his modesty and humility and a kind of simple kindness.' In a later letter David Cecil mentioned Hardy's 'sincerity and tenderness of heart'.

On his deathbed Hardy asked his wife to read one of his favourite poems, Walter de la Mare's 'The Listeners'. He had written to de la Mare (1873–1956) on 1 November 1918 thanking him belatedly for his generous review of *The Dynasts* in the *Bookman* (June 1908), a review 'such as only a poet could write'. He goes on, 'If I saw it at all at the time it came out . . . your name did not convey to me as it does now any of those delightful sensations of moonlight and forests and haunted houses which I myself seem to have visited, curiously enough . . .' (*CL* V, p. 284). In the 1920s the de la Mares made a number of visits to Max Gate. They were there on 16–17 June 1921 and again on 26–27 May 1923. It seems likely that de la Mare in the following passages from *The Listener* (28 April 1956, pp. 756–7), has mixed together incidents from both the 1921 and the 1923 visits as the visit to Stinsford churchyard was in 1921, but he could not have met T. E. Lawrence at Max Gate before 1923:

> Hardy was not wholly in his novels, though all his novels were wholly within himself. After all, how much of anybody's life is far beyond the telling. Think only of a child. However that may be, Hardy is

not within my knowledge the rank immoralist the bishop who burnt his *Jude* supposed him to be. He made not the slightest attempt to twist or contort me into becoming an atheist. His 'pessimism' did not wrap me up in an evil cloud haunted by demons. Neither G. K. Chesterton's Hardy, nor, assuredly, George Moore's, made the faintest appearance in my happy days with him.

We actually met on Dorchester station's down platform. He showed a child's satisfaction and a rare courtesy almost peculiar to himself, in his immediate apology that in spite of every effort he had failed to get me a cab. . . .

And so at length we came to his house, Max Gate. It had been of his own design and building; indeed, his first book [article] had been entitled *How I Built Myself a House*. It was not in the least like 'The House Beautiful', but resembled that style of writing which he said you must not make continuously flawless, since, then, it may become too much of a strain on the reader! What, however, would have redeemed, for me at any rate, sheer downright impossible ugliness was the fact, which he confided to me that when the builders were cutting the approach to the house they had, by accident, chopped off the skull from a Roman skeleton . . .

In the hall of the house there hung a portrait of the first Mrs Hardy, her golden ringlets bedangling her fair cheeks, and it was here I met Florence Hardy who became the very kindest of friends. The next morning she picked white clambering roses from the bush beyond the doorway for her husband to lay on his first wife's grave. And then to the churchyard itself he and I made our way – across the dusty parched downs in the bright, hot sun . . .

In the churchyard he pointed out to me the gravestones of some of the old friends who appeared in his poem entitled 'Friends Beyond' (*CP* 36):

William Dewy, Tranter Reuben, Farmer Ledlow late at plough
And the Squire, and Lady Susan, lie in Mellstock churchyard now!

There, too, lay a schoolchild [Fanny Hurden], who indeed was once his sweetheart and whom, in a sweethearts' quarrel, he had pushed back on to the stove behind her – burning her hands. It was the one thing in life he told me that he could never, never forgive himself. And there had never come the opportunity, since she had died young. . . .

The lyrics in embryo that he must have squandered on me in those few most precious talks! Whatever he said was somehow what *he* said. And he alone could have said it so simply, so ordinarily. Why then so strangely and memorably – indelibly? It was all so wholly in keeping. The very next afternoon, for example – a Sunday – he told me rather diffidently after lunch, but with Florence Hardy's nod of concurrence, that a prince was coming to tea. I did not turn a hair, I hope; nor ask which prince. I merely ran through, as far as I could, the complete Victorian Royal Family and decided against each one of them in turn. Then I remained on tenterhooks.

Round about four there came a ring at the bell. And as if a Jinnee had trumpeted in my ear, I realised instantly that on the doorstep was Colonel Lawrence. And Colonel Lawrence was, of course, a Prince of Mecca...

One of the most valuable of the Monographs is No. 7, 'Motoring with Thomas Hardy' (1963) by Harold L. Voss (1891–1966). The Voss and Hardy families had known each other for many years and, because of this Hardy seems to have treated Voss more as a friend than as a hired chauffeur with some interesting results:

> I was born in Dorchester in the year 1891 and have lived there my whole life. From boyhood I had known and heard talk of Thomas Hardy. His father was a builder and at one time employed six or seven workers. My grandfather was also a builder and ornamental plasterer. I remember hearing how in, I believe, 1887 my grandfather made plaster casts of the heads of the last two men, Stone and Preedy, to be publicly hanged at Dorchester. Hardy's father and my grandfather sometimes combined forces to tackle a building job that either had to be completed quickly or would have been too big for either builder separately. At the end of the job they would share the spoils. Yes! I and my family knew Tom Hardy well.
>
> In 1912 I went to work for Tilley's Garage at Dorchester, and within a few months of entering the firm's employ I was selected to drive Mr Hardy, and became his most regular hired chauffeur from then until 1914 and again from 1919 to the year before his death in 1928. When I was not available either Bob Scott or Dick Shipton would drive him. Thomas Hardy never owned a motor car. He always hired one.
>
> During the summer it was usual for me to drive him on Mondays and Thursdays. If a whole day trip, I called at Max Gate at 10.15 a.m. and we returned by 7.30 p.m. Only once do I remember having to take him out on a Sunday, and that was when he was invited to lunch by St John Hornby at Chantmarle.
>
> He preferred to be taken for drives in the remote districts away from towns and main roads. He enjoyed visiting the then unspoilt

villages of the Dorset countryside. He liked an open touring car and disliked fast driving. Twenty-five miles per hour was the fastest speed he would allow me to travel. He always sat in the front with me and chatted about the places we visited, and the houses and inns we passed. During the drives he frequently spoke of incidents in his younger days, as the place or scene reminded him. Once, I remember, he said to me as we motored out of Dorchester towards Piddletown, 'When I was a boy I often had to walk into Dorchester with a message for your grandfather and wait for an answer, and your grandfather would give me a threepenny bit for my trouble.' On another occasion he told me how he and his brother Henry, on their Sunbeam bicycles, had cycled all over England visiting cathedrals. On the tour they had put up at village inns, and had much enjoyed drinking shandy – ginger beer and ale. ...

One of the drives that I know gave him great pleasure was to Sturminster Newton along byeways and side roads, returning by a different route and leaving the selection to me. We often did this trip.

In the first week of October 1927 I drove him to Ilminster to visit the church. He had with him then a clergyman, and took him to see something (a tomb, I think) in the church. This was the last time I drove him.

If he had visitors he liked to take them to Bath and show them the pump room and Roman baths. He also enjoyed visiting Ilchester to look at the site where the county gaol once stood and criminals were hanged. I remember well the last visit to Ilchester in 1926. We had just been to Ham Hill to see the stone quarries, where Hardy had said to me: 'I have done architectural work in which many tons of the Ham Stone were used, but until today I had never seen the quarry.' ...

Thomas enjoyed a picnic in the summer, some favourite haunts being Badbury Rings; Lydlinch Common near Sturminster Newton, where he would visit the church; Blagdon Monument, and Holme Lane, Stoborough. For these jaunts a hamper of food with thermos flasks of tea and coffee were taken. For an afternoon drive the 'Cross in Hand', on Batcombe Down, was a particular favourite and he would take many of his friends there. I stopped the car at the side of the road, and Hardy and his guests got out and, if dry, sat on the grass and talked or, if wet, they sat in the car and chatted. I used to disappear for a smoke whenever possible.

The 'Pure Drop' at Marnhull was an inn for which he had a great fondness. Even if we did not enter for a meal I always had to stop there so that he could look at it. He really loved the old Dorset inns, and was also very fond of 'The Royal Yeoman', a thatched inn at

Grimstone. This inn caught fire and was burnt to the ground and the next day I had to motor Hardy over to see the ruins. He stood in front of it looking very sad and thoughtful. The inn was rebuilt without a thatched roof, but his interest had gone and never again did he want to stop and look. Whenever he heard of any damage or alteration to one of his favourite old buildings he would want to visit it and see for himself what changes it had suffered. If the changes had altered its character he would lose all interest in it . . .

I never saw Thomas Hardy in a temper. When I called at Max Gate to collect him for a drive he would greet me with a slight smile and a quiet 'Good morning.' He was a real gentleman; nothing harsh, never flurried, always calm, and very interested in the scenes and sights on his drives through the countryside, and his journeys back in time to childhood days which, as I have already said, he often referred to nostalgically. I think the old boy lived as much in the past as he did in the present.

Writing to Florence Henniker on 2 July 1921 Hardy told her, 'We have had a few pleasant people calling – poets mostly: I am getting to know quite a lot of the Young Georgians, and have quite a paternal feeling, or grandpaternal, towards them. Siegfried Sassoon has been, Walter de la Mare, John Masefield, and next week Mr and Mrs Galsworthy are going to call on their way to London. We have also seen the Granville Barkers. All this is by reason of the car fashion of travel, which seems to make us almost suburban' (*CL* VI, p. 93). Introductions to Hardy were passed on from one young writer to another, and one who took early advantage of this was the novelist E. M. Forster (1879–1970) who visited Max Gate in 1922, 1923 and 1924. The first visit was on 19 July 1922. His letter to his mother on that day (*Selected Letters of E. M. Forster*, Vol. 2, London 1985) is worth publishing because of its satirical humour and amusing exaggeration:

> Simple, almost dull tea at the Hardys. – nice food and straggling talk. I am to lunch there to-morrow 'but the cook only came today I don't know what it will be like' says Mrs H. gloomily, and then we proceed to a performance of Midsummer Night's Dream in the Rectory garden, of which likewise little is expected. T. H. showed me the graves of his pets, all overgrown with ivy, their names on the head stones. Such a dolorous muddle. 'This is Snowbell – she was run over by a train. . . . this is Pella, the same thing happened to her. . . . this is Kitkin, she was cut clean in two, clean in two –' 'How is it that so many of your cats have been run over, Mr Hardy? Is the railway near?' – 'Not at all near, not at all near — I don't know how

it is. But of course we have only buried here those pets whose bodies were recovered. Many were never seen again.' I could scarcely keep grave – it was so like a caricature of his own novels or poems. We stumbled about in the ivy and squeezed between the spindly trees over 'graves of ancient Romans' he informed me; 'sometimes we are obliged to disturb one.' He seemed cheerful, his main dread being interviewers, American ladies, and the charabancs that whirr past while the conductor shouts "'Ome of Thomas 'Ardy, Novelist." He went in a char a banc [sic] once, but 'I didn't much like it – I was the last to mount and had to sit at the back and was thrown up and down most uncomfortably.' – Thus the visit wore away, though he talked every now and then about his books: a sign of favour, I believe – I never pressed him to it. They were both very pleasant and friendly.

Only four days after writing those words he was telling Virginia Woolf that Hardy was a 'vain, quiet, conventional old gentleman' whose 'great pride is that the county families ask him to tea . . .' (Letter from Virginia Woolf to Janet Case dated 23 September 1922)

On 27 September 1923 in another letter to his mother he describes himself as 'Just going to lunch at Max Gate – sitting on a stack of straw in a field outside.' On 25 March 1924 in a letter written on Max Gate notepaper, he tells his 'Dearest Mummy' that he has just been for tea at Max Gate, having had lunch with them yesterday, and 'They were both so friendly and kind.' The Hardy hospitality was repaid on 21 June 1924 when the Hardys came to tea at T. E. Lawrence's cottage, Clouds Hill. The following is from another letter to his mother, dated 22 June 1924:

> The Hardys came to tea yesterday, both well and cheerful. She has read my book twice herself and now reads it to him. He is most complimentary, which pleases me the more since he has never mentioned my work to me before. 'Well get on with your studies,' was his parting shot, as somewhat entangled in Wessy's chain he got into the taxi.
> Mrs H. very gloomy over Isle of Wight journey 'longer than London.' But she is a pessimist – more so than her husband, who grows gayer as the years increase.

On 11 January 1928 *The Times* published a letter from the Revd Albert Cock (1883–1953), Professor of Education and Philosophy at University College Southampton. He had been in correspondence with Hardy about his plan to establish a Wessex University with a Hardy Chair of English Literature, something that sadly has never come about. In his letter

168   *Thomas Hardy: Interviews and Recollections*

Professor Cock describes a visit to Max Gate in 1922 during which he expressed his gratitude for the note of deliverance offered in the last line of *The Dynasts*. Hardy shook his head and said, ' I should never write that now.' 'Why not?' asked the Professor. Hardy replied 'Versailles!'

Eric Austin Hinton (1899–1974) was a student at Birmingham University when in 1921 he wrote to Hardy about a thesis he was writing on Hardy's poetry. In the summer of 1922, or possibly 1923, he and a friend were on a walking tour of Dorset and managed somehow to get an invitation to tea at Max Gate. Subsequently, he wrote down some detailed notes of that meeting and here are some extracts with the headings given by the writer:

CHESIL BEACH   Had seen waves break over and through the beach: a wonderful sight: had authentic evidence of ship being carried right over the beach: doubted by Mrs Hardy he replied that he had spoken with one of the sailors who was on her.

POETRY   Believes he has written poetry longer than prose: attempted in one poem onomatopoeia – the imitation of water through a mill (*CP* 426): a critic said it sounded like 'chukking' of milk in a churn which Hardy said exactly resembled the sound he wished to imitate: re. the poem 'The Temporary The All' (*CP* 2), he remarked that a critic had not been able to find any metre in it. Hardy said they were correct Sapphics if not good ones – a difficult metre: H [Hinton] suggested the misrepresentation by misquotation, Hardy instanced a humorous poem on love which was quoted without last and most important stanza by a newspaper to prove all his works were tragic: Noyes in a lecture referred to a phrase about the 'imbecile God' (?) also without quoting context thus misrepresenting Hardy's view: he apologised when Hardy wrote to him; he had sometimes an entirely different view half-an-hour after writing a poem: e.g. he sometimes speaks of a personal God which is entirely emotional: ... H thought that it was greatly due to Hardy the opinions on suitability of reading etc. had changed and that we could see the change of common thought in his prefaces to his works: seemed to suggest that his poems were a later and more complete exposition of his attitude than his novels: he mentioned that *Dynasts* was published in three instalments and that the criticism of first was adverse, of second doubtful and of third favourable ... most critics, he thought, were inexperienced: pointed out that of course in his poems expression is given to inconsistent and frequently conflicting ideas: but significantly remarked that concordance of ideas was for philosophers not for him: he seemed to speak from the attitude of a seer ...

WALTER DE LA MARE   He introduced subject and asked us what we thought of him: H suggested that he was limited in sphere and that there was a ghostly atmosphere in his work: Hardy agreed but said that he was very perfect within that sphere: Mrs Hardy agreed: H suggested that he repeated himself and Hardy thought it was possibly due to the fact that he had to write for money: he thought it better that a man should have something else to fall back on but was sorry that Matthew Arnold had had to work so hard as a school inspector: . . .

DIALECTS   He spoke of the richness of Dorsetshire dialect and was at great pains to explain that they had an additional demonstrative 'thik' = 'that one' e.g. that corn, thik wood: Mrs Hardy spoke of hearing a child say 'thik toy': several people who had written Dorset novels had made the mistake of saying 'you be' which is never heard in Dorset: he thought dialect dying out although it was a real speech and not a corruption: he spoke of men performing plays founded on novels not knowing meaning of the words they used: the young people of today did not understand many words Barnes uses: . . .

PHILOSOPHY   He did not consider it fair to demand a reasoned and consistent philosophy from the poet – *'unadjusted impressions'*: the poet voices the general view of his age: he should not attempt to recreate past ages: Will – does not bear a strictly theoretical or philosophical interpretation: a poet must use the best possible word for his purpose: he suggested as alternatives 'Urge' or 'Force' both of which were scarcely possible in poetry: the word 'will' common in a school of philosophy of which Schopenhauer, Hartmann, Nietzsche are chief exponents: he had read the first two but would not say if he owed anything to them, despite that fact that the words 'immanent will' are common and that H had seen it asserted by Gosse on his authority that he owed no debt to Schopenhauer: the philosophical terminology of the *Dynasts* only used because it predominated in this age: he had always endeavoured to use the current philosophy of his time. H questioned him about the apparent incongruity between a supreme 'Unconscious Will' creating conscious human wills: the same question had been put by Noyes: he replied that (a) on what authority do we regard the supreme and ultimate power as one and indivisible: 'may not one effect be produced by a thousand causes' (b) May not intelligence be possibly produced in a manner analogous to explosion produced by gunpowder and a light or a colourless liquid being produced by the mixture of two colourless ones i.e. chemically . . .

WEYMOUTH   A very interesting old town: K [Hinton's friend] enquired about truth of legend that George III never came to Weymouth after cutting of figure [on hillside in chalk]: Hardy had never heard of legend but George did not go to Weymouth after 1805, whether for that or another reason: Mrs Hardy suggested that George was perhaps already mad and Hardy that it was too dangerous owing to French frigates: he said we should go into Weymouth the way George used to go and should see Weymouth as he used to see it.

FILM   He had been present at the filming of a scene from one of his novels at Maiden Castle instead of the 'Ring'.

WEYMOUTH   He mentioned that the figure of George III was getting very indistinct and Mrs Hardy suggested that perhaps the horse was already there and the rider added: Hardy described how these figures were made.

Austin Hinton subsequently became Librarian of Coventry and then Newcastle. The text above has not previously been published, and is printed here by kind permission of his daughter, Miss Vanessa Austin Hinton.

Edmund Blunden (1896–1974) was another of the young poets and writers who made the pilgrimage to Max Gate. He had sent Hardy a volume of his verse in 1920, and another in 1922, and was invited to Max Gate for a visit from 15 to 17 July 1922. Siegfried Sassoon and E. M. Forster also signed the Visitors' Book on 15 July. The *Life* (p. 450) records that the three of them accompanied Hardy to an amateur performance of A *Midsummer Night's Dream* on the lawn of Trinity Rectory. Strangely enough, Blunden's 'Notes on Visits to Thomas Hardy', passages from which follow, make no mention of this:

> Reached Max Gate about four; Mrs Hardy immediately introduced me to T. H. An artist, Mr Hill, was present, commissioned to make a portrait for John Lane's new edition of Lionel Johnson's book on Thomas Hardy. T. H. had been sitting all day, but did not appear fatigued. The pleasant, large sitting-room was dominated, grandfather-clock and all, by a small portrait of Shelley. Tea and war reminiscences. T. H. recalled his visits to the commandant of a local camp for German prisoners. Said (with enjoyable gravity) that the commandant and he moved freely among the thousands of prisoners, 'and yet they might have turned on us at any time and neither of us was carrying arms.'
>
> After tea Mr Hill took his leave. Mr Hardy proposed a walk... We walked uphill and down to Winterbourne Came at a fine pace.

T. H. spoke, not very favourably of modern reviewers: he urged me to write on the stupidity of hasty reviewing. If he were meditating an essay on Shelley he would give a month to it, but the present reviewers disposed of a new volume in a day or so. He thought none of the reviewers of his *Late Lyrics* had read the volume through; said they had chosen for quotation only pieces which he had included with doubts – had indeed put in only to lighten the volume as a whole.

Through Came Park and its avenue we reached William Barnes's little but beautiful church; stood by Barnes's grave . . . Something made him recall to me Hawker of Morwenstow and his six cats, which occupied a front pew. I was admiring as a piece of calligraphy a black-letter inscription over the rood-screen. T. H., with technical and indifferent eye: 'Yes, it's correct church text.'

On the way home I asked if he did not like Barnes as a poet, not only in dialect, but in common English as well; this made him break in with enthusiasm, 'There's another great wrong done by the critics – they checked Barnes.' And he continued praising Barnes's volume of *Poems in Common English*, and deploring the dull criticism it received . . .

By this, we were almost at Max Gate. It had rained a little. He urged me to change my suit: 'You're younger than I am, as I said before.' Dinner in another comfortable room, with leafy light around us; solid sets of books here, and one oil portrait of T. H. Afterwards there was earnest talk round the fire – although it was July, a fire was welcome! T. H. acknowledged himself a book-hunter; in the pre-Kingsway days he had haunted Bookseller's Row, which he would have properly named, Holywell Street. The name Grub Street, too, he said, he had long wished to see perpetuated, even though only in the form of 'Milton Street, formerly Grub Street' . . .

Sunday, July 16th

Cloudy and chilly. I took myself off to Dorchester in the morning. The afternoon we spent at the fireside. With allusion to my having been a Bluecoat boy, T. H. said, 'It's a great wonder that I didn't go to Christ's Hospital.' His mother knew a governor of the School, and a nomination was the natural prospect for him; but the Governor died when he was still very young. He remarked on the presumed attitude of the Coleridges towards S. T. Coleridge – 'Probably ashamed of his blue coat'; said that an enthusiast visiting the family at Ottery St Mary had spoken of S.T.C., and found 'an icy silence.' On my noticing the architect Pugin as a Blue, T. H. praised him warmly. Mrs H. observed that if she had a son she would as readily send him to school at Christ's Hospital as anywhere...

He advised me to write a history of old wars in the light of experience gained in the new one, and soon pitched on Marlborough as a fruitful subject. In zeal he hurried upstairs for the required volume of the *Dictionary of National Biography* and explored the bibliography there given to ensure that the work had not been forestalled.

I kept the plan before me, but not long afterwards a work on Marlborough appeared and prevented me.

He also ran for another volume of *D.N.B.*, in order to find out who Ebenezer Jones was. He had been reading aloud with great happiness the lyric, 'When the world is burning', and afterwards I spoke of the author as a Chartist and unhappy genius; this set T. H.'s imagination off. Reading in the *D.N.B.* that Jones was a mounting spirit crushed by public apathy and critical clumsiness, T. H. was moved, and brooded for some minutes.

The Queen's Doll's House Library being at that time in preparation, I spoke of it. T. H. was not exactly pleased with the way in which it was being collected. He said that at first 'a Tradesman' had written requesting his contributions, but he ignored the letter. Then some months after 'a Princess had, with her own hand, written and turned the request into a petition', proposing to have a copy of one of his poems made, which he might sign. He consented, but had heard nothing more.

(*The Great Victorians* London 1932, pp. 236–41)

One other recollection attributed to Blunden needs mention. In Seymour-Smith's *Hardy* (London 1994) he writes on p. 38 that Hardy 'at the age of eighty-five told Edmund Blunden – and Blunden himself said it to this author as he did to others – that "sexual desire could be a great problem for an old man." He then mentioned that he had been capable of full sexual intercourse until he was eighty-four.' Another visit of Blunden, together with Sassoon and T. E. Lawrence, to Max Gate on 9 August 1924 is recorded in Hardy's *Personal Notebooks*, so it is possible that Hardy may have taken Blunden aside and discussed intimacies of his sexual life with him, but knowing what we do about Hardy this takes some believing.

George Herbert Clarke (1873–1953) was Professor of English Literature at several American universities and came to England in the summer of 1922 with the intention of visiting several famous writers and then writing articles and/or a book about these interviews. He met Conrad on 6 August, Hardy on 11 August, Galsworthy on 6 September and John Masefield on 9 September. In the interview with Vere Collins (see pp. 136) on 19 August 1922, a few days after the Clarke visit, Hardy is reported as saying, 'Several American professors have urged me to write them [his memoirs]. They come to see me from all parts of America. I had one all the way from Tennessee. They ask all sorts of questions about one's private life.' Clarke was the professor from Tennessee and Hardy liked him enough to give him nearly an hour of his time. The following passages of Clarke's notes are extracted from *Douglas Library Notes* (Queen's University, Kingston, Ontario, Autumn 1964, pp. 8–10):

Called upon him and Mrs Hardy at Max Gate, Dorchester, August 11, 1922, at 4.30 p.m., stayed for tea and left at 5.20.

Mrs H, before he entered, explained that holiday-makers were not particularly desired, but that 'American professors of Literature', who naturally had a real interest in H's work, were welcome. She said that Mr H did not like to be asked for his autograph, because assent was sometimes abused – she knew of one case where a book so autographed was immediately sold ...

Mr Hardy was most kind in his greeting. He is of somewhat slight stature, with a really *beautiful* face, nobly old – a grave brow, serene eyes, pleasant smile, roman nose, mobile mouth – a face of dignity but of goodwill.

The Dynasts. We discussed various points. He explained that much criticism had been directed against its length, but that the great difficulty was *condensation*, which he had constantly sought and, he thought, achieved. I expressed my great admiration of the drama, and especially of its fidelity to its own impetus. He was gratified, he said. He told me of the Oxford (and antecedent London) performances – how the philosophy was cancelled & an objective twenty or so scenes developed – the energy and pleasure of the undergraduates who arranged it. Why, he wondered, did not America try a similar experiment. He thought it might go well in America. His pronunciation was Dinasts (a quick slurring of the last syllable). I remarked on the persistence of the Spirit of Pity & the Spirit of Irony (and I should have added, the Sinister Spirit) in "And There was a Great Calm" (*CP* 545) – the Armistice verses.

His 'Apology' for *Late Lyrics & Earlier*. I said that I was struck by the phrase 'evolutionary meliorism' as against 'pessimism' in that 'Apology' & preferred it to my own phrase 'pitying ironist'. He said that he had not carefully considered it, indeed had written the 'Apology' somewhat hurriedly (in bed, I understood him to say). In any case, I said, his admirers were glad that he had made a definite and authoritative statement as against the facile journalism that likes to sum him up as a 'pessimist'. He smiled, & spoke of the variousness of humanity, the difficulty of being understood ...

He assented to the remark that great expression by one man in prose and verse must be better in the latter than the former. Verse is so much more *condensed*. As the world ages, and there is less *time*, poetry will again come into its own, he believes...

I regretted Mr H's inability to come to America, and compared his poem 'On an Invitation to the United States' (*CP* 75). He replied that although he had not come, the Americans who came to see him kept him in touch with the U.S. & that perhaps he saw its best without having to see its worst, by seeing them. I wished that it might be so. He had not himself travelled much. Western Europe. But see the great cities of Europe, he said. They give quintessence.

The editor has a difficult task when it comes to Newman Flower (1879–1964), publisher and chairman of the publishing house of Cassell & Co. He was a Dorset man and claims that as a youth in his teens he lay in the bracken near the Bockhampton Cottage to catch a glimpse of Hardy on his way to visit his mother. He met Hardy, he tells us, about the time of his second marriage (1914) and subsequently visited Max Gate whenever he was in Dorset. On the strength of this he wrote article after article about Hardy over a period of more than forty years, all using very much the same memories and very often the same words. His autobiography *Just As It Happened* (London 1950) was known to many of his friends as *Just As It Didn't Happen* because of many errors of fact such as that Hardy owned a motor-car and that because of problems with his first wife, Emma, he lived 'his future life in his study' and built an outside stairway to his study in order to avoid her. However, it is indisputable that he knew Hardy well and that some of his memories are worth keeping:

> It was before the first World War that I went to see him on a strange mission. He had just married again, and his second wife – exactly my own age – came into the room with him as if to protect him from one of these vague unknowns who were always ringing the bell.
> My call upon Hardy was made in order to get something for nothing. Not for myself, but for a cause in which he was deeply interested – the Society of Dorset Men in London. I was editing the Society's Annual as a hobby at that time. So I went to Hardy and asked him to give me a poem for the next year's issue. He gave me the poem, and something that was far richer – his friendship till the end of his days.
> I saw him standing before me, a very little man, with a great dome forehead. A very little man with a pricked moustache, and deep-set

eyes, a curved nose, and small white hands with short stubby fingers. I have never yet seen what I would regard as the perfect photograph of Hardy. But a Russian sculptor named Youriévitch made a bust of him in 1924 which has always seemed to me the best portrait. The sculptor beat the camera. He made Hardy as he was. When at a later stage Hardy gave me a photograph of that bust he said: 'The Russian has put in that large curved nose without mercy.'

At that first interview we discovered that our two families had belonged to the same patch of Dorset soil, back and still further back, through the generations. And the link through a patch of soil can be greater than the blood link. From that day I went regularly to Max Gate.

I saw the later years sweep past Hardy and, in their passing, leave but slight trace upon him. He appeared to grow no older. The body, the mind of him became 'fixed'. Life in passage ceased to make its marks upon him. He remained agile from year to year. There was no sign of waning physical strength. In his brain were the same blazing fires...

In those days [1862–7] Hardy spent much of his time in London. He was studying architecture, and lived in the Adelphi. He told me that he used to eat his mid-day meal at a little coffee-shop in Hungerford Market which stood by the present site of Charing Cross Station. Charles Dickens frequently went to the same coffee-shop for his lunch. Hardy watched Dickens perch himself on a high stool at the counter. Many times the urge came to him to speak to one whom he regarded as the master.

'Once,' he said, 'I went up and stood at the vacant place beside the stool on which Dickens was sitting. I had eaten my lunch, but I was quite prepared to eat another if the occasion would make Dickens speak to me. It would be a reward more than fitting for the torment of a second helping. I hoped he would look up, glance at this strange young man beside him and make a remark – if it was only about the weather. But he did nothing of the kind. He was fussing about his bill. So I never spoke to him.'

Today the ashes of Hardy lie but a few feet away from the remains of Dickens in Westminster Abbey. Two great writers who met but never spoke...

I remember once discussing capital punishment with him, and the process of mental rather than physical torture which it involved to those other than the criminal. We were wandering round and round his garden probing in our talk into the rudiments of right and justice, cruelty and blame. We knew – I think we knew – that we were only beating round and about a law as immutable as the place of the stars, or the tragedy of *Tess* which belonged to and was part of the same immutability.

He stopped suddenly and said:

'I have seen some awful things, but what impressed me more than all else is something my father once told me. My father saw four men hung for *being with* some others who had set fire to a rick. Among them was a stripling of a boy of eighteen. Skinny. Half-starved. So frail, so underfed, that they had to put weights on his feet to break his neck. He had not fired the rick. But with a youth's excitement he had rushed to the scene to see the blaze. . . . Nothing my father ever said to me drove the tragedy of Life so deeply into my mind.'

I think one of my happiest memories of Hardy was a gay day of Dorset adventure [11.9.22]. I always went to see him when on my paternal patch of soil. I happened to be at Weymouth on this occasion, and we fixed up a picnic on the telephone. It was the best picnic I ever knew. We called for him – my wife Eve, my son Desmond, and myself – with a well-primed luncheon-basket on the back of the car. He was afire with life that morning. He climbed in beside me at the driver's seat, and Florence Hardy joined the company in the back.

'Now, T. H.,' I said: 'where do you want to go?'

He hesitated as we steered out of the Max Gate drive. Then said he would like to go to some of the spots associated with his novels. Possibly he had read my thoughts.

We drove off towards Sturminster Newton. Here was a village unspoiled: one of the most lovely of the Dorset hamlets. We parked the car in a side street, and Hardy and I walked off in search of a little villa he wished to see.

We reached the river with its bridge across which the Dorset poet William Barnes used to pass on his way to the village school. Then we found the villa.

We stood outside the garden; then went in. Hardy seemed fascinated by the place. He stood looking at it in silence. I glanced at him presently and saw that his eyes were fixed upon the house. He pointed to a side window and said: 'In that room I wrote *The Return of the Native*.'

He began to look around him. At his side was a vast monkey-puzzle tree. The tree had some attraction for him. He began to stare at it from root to its uppermost point. Presently he exclaimed as if to himself:

'How it's grown! I planted that tree when I came here. It was then a small thing not so high as my shoulder.' He waited a moment as if thinking. Then:

'I suppose that was a long time ago. I brought my first wife here after our honeymoon.... She had long golden hair.... How that tree has grown! But that was in 1876.... How it has changed....'

He paused, still staring at the tree – then remarked: 'Time changes everything except something within us which is always surprised by change.'

He said no more. He seemed to want to get away from the place as if something so richly dead disturbed the tranquil of his mind by remembrance. He stopped to play with a mangey ginger cat on the bridge. Then we rejoined the car, and drove towards the Hintock country of *The Woodlanders* ...

We got out at the foot of High Stoy, that hill of soft and lovely proportions, drew the car apart from the road and went in among the trees. High Stoy! No hill in Dorset has been so immortalised by Hardy, and for its beauty, few better devised by God.

Hardy sat on a fallen tree, and Desmond beside him. We began our lunch. Hardy ate lobster. Ultimately he thought he would like a glass of port! Port wine and lobster when one is in the eighties! And he seldom touched wine!...

'Now,' he said, 'I'm going to climb High Stoy!'

His wife told him it was foolishness. She and I suggested that he should sit in the shade of the beech-trees. But he would not listen.

'I haven't been up High Stoy for many years, and I shall never go up it again,' he said. 'I am going to climb High Stoy!' He shuffled himself from the fallen tree and prepared for action.

We went up High Stoy – he and I and Desmond. The latter in the full vigour of youth reached the summit first. When we reached him after several halts, Hardy stood in the wind, his hat in his hand, looking over that piece of Wessex which had known no pattern of change through the centuries, and which he had made famous.

He turned to me presently and said: 'I shall never see this again.'

He never did. (pp. 81–104)

Brigadier-General J. H. Morgan (1876–1955) was introduced to Hardy by Edward Clodd in December 1903. He was successively journalist, lawyer, and then held high office in the army during the First Great War serving on several Commissions looking into such matters as the conduct of the Germans in the field and the disarmament of Germany. It was he who told Hardy that he was convinced that Germany had no intention of disarming, a remark which led Hardy to comment to

Eden Phillpotts 'that only a phantom peace rose from the accumulated bitterness of Versailles and that men were sowing another crop of dragons' teeth rather than the fruit of the olive.' Here is a reminiscence by Brigadier Morgan from an experience in October 1922 when he walked with Hardy to Stinsford churchyard:

> ... talking by the way through the meadows of the eternal riddles of human destiny, chance, free will, immortality, whence we arrived at the subject of religion, and the Church of England. Thereupon he said, 'I believe in going to church. It is a moral drill, and people must have something. If there is no church in a country village, there is nothing.... I believe in reformation coming from *within* the church. The clergy are growing more rationalist and that is the best way of changing.' Pressed to charge the clergy, in that case, with casuistry in subscribing to articles in which they did not believe, Hardy would have nothing of it. He looked on it as a necessity in practical reform. And as he laid his flowers on the grave of his first wife, he began a long talk on the theme, 'The liturgy of the Church of England is a noble thing. So are Tate and Brady's Psalms. These are the things that people need and should have.'

(From *Thomas Hardy* by Edmund Blunden, London 1967, pp. 164–5)

It should be possible here to include some observations on Hardy by Sir Sidney Cockerell who had met him in 1911 while trying to beg manuscripts of famous writers for his Fitzwilliam Museum at Cambridge, and in the remaining seventeen years of Hardy's life visited Max Gate forty-two times. *Collected Letters* contains more than seventy letters from Hardy to Cockerell, and Hardy entrusted Cockerell with the disposal of his manuscripts, the Fitzwilliam Museum, of course, getting two of the best, and Cockerell himself picking up one or two choice minor items. But there is surprisingly little written by Cockerell about Hardy that is worth publishing.

Charles Morgan (1894–1958), novelist and playwright, met Hardy first when as Manager of the Oxford University Dramatic Society he looked after Hardy during his visit to Oxford to see a performance of *The Dynasts* in February 1920 (*Life* pp. 432 and 524–7). He wrote to Hardy on 11 November 1922 asking for permission to call at Max Gate, and the visit took place a few days later. An account of both Hardy's visit to Oxford and Morgan's visit to Max Gate was written by Morgan in 1929 at Florence's request, and then inserted by her in the second volume of 'her' *Life* of Hardy:

> ... going to Dorchester in 1922 to see the Hardy Players perform a

dramatization of *Desperate Remedies*, I was invited by him to Max Gate, where we sat round the fire after tea and he told me of his early days in London, and how he would go to Shakespearian plays with the text in his hands and, seated in the front row, follow the dialogue by the stage light. He told me, too, that he had written a stage version of *Tess*, and something of its early history; how, after the success of the novel, the great ones of the earth had pressed him to dramatize it; how he had done so, and the play had been prepared for the stage; by what mischance the performance of it had been prevented. Where was it now?

In a drawer. Would he allow it to be performed? He smiled, gave no answer, and began at once to talk of criticism – first of dramatic criticism which, he said, in the few newspapers that took it seriously was better than literary criticism, the dramatic critics having less time 'to rehearse their prejudices'; then of literary criticism itself – a subject on which he spoke with a bitterness that surprised me. The origin of this bitterness was in the past where, I believe, there was indeed good reason for it, but it was directed now against contemporary critics of his own work, and I could not understand what general reason he had to complain of them. He used no names; he spoke with studied reserve, sadly rather than querulously; but he was persuaded – and there is evidence of this persuasion in the preface to the posthumous volume of his verse – that critics approached his work with an ignorant prejudice against his 'pessimism' which they allowed to stand in the way of fair reading and fair judgement.

This was a distortion of facts as I knew them. It was hard to believe that Hardy honestly thought that his genius was not recognized; harder to believe that he thought his work was not read. Such a belief indicated the only failure of balance, the only refusal to seek the truth, which I perceived in Hardy, and I was glad when the coming of a visitor, who was, I think, secretary of the Society of Dorset Men, led him away from criticism to plainer subjects. When the time came for me to go, seeing that he proposed to come out with me, I tried to restrain him, for the night was cold; but he was determined, and Mrs Hardy followed her own wise course of matching her judgement with his vitality. So he came down among the trees to the dark road, and I saw the last of him standing outside his gate with a lantern swaying in his hand. I shall not know a greater man, nor have I ever known one who had, in the same degree, Hardy's power of drawing reverence towards affection.

He was not simple; he had the formal subtlety peculiar to his own generation; there was something deliberately 'ordinary' in his demeanour which was a concealment of extraordinary fires – a method of self-protection common enough in my grandfather's generation, though rare now.

There are many who might have thought him unimpressive because he was content to be serious and determined to be unspectacular. But his was the kind of character to which I lay open. He was an artist, proud of his art, who yet made no parade of it; he was a traditionalist and, therefore, suspicious of fashion; he had that sort of melancholy, the absence of which in any man has always seemed to me to be a proclamation of blindness.

There was in him something timid as well as something fierce, as if the world had hurt him and he expected it to hurt him again. But what fascinated me above all was the contrast between the plainness, the quiet rigidity of his behaviour, and the passionate boldness of his mind, for this I had always believed to be the tradition of English genius, too often and too extravagantly denied. (*Life* pp. 527–8)

Hardy became acquainted with St John Ervine (1883–1971), novelist and playwright, in 1921 when Ervine was much involved in the presentation by a hundred and six younger writers of a first edition of Keats's poems to Hardy on 2 June, Hardy's birthday. Later in the twenties there was correspondence between them about the possibility of Ervine revising Hardy's dramatisation of *Tess* for the stage. Hardy's 'Personal Notebooks' record a visit by him on 7 April 1923, and on New Year's Eve 1923 Hardy and his wife had lunch with Ervine at the Royal Hotel, Weymouth. The following recollections were part of the BBC radio programme, 'Hardy and His Friends', broadcast on 19 February 1955:

> I knew him only in his old age, but I met him often and was frequently alone with him. I never once heard him utter a word of despair. The deepest impression he made on me was of great serenity of mind, and I should describe him as a stoic who faced existence with courage and fortitude. He didn't ignore pain, but neither did he ignore pleasure. His novels are full of characters who contend with calamity and are not daunted by disaster. When an overzealous dog drives Gabriel Oak's sheep over the edge of a precipice, Gabriel doesn't sit down and moan like a modern young man that he's been frustrated by fate: he tidies up the shed in his sheepfold, and then taking his stick in his hand, walks onto the high road and starts his life again.
>
> Hardy was a small man, with delicately drawn features, which easily eluded photographers and portrait painters. But his delicate appearance did not denote either a feeble body or a weak will. He was tough and his mind was not easily moved from its purpose. He was

uncommonly courteous, though he let no one take liberties with him, and he was the only great man I have ever met who seemed to have no fads except perhaps his objection to being touched. His conversation was good without being brilliant, and he was always at his best with one or two people that he knew well. A large company silenced him. He didn't fade out of such a group, he withdrew from it, although he was still there.

Once, when he came to lunch with me in Weymouth, I heard him make a remark that might have been called 'characteristic' of his alleged gloom. "I never come into this hotel," he said "without remembering someone who is dead." But he was an old man then, and only that morning had heard of the death of a close and much loved friend. [Sir Frederick Treves had died on 10 December] And isn't it natural for an old man to remember the dead more than the living?

The following recollection of Major-General Sir Harry Marriott Smith (b. 1875) probably dates from the mid 1920s. The Major-General lived in a house close to Max Gate which in 1968 became The Trumpet-Major pub and restaurant. Hardy must have had a shock at the proposal to 'shuffle' off his distinguished guests to a Major-General unknown to them, but extricates himself from the offer with a kind duplicity. The text here is from the BBC radio programme of 1955 mentioned previously:

I can remember when I came to live in his neighbourhood. He was then already old, and there was a constant stream of young and old authors and artists coming to see him, and I did suggest to him that he might find it convenient to shuffle them off on to me, or that I would enjoy their company and their conversation. "Oh, no," he said "you know, they are an uncommon dull lot." I said "But surely, Barrie and Shaw...." "They'd bore you stiff," and all this with a sparkle in his eyes, and a kindliness which was characteristic of the man.

About his deeper thoughts he would sometimes speak. What struck me as a soldier was the indomitable courage with which he always refused to blur in any way the ugly facts of the world. The suffering came home to him so nearly and so hardly that he found it difficult to forgive the powers that directed our existence, for the pain and the grief that he saw all around him. He would not accept my own view that the suffering of others could be exaggerated – that there was a limit to human suffering, and that we did not, could not expect to know the whole of the plan of the universe. "No," he said "we've got to face it, we are up against a power which may be indifferent, may be malignant and is extremely unlikely to be benevolent."

Well, I bought *The Dynasts* in 1915 between the retreat from Mons and the landing in Gallipoli and I still think it is the greatest book that has been written during my lifetime. I often tried to get him to talk about it, and how he acquired this astonishing knowledge of Napoleonic law [lore?], and an almost uncanny knowledge of how soldiers thought and how they behave. I remember instancing the picture he gives of the retreat to Corunna, and the stragglers – the desperation, the contemptible characteristics that are produced by these circumstances, and the one or two heroic figures standing out like beacons among the rest. He said "Oh, well, I just knew it. I didn't read that anywhere, I just knew it." And I think that he did: he had that insight which is really a form of genius.

T. E. Lawrence ('Lawrence of Arabia', 1888–1935) had an introduction from Robert Graves to Hardy, and he made the first of many visits to Max Gate in March 1923. He was then serving as a soldier under the alias 'Private T. E. Shaw' at Bovington Army Camp, an important centre for tank training, only a few miles from Max Gate. He and Hardy took an instant liking to each other. Although Hardy knew all about the pity of war he had a great admiration for soldiers, and 'Colonel Lawrence', as Hardy called him, was a frequent and welcome visitor during the two and a half years he was stationed nearby. For Lawrence, Hardy was 'above and beyond all men living as a person' (Letter to Florence Hardy 16 April 1928), and for Florence, Lawrence was 'one of the few entirely satisfactory people in the world' (Letter to Sydney Cockerell 11 April 1924). The two following extracts are taken from *The Letters of Lawrence of Arabia* (London 1964):

8.ix.23
... The truth seems to be that Max Gate is very difficult to seize upon. I go there as often as I decently can, and hope to go on going there so long as it is within reach: ... but description isn't possible. Hardy is so pale, so quiet, so refined into an essence: and camp is such a hurly-burly. When I come back I feel as if I'd woken up from a sleep: not an exciting sleep, but a restful one. There is an unbelievable dignity and ripeness about Hardy: he is waiting so tranquilly for death, without a desire or ambition left in his spirit, as far as I can feel it: and yet he entertains so many illusions, and hopes for the world, things which I, in my disillusioned middle-age, feel to be illusory. They used to call this man a pessimist. While really he is full of fancy expectations.

Then he is so far-away. Napoleon is a real man to him, and the country of Dorsetshire echoes that name everywhere in Hardy's ears.

He lives in his period, and thinks of it as the great war: whereas to me that nightmare through the fringe of which I passed has dwarfed all memories of other wars, so that they seem trivial, half-amusing incidents.

Also he is so assured. I said something a little reflecting on Homer: and he took me up at once, saying that it was not to be despised: that it was very kin to *Marmion*.... saying this not with a grimace, as I would say it, a feeling smart and original and modern, but with the most tolerant kindness in the world. Conceive a man to whom Homer and Scott are companions: who feels easy in such presences.

And the standards of the man! He feels interest in everyone, and veneration for no-one. I've not found in him any bowing-down, moral or material or spiritual....

Yet any little man finds this detachment of Hardy's a vast compliment and comfort. He takes me as soberly as he would take John Milton (how sober that name is), considers me as carefully, is as interested in me: for to him every person starts scratch in the life-race, and Hardy has no preferences: and I think no dislikes, except for the people who betray his confidence and publish him to the world....

For the ticket which gained me access to T. H. I'm grateful to you – probably will be grateful always. Max Gate is a place apart: and I feel it all the more poignantly for the contrast of life in this squalid camp. It is strange to pass from the noise and thoughtlessness of sergeants' company into a peace so secure that in it not even Mrs Hardy's tea-cups rattle on the tray: and from a barrack of hollow senseless bustle to the cheerful calm of T. H. thinking aloud about life to two or three of us. If I were in his place I would never wish to die: or even to wish other men dead. The peace which passeth all understanding; – but it can be felt, and is nearly unbearable. How envious such an old age is. (To Robert Graves, pp. 429–30)

12.iv.25

Clouds Hill Moreton Dorset

I waited till I'd seen old T. H. again (yesterday): to revive my memories of what he said. The old man never gives judgements upon live writers: so don't quote it. He would not talk to me if he thought I made notes.

Unfortunately a Mrs [*name omitted*] butted in & spoiled my preparation. His memory for recent events is getting patchy: and it is no good springing a question upon him.

He said '*The Fables* [La Fontaine's *Fables*, translated by Edward Marsh].... oh yes.... I thought they were excellent reading. Good.'

Then he went on to talk of the rat which found oysters upon the sea-shore, & thought they were ships.... and the quote from Rabelais. It was going to be quite worth reporting.... and then this old hen butted in: & when she had stopped, & I asked again, he had forgotten that he had read the fables. The truth is that a film seems to slip over his mind at times now: and the present is then obscured by events of his childhood. He talked next of seeing Scots Greys in a public house in Dorchester drinking strong ale, whose fumes made him (aet.6) drunken.

I'll try again in a fortnight or so. I generally see him every other Sunday....

(To Edward Marsh, pp. 473–4)

On at least one occasion (16 June 1924) the Hardys were asked to tea at Clouds Hill, Lawrence's little hide-away cottage at Moreton near Bovington Camp. E. M. Forster was staying with Lawrence as he did occasionally during those years, and according to Lawrence, was coming 'to cheer me up'. Lawrence said goodbye to Hardy for the last time in November 1926. He had been posted to India. It was a sadness to Hardy that, feeling the cold, as Lawrence was going, he rushed indoors to get a shawl. When he returned Lawrence was just disappearing on his motorcycle. Hardy said that 'he did hope Col. L. did not think he was tired of waiting and went in. He said he always liked to have the last look – Col. L. always looks back, he says, as he departs' (Letter from Florence Hardy to E. M. Forster of 22 November 1926).

In November 1922 Hardy was elected to an Honorary Fellowship of Queen's College, Oxford, and on 25 June the following year Florence and he paid a two-day visit to Oxford and stayed at his College. Godfrey (later Lord) Elton (1892–1973), historian and writer of novels, wrote an account of that visit which was published in *Horizon* (Spring 1965, pp. 62–4), and from which the following extracts are taken:

> The volume of traffic in Oxford's High Street on a July afternoon in 1923 was naturally nothing like what it would be today, and it could move a lot faster. Which meant that from the steps in front of the college we might hope to spot a car slowing down before it drew up at the college gates. 'You'll find that they will be punctual,' said my companion confidently.
>
> I did not feel so certain myself, for people are by no means always punctual in dreams, and I had not yet altogether shaken off the impression that we were involved in a stimulating but faintly embarrassing dream. For we were waiting to receive Mr and Mrs Thomas Hardy...

Punctually almost to the second, the Hardys' car drew up, and a smallish, frail old gentleman in tweeds was clambering out of it. Alert, birdlike, and unassuming, he might have been an exceptionally intelligent retired farmer, but certainly not a literary giant, and still less a thwarted student; and it was with such polite small talk as might have been exchanged with a retired farmer that we occupied the crossing of the front quadrangle to the Provost's lodgings . . .

Next morning the Hardys were ritually conducted around the principal sights of the college by a small posse of four Fellows, headed by the pro-Provost. No one could have been better qualified that the pro-Provost to provide factual information, for he possessed a photographic memory . . . But this morning, I couldn't help feeling, he was almost too informative. We would pause before the Grinling Gibbons carvings in the Library or Garrick's copy of the First folio or the contemporary portrait of one of our more distinguished Old Members, King Henry V, and Hardy would gaze reflectively at it and seem about to speak, when a fresh spate of information would break over his head. One recalled the observation of a rustic character in *Under the Greenwood Tree*: 'He can hold his tongue. That man's dumbness is wonderful to listen to,' but Hardy's, it was to be feared, had been to some extent involuntary.

However, when the tour was completed there was half an hour or so to spare before lunch, and Hardy asked me to go with him and Mrs Hardy into High Street, where he was anxious to see the famous curve from the most revealing viewpoint. (Had not the carter assured young Jude that 'there's a street in the place – the main street – that ha'n't another like it in the world'?) As usual, bicycles as well as cars were pouring down toward Magdalen Bridge, and Hardy remarked that about 1900 he had done a lot of cycling and believed that he could do it still if it were not for the motor traffic, of which, he confessed, he would be somewhat apprehensive. Once, he said, when bicycling from Bath to Bristol, he had skidded and fallen on the muddy road; and then going into a second-hand furniture shop, he had seen a first edition of Hobbes's *Leviathan* lying in a basin, and when he asked the price, the woman in the shop had eyed his muddy clothes and replied, 'Would sixpence hurt 'ee?' He displayed little fear, however, of the cars now swirling past us: too little indeed, it seemed to me, when we crossed the street for a better view of All Souls. Hardy's eye travelled appreciatively along the majestic arc from Queen's to Brasenose. Was he recalling how often the youthful Jude had climbed the hill to gaze at the distant city, seen as a faint halo of light in the night sky, and called it 'the heavenly Jerusalem' and 'a castle, manned by scholarship and religion'? Evidently not, for he remarked thoughtfully that it was by way of Oxford that Shakespeare had travelled on his first journey from Stratford to London, and that he had put up at Carfax; by which road would he have entered the city? 'Just fancy *him* being here!' he murmured. We had some minutes in hand before lunch, and Hardy's thoughts were evidently still running on literature rather than learning. Would it be possible to see the Shelley Memorial? he inquired. Shelley, like Jude, it occurred to me, must have got a good deal less out of Oxford than he had hoped for. I could not remember having seen the memorial myself, but I knew that it was conveniently close at hand, somewhere in University College, and without disclosing my ignorance to the Hardys, I led them throught the college gate and made unobtrusive inquiries in the porter's lodge. Hardy did not seem to be very favourably impressed by the memorial when we had reached it, and perhaps the effigy of a naked man spread out on a slab does suggest a failed cross-Channel swimmer rather more than either the undergraduate who was suspended for atheism or the author of the *Ode to the West Wind* ...

... the Hardys invited me to accompany them in a hired car which was to take them sight-seeing where they pleased. I was only too well aware that in respect to dates and architecture my local knowledge might prove sadly unreliable on an intensive tour of the university in company with one who, like the young Hardy, had been trained as an architect or, like the young Jude, must have eagerly accumulated heterogeneous information as to the colleges. I was somewhat relieved therefore, as well as somewhat surprised, when once again his inclination proved to be toward literature rather than the university. We would drive to Boars Hill, a mile or two to the south, he proposed, to call on the Masefields. John Masefield was not then poet laureate, of course, but his *Widow in the Bye Street* and *The Everlasting Mercy* had excited the young shortly before the war, and in 1923 almost any undergraduate with literary leanings could quote 'Quinquiremes [sic] of Nineveh from distant Ophir...' Mrs Hardy remarked that Masefield had always sent her husband his books, with the solitary exception of *Right Royal*, which, they concluded, he had felt to be not up to standard. Of the younger poets, Hardy said, he liked Siegfried Sassoon best. This suited me, and I asked what he thought of another of my favourites, James Elroy Flecker, but he seemed hardly to know of him. However, they had been seeing a good deal of Colonel Lawrence, of Arabia, recently transmogrified into Private Shaw. Lawrence was stationed near Dorchester and used to ride over to Max Gate; and Hardy described how once Lady Crewe and some peer or other were in the house when Lawrence arrived, and he had refused to come in while they were there and had drawn himself up stiffly to attention against the wall of the porch as they passed him when departing.

So far as I know, the Masefields had no warning of our advent, but they were at home, and I admired their almost instantaneous control of the incredulity with which they must have heard their maid announce Mr and Mrs Thomas Hardy... Masefield inquired of their drive to Oxford. Hardy said that they had paused at Fawley (the Hampshire [sic; Berkshire] village which, as 'Marygreen', was Jude's birthplace and had provided him with a surname), but he mentioned the book with a deprecatory air, and twice referred to Jude as 'that fictitious personage.'...

When we were being driven back toward Oxford, Mrs Hardy said something about the advantages of cousinship being that one could make what one pleased of it, and I remarked that Sue Bridehead, Jude's *femme fatale*, was his cousin. Hardy, who was holding a red rose which Masefield had presented to him as we left, replied mysteriously, 'I ought to have made them second cousins.'

As we approached St Aldate's the clock was striking the hour in Christ Church, the 'Cardinal College' from which Jude had counted the hundred and one strokes at nine o'clock on his first night in Oxford, but Hardy made no reference to that doomed assault on the university: he only remarked that a pre-Reformation bell in their village church was cracked and that, despite their vicar, he hated the idea of its being recast; 'Just think of all the people it has called!' He had told the vicar, he added, that he would, at least and at last, be a member of his flock when he was dead; on which Mrs Hardy, who was his second wife and many years younger, commented hastily that he probably would not, since Mr Cowley was not likely to stay with them much longer. Hardy now asked that we should visit the Martyrs' Memorial, and I am afraid that I asked him to repeat himself, thinking that I must have misheard him. For amidst so much that was ancient and academic, the choice of that unimpressive neo-Gothic structure seemed inexplicable. 'Erected by public subscription' in 1841 as a counterblast to the high Anglicanism of Newman, Pusey, and Keble then spreading through the common rooms of the university, the memorial commemorates the three Protestant bishops burned at the stake three hundred years earlier in the reign of Queen Mary. I could not believe that Hardy was deeply interested either theologically in the controversies of the Tractarian era, or architecturally in an uninspired pastiche. However, we were duly driven to the south end of St Giles, and after pensively surveying Sir Giles Gilbert Scott's crocketed pinnacles, Hardy observed that somewhere nearby a small cross in the pavement marked where the stake had actually stood...

I went straight home to leaf through my *Jude*. Yes, Jude's first meeting with Sue, while his hopes were still high, had been beside the memorial, 'at the cross in the pavement which marked the spot of the Martyrdoms,' and it was past the memorial that he staggered with Arabella in his hour of despair. Something surely in that fictitious personage, although not his exclusion from the university, still mattered much to his creator.

The Hardys were driven back to Wessex next morning. He never slept away from home again.

Elton subsequently visited Max Gate on 9 April 1926 and 1 September 1927.

May O'Rourke (1897–1978) first met Hardy in July 1918. A friend had sent him a book of verse she had written and this resulted in an invitation to tea at Max Gate. Talking of Stinsford church she described it as 'a Gray's Elegy' sort of place, and she describes his reaction thus: 'He looked at me, and face and voice had changed completely: "It *is* Stoke Poges!" he said quietly. I can never find words to convey what I saw in him then; this was not my pleasant host, this was Hardy as he would be seen in Elysium; the authentic dignity of his kingship as a poet simply transforming his face and mien. It passed in a flash, but it remained unforgettable. In later years I had many enriching awarenesses of Hardy's human personality, but that one strange moment of vision never came again'. . . .

Five years later, on 27 March 1923, May O'Rourke began work at Max Gate as a secretary and she was close to the heart of Max Gate for the last five years of Hardy's life. Monograph No. 8. 'Thomas Hardy: His Secretary Remembers' (1965) is a valuable addition to our knowledge because of this and because of her clear, balanced, sensitive description of her life at Max Gate during that period:

> As a dwelling of a poet, designed by himself, Max Gate seemed to me strangely inappropriate. An architect friend has assured me that I overlooked what is praiseworthy in it: despite this, to me it was always, externally, a dull dispirited house – the solidification in brick of Hardy's intermittent mood of hopelessness at the ugliness in life.
>
> Once inside Max Gate, the exterior was forgotten; and I grew to love my own corner in the dining-room, where the trees waved green fans of leafage beyond the window, and played a strange, fugal music when the inshore wind swept across the fields of Came . . .
>
> I had as well the equally wordless companionship of Emma Lavinia Hardy, his first wife, whose portrait in oils drew my thoughts often enough, since she already lived for me in the poignant elegiac poems

which Hardy wrote after her death. It is a painting of average quality, but I thought it showed premonitory signs of what her later existence would reveal. The eyes do not look, so much as peer out apprehensively – the mouth hints at obstinacy, but even more of nervous tension. In the years since these impressions formed in me, enough has come to light to confirm them. It is happier to recall one recollection of her, for which I am indebted to Mrs E. M. B. Weber. The Hardys were frequent visitors to her home [Birkin House, Dorchester] when she was a child, and were welcomed and liked by the children. Her recollection is a pretty one – of how the birds, whom Emma Hardy loved, would alight happily along her outstretched arm, remaining there confidently. This glimpse reveals her as someone with whom a child or a bird would feel happily at home; and I, for one, welcome this new aspect of that sad and shadowed lady. Florence Hardy also spoke warmly and appreciatively of the first Mrs Hardy, who, she told me, had always been very kind to her.

When the first tentative days at Max Gate were over, Florence Hardy and I found that we had much in common, and we chatted at odd moments, frequently enough, as she was around and about while Hardy worked in his study upstairs. I enjoyed being with her, and liked seeing her in a relaxed mood, with those great dark eyes (made more sombre by Rossettian eyelids) sparkling into sudden, youthful gaiety. Hardy observed our growing friendship serenely; indeed, he would have been surprised and perturbed if the secretary, introduced at his suggestion, had lacked warmth towards the lady of his household . . .

Hardy had the sound characteristics of the greater Victorians, notably their steady self-discipline. He had a respect for order, for a pattern of living to be followed with resolution. He went to his study every morning at ten o'clock, as punctually as a city man to his office, and worked there for a fixed time. 'I may not write a word for a fortnight,' he said to his friend Newman Flower; 'but it is discipline – on one of those mornings of discipline the mood comes – and I write.'. . .

He came down to lunch, returning upstairs afterwards for a rest. Then came his daily exercise, a walk with Mrs Hardy and Wessex. Sometimes they would walk over to Stinsford churchyard, where Hardy would bring small posies of flowers which he had made himself, to lay on the family graves. Or, more frequently, they would choose the sloping fields facing Max Gate; a stubbled track which, as Hardy would recall, he had followed one October day to take part in William Barnes' funeral. Memories, ghosts – these cannot have failed to accompany him wherever he went. But when he came into the lamplit room, later, to relax and take tea, Hardy left this grey retinue outside.

When the evening closed in and dinner was over, Mrs Hardy would read aloud to him; the choice ranged from memoirs, history, and biography, and his familiar loves among the English poets, to the latest modern works. It was part of the invincible freshness in Hardy's mind that he turned eagerly to the young, new writers, and observed their experiments without prejudice. The past lay upon him like a garland, not as a fetter...

In September 1924 Florence had to go to London for an operation on her throat. May O'Rourke continues:

> There is no doubt in my mind that when Florence Hardy returned after her operation, a grim bogy was then and henceforth never far away from her. Anyone who has lived with a grave fear will understand how it could discolour and distort life for her; and how secret efforts at repressing that fear may emerge before others in inexplicable depression, and bleak, difficult moods. In my own case, I hasten to add, these were only intermittent and rare; and when she had realised their occurrence, swiftly and warmly regretted. But she did not realise that there was in herself an emotional insecurity, and a possessive love, too easily alerted, possibly, when no real menace to her happiness existed...
>
> So far my picture of him may appear, to some, over-glazed with sweetness and light. I have written of him as I saw him – 'in his habit, as he lived'; scrutinising every phrase lest I had failed in the writer's obligation to record truly what has been truly observed. And I know that I could not portray him otherwise. I cannot daub in a morose aspect, where I saw a pensive one: the gloomy, cynical Hardy, as seen by other eyes, was never revealed to mine...
>
> One day we were all out in the garden when he asked me suddenly if I knew a poem about the execution of Mary Queen of Scots, which had been popular in his youth. I did not know it. 'Would you like me to say it to you?' he asked. I agreed warmly, and he stood before me, his hands folded like a child, and recited the numerous verses without hesitation. It was good narrative verse, but not more than verse – and my face lengthened visibly. When he had finished, Hardy looked at me gently and quizzically, and he said:
>
> 'It's not poetry – it's not poetry! – but it's none the worse for that!'...
>
> I have gleaned my memories of Hardy as closely as I could, but a few still remain to be gathered in. I had noticed with admiration in his poems how the carefully spaced lines and stanzas, grouped in proportion, recalled that architecture had been his profession before

writing. One day I ventured to tell Hardy how I had noticed this feeling for design in his verse. He was interested, and I think, pleased; and he asked if I would like him to show me how to do it with a poem of my own. One lay near at hand, so Hardy settled down to loosening the tight pattern I had achieved, it seemed to me, setting the words free as he moved a line a little further in, another line a little further out, till the balance he sought was achieved.

So many who knew him have spoken of his simplicity, and I can add a memory to theirs. When he had given me a poem to type, he would come down to collect it later, and enquire: 'This will do, won't it? Do you like it?'...

My visits to Max Gate were, normally, three times a week, that is when there was a lull in urgent correspondence, or the final draft of one of Hardy's poems not completed. Then a spate would suddenly flow in, and I would be needed all day; on these occasions Hardy would be present at luncheon, but only corporeally, as his mind was still intent on the work of the morning. Therefore we spoke little, leaving until tea-time that easy to-and-fro of good conversation which I found so delightful. Hardy talked simply and as a rule, briefly, however memorable the thought expressed. He did not startle you often with a flash of wit, but he charmed you frequently with his quiet humour, and the lash of sarcasm was never his. He would check any unkindly trend in a conversation by a sudden, chilly silence; and I saw once, with one visitor, how his eyebrows contracted and his expression became admonitory, at a phrase in which he found unpleasant implications. One memorable trait must be recalled here. I wish that I could breathe into these pages the voice of Thomas Hardy, gently pitched, never rough or husky with age, and full of colour and warmth when he was interested or moved. His face was very expressive, and it would flush rosily with pleasure – or even diffidence – for at times he revealed the charming shyness of a child...

In the last year of his life Hardy was inwardly jaded by the weight of his eighty-seven years.

Although he kept to his daily routine, as the dark winter days closed in his wife, at least, must have had her own disquieted thoughts. One day in December, he seated himself as usual at his writing table, only to find that now his work was beyond him. So the pen was laid aside, where poetry was concerned; he used it finally, to write a splendid signature on a cheque for the Society of Authors, two days before he died.

May O'Rourke took part in the 1955 BBC broadcast and her short contribution deserves preservation:

I typed all his manuscripts for him. When I say 'all his manuscripts', there is one exception that I would rather like to tell you about... Hardy was an agnostic, and I am a Catholic. It might have been rather a tricky situation. Two things could happen – Hardy could have done, and many people would have done, just ignored it, after all what would it matter what his secretary was? But that was not Thomas Hardy. His generation had a very protective sense towards younger people, and one of the things that I remember with deep gratitude is that Hardy went to the greatest pains to see that my faith was safeguarded. To this extent that when he wrote a poem to the memory of a friend who had died, one line was rather tragic and expressed the finality of death, and when I was asked to type that poem, that line had been changed: there was absolutely nothing in that poem that could affect my faith.

It's quite clear from his writings that he was intensely preoccupied with religion. I have always thought that the Christian inheritance came into play in Hardy's personality and character to the fullest extent: he was charitable in speech: he was humble. Of the speculations in his poems, I think they were a kind of inverted faith. A man whose sympathies are with humanity, and after all humanity is a suffering thing, a man who had somehow failed to find in Christianity the solution.

Reference has already been made to the Prince of Wales's visit to Max Gate on 20 July 1923. Two further stories which circulated in Dorchester at that time were that Florence wrote to the Prince's secretary to ask what she should give him for lunch and received the reply, 'chicken and whisky', and that the Prince told Hardy, 'I believe my mother has read one of your books.' (Monograph No. 12, 1963)

There are still people alive who claim to have known Hardy in their youth. Their memories of seventy years or more ago and the obvious desire that some have to claim acquaintance with the famous, make what they have to say often of doubtful credence. In a television programme on William Barnes two of three years ago a man who obviously couldn't forgive Hardy for being so great that he tended to push Barnes into the shade said that he knew Hardy well, and he was a bad-tempered, gloomy old man. He didn't reveal that he was just seven years old when Hardy died. He was just passing on the received opinion among many Dorchester locals that Hardy was no good. In my own interviewing of those who, seventy years later, claim to remember Hardy I have found the most convincing to be those who remember just one incident which is as sharp today as it was then. While working on this book I have talked with a number of such people, and what they had to say was first-hand evidence of Hardy's interest in and kindness to the young.

In July 1923 John Cave was a boy aged about twelve living at Winterborne Monkton where he was being tutored by the vicar, the Revd Lionel Harrison. Round about the time of the Prince of Wales's visit to Max Gate he was taken by his tutor, who knew Hardy, on a number of visits to Hardy. He sat listening to his elders talking and regrets that he remembers nothing of it. But he does remember Hardy saying to him at the end of one visit, 'Boy, tell me about the roofs you saw on your way here.' In confusion he could remember nothing and had to tell Hardy so. A week later, at the end of a similar visit, he was all ready for the same question having looked carefully at all the roofs on the way there. 'Boy,' said Hardy, 'tell me about the trees you saw on the way here.' Once again he was able to say nothing, at which Hardy said, 'Boy, you *see*, but you do not *observe*!'

Norrie Woodhall, now ninety-four, is Gertrude Bugler's (see p. 209) sister and acted in several of the Hardy Players' productions. She liked Hardy, found him a kind man who, in the 1920s, still retained all his faculties and was intensely interested in life. One particular kindness was remembered. In 1924 she had the part of 'Liza-Lou in the Players' production of *Tess*. He came across to her during a rehearsal and said, 'I haven't given 'Liza-Lou much to say, have I?', and he straightaway wrote on her script 'I am so glad you have come home.'

Aileen Hawkins gives her own account of her meeting with Hardy in 1927:

> I was a Girl Guide and Miss Fisher was our captain. She knew that I wrote poetry and she asked me if I would write two poems and an essay for my author's badge. Florence Hardy was her friend, and Miss Fisher had asked her if she would be the examiner.
>
> I remember the day that Miss Fisher and I walked to Max Gate. We were shown into a comfortable room with a brightly burning fire. Thomas Hardy came into the room looking very frail, but his smile was warm. He talked to Miss Fisher and she said "This is Aileen." He patted me on the head, or rather on my hat, for I was dressed in my guide's uniform. He sat opposite me by the fire. I only spoke when I was spoken to, as my grandma's words always were: "little girls should be seen and not heard when grown-ups are talking." Miss Fisher asked Thomas Hardy if he had read my poems, and he told her that he had and thought they showed a great love of beauty. Then he stared into the fire, and Florence Hardy and Miss Fisher were in conversation. I thought he looked sad, and I thought of my grandma's words: "a smile is a wonderful gift, and it costs nothing",

so every time he looked my way I gave him a beaming smile, and he smiled back. His eyes twinkled when his wife asked Miss Fisher for the certificate to sign. Miss Fisher and I thanked her. It was time to say goodbye, and Thomas Hardy stood up and shook my hand and said: "You've got a lovely smile, my dear." It was cold coming from the warm, stuffy room, and as we faced the cold wind I thought how nice Thomas Hardy was. I really didn't think of him as being famous at all.

Dorothy Phillips was a young girl living in the Dorset village of Sydling St Nicholas who, one day in 1927, was having trouble in doing up the many buttons on her boots. Hardy, who was visiting a Lady Ashburnham, who lived in Sydling, happened to be passing by and produced a button-hook which he gave her as a present. Her mother was horrified and saying, 'He's no good, that man' insisted she took it back to Lady Ashburnham who kept it until Dorothy was sixteen and the 'wicked old man' dead, and then gave it back to her. She has it still.

Finally, there is Meriel, Lady Salt, who told her story on a BBC Dorset FM programme, and repeated it to me in 1996:

I knew Thomas Hardy simply as an elderly friend of my parents, who used to come to tea sometimes on a Sunday. I must have been about five or six, and I had my first bicycle, which in those days was called a fairy bicycle, with small wheels. He obviously saw me struggling to mount it, so he called me over, and he said "Take my advice, go out into a quiet lane where there is a nice grassy bank. Lean your bicycle against the bank, climb up the bank and then lower yourself onto the saddle, and put your foot on the outside pedal which is up in the air, and then push off with your foot against the bank, and start pedalling. Then if you do start falling, you'll fall against the soft bank again." And I did do that, and succeeded, but of course I had no idea until long after he'd died that he was anything special. He was just a kind old gentleman. It was the only time, I think, that he ever spoke to me.

Marie Stopes (1880–1958) achieved fame by her advocacy of sex education and family planning. She was a courageous reformer whose books such as *Married Love* (1918) did much to break down barriers of ignorance and silence. In the 1920s she bought a disused lighthouse at Portland Bill for summer residence, and also purchased the cottage described in Hardy's novel *The Well-Beloved, as* 'Avice's Cottage'. If Hardy's visit to the lighthouse was made on the day after the visit of the Prince of Wales, then it was on 21 July 1923, and here is her account of it as it appeared in *John O'London's Weekly,* 27 December 1940 (pp. 329–30):

There was a day in the late summer of 1923 when every Briton who took a newspaper read of a visit paid by the Heir to the Throne to our greatest writer, Thomas Hardy, in Dorchester. Most of the national newspapers had streamer headlines to the effect that the Prince of Wales had to go personally to Max Gate, Hardy's home, because the veteran novelist never went out of it to visit anyone. On that morning I stood in my lighthouse tower reading the captions in the popular papers telling of the historic visit of the day before, and I smiled. For that afternoon I was expecting Thomas Hardy to visit me. That afternoon he and Mrs Hardy drove twenty miles to have tea with me.

The newspapers had said how they wished they could have told their readers what that historic conversation between the Prince and Thomas Hardy was about – but no one knew! Well, I could have told (but I never have), for Thomas Hardy that day told me every word of it as he drank tea in the round stone tower of my little old Dorset lighthouse on Portland Bill.

Hardy told me that having tea in that tower fulfilled one of the longings of his youth. The lighthouse is mentioned in his novel, *The Well-Beloved* (all about the Isle of Slingers), but he had never been in it. After tea he climbed up on to the roof of the tower and eagerly looked towards every point of the compass over the magnificent stretches of land and sea that are limited only by the blue haze of the circular horizon. Hardy walked round the house and tower, and then my husband photographed him in the sunshine.

There was no trace of 'Hardy the pessimist' in him that day; he was Hardy, the eager, happy boy, the amused and sympathetic observer. How his eyes twinkled as he told me about the Prince's visit on the previous day, and how kindly the tone of his voice as he called him 'that poor boy!'...

He was hurt by some people as well as bored, and the chief hurts I encountered in him were connected with his poetry. He cared about it far more than he cared about his prose: he autographed his poems for me one day, saying: 'They are all that will live – all I *want* to live.'

Hamlin Garland (1860–1940) was an American novelist and writer, best known for his realistic studies of the Middle West, and described by Denys Kay-Robinson as a writer of almost endless trivia. With an introduction from William Dean Howells, another American novelist and, for Hardy more important, editor, Garland had first called on Hardy in London in the summer of 1899. In his account of that meeting he described Hardy as 'small and blond, with a fine head and full brown beard', whereas Hardy had not worn a beard since 1891. He goes on to say that Hardy's 'lack of humour, his blunt, plain speech, his scientific outlook on the world all reminded me of Burroughs'. Could he have mixed up Hardy with someone else, one wonders, because what Garland was doing was what Hardy abhorred? He was visiting one writer after another in order to write articles and/or a book about them.

Garland included Hardy once again in his English tour of 1923 and signed the Max Gate Visitor's Book on 16 August. Here are some passages from his account of that visit in *Afternoon Neighbours* (New York 1934, pp. 85–93):

> A maid who met us at the door said that Mr and Mrs Hardy were awaiting us. As we entered the drawing room, a thin, gray wisp of a man with a very broad brow and a pointed chin rose to meet us. This was Thomas Hardy, but I confess I would not have known him outside his home, so shrunk, so slight had he become since our last meeting. His hand was weak and cold, and in his eyes was the wistful look of age. This feebleness was distressing to me, for I remembered him as an alert and vigorous man of middle age. The expression of his face was that of a poet who faces death, a philosopher with no hope of life beyond the grave – a look such as John Burroughs had in his final year of life.
>
> Mrs Hardy, a pale, serious woman much younger than her husband (she was a second wife), drew my wife aside, leaving the poet to me; and for more than an hour we talked, rapidly and intimately, of the men and subjects which naturally come up in such a meeting.
>
> 'It is a long time since our last meeting,' I began as we took our seats. With sad intonation he replied, 'Yes, it is many years.'
>
> I asked him how long he had lived in this house, and he replied, 'Over forty years. I built it myself. It is my only home, and I seldom leave it – even for a day.'
>
> Mrs Hardy, overhearing this, said, 'That is one of my crosses. I would like to get away from Dorchester now and then, but Mr Hardy will not consent to accompany me. We see no one, except when someone comes to call. Sir James Barrie asked us to visit him recently, but Mr Hardy would not consider even that – much as I desired it.'
>
> My wife spoke of our recent visit to Barrie at Stanway, and I described the splendid old mansion in which we found him living. 'It was like going back for a few days into seventeenth century England,' I said. 'Like living a story.'
>
> To this Hardy replied, 'I didn't know Barrie lived like that. I know his London home – I sometimes stay with him there. I can not understand how he endures life in London. His place is in the very centre of the theatre world, and every one tries to see him. He has a watchful doorman, but even so I do not see how he avoids unwel-

come visitors. You know how persistent certain theatrical folk are!'... 'As Mrs Hardy says, I see no one except those who come from a distance to see me. Many nice Americans take the trouble to call. Recently, several professors of English literature came down from London. One of the latest of these tourists left a book he had written on 'The Technique of Thomas Hardy.' Upon reading it, I found he had made no reference to me as a poet. There isn't any technique about prose, is there? It just comes along of itself.'

To this amazing statement (which affected me as the judgment of an artless artist) I made no reply, for Hardy's prose has precision as well as music.

He went on, 'For more than a quarter of a century, I have devoted myself to the writing of verse. For years I haven't so much as glanced at one of my novels. I don't know what I would make of them now'...

Notwithstanding his attitude toward his fiction, I persisted in talking of it, and I found him willing to discuss the latest edition of his novels, which as a source of income he was obliged to respect. At last I said, 'I have been told that in your novels you made the fullest use of the actual scenes and characters of this region, and that 'Casterbridge' is really Dorchester. Is that true?'

For some reason he did not relish this question, and if I could have recalled it, I would have done so. He evaded my query by saying, 'You must remember that the periods of which I wrote in *The Return of the Native,* in *The Trumpet-Major* as well as in *The Mayor of Casterbridge,* are those of my father's time rather than my own. They are in effect historical novels.'...

He then passed to a discussion of Bret Harte. 'I suppose the "Harte tradition" still hovers over California, just as the "Dickens tradition" still broods over London. None of the recent writers of California stories are able to ignore Harte any more than our London novelists can rise clear of Dickens. I know no writer, not even George Gissing, who has reported the people of London as I see them. I have never been one to see human beings as caricatures. To my way of thinking, the fiction of California is false. It must all be rewritten in an entirely different spirit from that of Harte. Harte loved to tell the story of a dashing, romantic villain and end by investing him with some absurd touch of moral sentiment.'

It was evident that Hardy did not know the later fiction of the Pacific Coast, and I made no attempt to enlighten him. He came back to his verse, which alone had vital interest. 'I have written verse to please myself,' he declared with an accent of pride. 'I wrote *The Dynasts* without regard to the public, and I was quite amazed at the hit it made.'

As I had never been able to read *The Dynasts* and could not believe that it had made any such hit as he imagined, I remained silent. Furthermore, I refused to join in deprecating the novels which had enabled him to live in comfort and honour for sixty years. . . .

He said nothing of the high honour which the Prince of Wales had paid him in coming to Max Gate. His reticence concerning this tribute was as marked as that of Barrie, who made no mention of the Queen's visit to Stanway, until my daughters drew it from him.

In reply to some remark of mine concerning Joseph Conrad, Hardy said, 'I am not acquainted with him. I never saw him but once, and that was at a public dinner. He is a great writer, a very great writer, but he is not English in any sense. I have read several of his works and was particularly impressed by his *Arrow of Gold* – a fine book.'. . .

In speaking of the Lowells, I mentioned Lawrence Lowell, President of Harvard, and was astounded to have Hardy hesitatingly inquire, 'Is that a girls' school?'

Whilst I laboriously explained the relative positions of Harvard and Yale, he listened politely but without deep interest. That he could be ignorant of this great university was astounding. Perhaps it should be set down as a weakness due to his advancing years. . . .

According to Mrs Hardy's report, Dorchester was not only non-literary, but lacking in social gaiety, a fact which Hardy welcomed. 'I am seldom distracted from my work. I do not walk or ride or work in the garden. I used to ride a bicycle, but I long ago gave that up. The truth is, I live a very secluded life – a hermit's life.'

Notwithstanding his confinement and his lack of exercise, he appeared to be in fairly good health for a man of his age. He had never been an impressive man physically. He gave little sign exteriorly of the genius he was. I found it necessary to remind myself of the books he had written in order that I might identify the man before me with the world-renowned novelist. To me he was only a small sad old man, and I found myself helping him out when, from time to time, his sentences trailed off into vague murmurings. Whether this incoherence arose from physical weakness or from lack of interest, I could not tell; but despite my sixty-two years I felt youthful by contrast with his age . . .

I brought up the question of his actual birthplace. 'I have been corresponding with the present owner of your ancestral cottage, and as it is only a mile or two away, I have planned to walk over there. I am interested to see your boyhood home and its surroundings.'

Again I caught on his face and in his voice a subtle expression of disinclination. He was not exactly displeased by my plan, but it was evident that he was not eager to have me carry it out. He mumbled something about its being a 'little old tumble-down place' which he hadn't seen for many years; and while he did not actually object to my going there, I could see that he took no joy in it. This, of course, increased my desire to see it. I felt that he undervalued it, as his admirers had persistently glorified it.

This is a revealing interview because it shows how Hardy could behave in the presence of someone who was boring him and wasting his time. The give-away is his question about Harvard, 'Is that a girls' school?' As in 1919 he had turned down an invitation to give a lecture at Yale University, he could no more have been ignorant of Harvard than one could be ignorant of Oxford if one knew Cambridge. One notices, too, the contradiction between Garland's opening description of Hardy as 'feeble' and his later 'he appeared to be in fairly good health for a man of his age'. Hardy, too, would have been irritated by the crass ignorance of the question '. . . Casterbridge is really Dorchester. Is that true?' It should be said finally that Florence wrote to Richard Purdy on 3 February 1935 *(Letters of Emma and Florence Hardy*, p. 326) protesting at Garland's recently published account of his visit to her, denying that she had ever used the phrase 'one of my crosses', and pointing out that T. E. Lawrence was present throughout the interview, but was not recognised by Garland. Lawrence described Garland as 'the worst kind of interviewer; one who comes in the guise of a friend'.

The painting of Hardy by Augustus John (1878–1961), now in the Fitzwilliam Museum at Cambridge, is said to have resulted in Hardy's saying, 'Well, if I look like that the sooner I am underground the better' and 'I don't know whether that is how I look or not – but that is how I feel.' John met Hardy on 21 September 1923 and he made several visits to Max Gate shortly afterwards. The painting was completed by the middle of October. Michael Holroyd in his *Augustus John*, Vol. 2, p. 95, describes it as 'the portrait of a shy man, full of disciplined emotion'. The following is extracted from John's *Chiaroscuro* (London 1952, pp. 134–5):

> In the dining-room of Max Gate hung a portrait of a young woman with blonde hair hanging down; the work, it would seem, of the local photographer: this was the first Mrs Hardy. Her husband's image, by an Academician, confronted her on the opposite wall. The walls of Hardy's study, where I painted him, were piled to the ceiling with books, mostly of a philosophical nature and many of them French. Hardy said 'lucidity' had always been his aim. He disliked obscurity in others and tried to avoid it himself. We attended a performance of *Tess* at Dorchester: Hardy, hearing that I was present, sent word

to invite me to meet him 'behind': I was thus able to watch the play from the wings. The title role was filled by a Mrs Bugler, a butcher's wife from Bridport [sic; Beaminster]. Hardy greatly admired this extremely handsome young débutante, who, flushed with success, was dreaming of taking to the stage professionally; but Hardy, in spite of her 'evident genius', 'didn't feel justified in encouraging her to take this step, 'for we all know the hazards of the stage,' he said. When Gwen Ffrangcon-Davies, with a company from London, played *Tess* at Max Gate, Hardy was moved to tears: his only criticism was, 'In Dorset, you know, we don't drop our aitches.' During the hours spent with the poet, the respect in which I always held him had deepened to affection. On my leaving him for the last time he gave me a copy of *Wessex Tales*, inscribed.

Ernest Brennecke Jr. (1896–1969), an American literary and philosophical critic and university lecturer, visited Hardy in November 1923 but he did not sign the Max Gate Visitors' Book and it has not been possible to find the exact date. In the letter quoted below Florence refers to an earlier visit, probably in May 1923. In 1923 he had sent a typescript of his book *Thomas Hardy's Universe* (London 1924) to Hardy, and it obviously found favour with Hardy as Florence, replying on behalf of her husband on 27 August 1923, wrote, 'As far as Mr Hardy can gather, you appear not to have stumbled into the pitfall which has been the undoing of some previous critics – that of assuming his inventions to be real personifications and experiences of his own' (*CL* VI, pp. 207–8). Hardy even at the age of 83 is still sensitive about the autobiographical nature of his novels. So far so good – but Brennecke, not content with his first book on Hardy, decided to do a biography of him. This incurred, as so many had done, the displeasure of the Master, who did his best to stop its publication in England, describing it to one possible publisher as 'a mass of unwarranted assumptions and errors', and 'an impertinence'.

The following passages are taken from that 'impertinent' book, *The Life of Thomas Hardy* (New York 1925, pp. 4–10). They have sufficient interest and originality to justify publishing them, but they need to be treated cautiously as at one stage of the book Hardy is described as smoking, ('He has lit a cigarette, holds it in steady fingers, puffs meditatively.'), which was something he never did. The use, too, of so many of Hardy's own words is suspect, as we know how Hardy felt about that:

> ... Hardy has come down. He is small, somewhat stooped; grave and kindly in manner. Deep-set brooding eyes look out from a frame-

work of wrinkled parchment. They look out dispassionately; yet they dominate. He wears a fuzzy sweater beneath a thick grey-green suit.

'People at last seem to be discovering the curious charms of this part of the country. Even on dull days like this, I daresay, one can love it.' His voice is even, vibrant, slightly high-pitched, with a strange questioning inflection to each cadence. It makes everything he chooses to say seem somehow tentative, unfinal.

'Granville Barker and his wife are thinking of settling around here. The lovely dignity of the countryside leaves its photograph on the people, you know. I've become convinced that climate really makes character. I'm sure your terrible, harsh West Virginia mountain country is really responsible for the overwhelming multiplied tragedy which you call your 'poor white' population. America is a tragic country; its tragedy is reflected in the countenances and manners of even the visitors who pass through England. But we get only vague inklings of the basis of it, such as the periodic outcropping of your Negro problems and other racial difficulties. I am too old ever to fathom this; I can only feel it vaguely, like a faint echo of a cataclysm on another star.

'I can't even always fathom quite the charm of the ancient church musicians about here. They serenaded me with some old tunes the other evening. That sort of thing carries me back to the fifties – even to the forties. I'm old enough to remember the gaudy Napoleonic military uniforms, with their long flapping tails. Their fascination has been a lasting thing. Dashing uniforms give me pleasant sensations.'

Slightly inconsecutive is the Hardy discourse, but quietly dynamic. Sometimes the gears of memory actually slip for a moment. Minor characters in certain of the Wessex novels, for instance, have become quite submerged.

About other things there are flashes which brilliantly, electrically illuminate the fading past. At the mention of Swinburne! ' I loved *Atalanta*,' he confesses, simply. 'I used to walk from my lodgings near Hyde Park to the draughting office every morning, and never without a copy of the first edition of the *Poems and Ballads* sticking out of my pocket . It was a borrowed copy. . . . If I'd only bought it at the time, it would be worth many guineas today.

'Tennyson and Browning both lived near me. For two years I read only poetry – no prose, except the newsprints – a curious obsession! Well, I still believe poetry to be the very essence of literature. . . . No editors even touched my verse for many years. Oh, yes, I sent much of it out; it invariably came back. And I destroyed a good deal of it.'. . .

'You have some mighty promising poets in America. Who is Louis Untermeyer? I'm very fond of his verse. It's keen. But he's not a rebel, is he? I don't fancy revolutionaries. I never moved in revolutionary circles, even in the sixties and seventies when Darwin set London aflame. Blomfield, my architectural master, was a clergyman's son, you see. I liked the artists best. I liked the quiet galleries.

'We've just been reading Dreiser's *Genius*. What does one think of it?'

Mrs Hardy, serving the custard and plum-pie: 'We think it ought to be suppressed – really!'

Hardy holds up a finger: 'Not because it's immoral. It may not be. But because there's no excuse for a writer's deliberate abandonment of any kind of form. One prefers – expects – some sort of structure, not a mere heap of bricks, no matter how excitingly red they may be. . . .

'Young Springrove, in *Desperate Remedies,* was actually drawn from life, it is true – but not from my life. It was a youth I once knew quite well. He's now dead, poor fellow' . . .

You find yourself back in the drawing-room. Hardy continues chatting amiably. He takes down from his shelves a heavy volume, turns the pages abstractedly. You venture to admire a Hardy portrait, facing the Shelley on the opposite wall.

'We like that one,' says Mrs Hardy, detached, half-dreamily. 'Another used to hang there. We tired of it. One day Mr Hardy tore it up.'

Mr Hardy allows himself a twitch of a smile, although he continues to look elsewhere.

'Now here,' he observes, proffering the book, 'is a fellow who has written about me with some enthusiasm. Only he has gone to my novels instead of to *Who's Who* for his facts. He's been impertinent in spots, you see. We've corrected him; I've pencilled some notes in his margins. Perhaps you'd care to look over them, if you're interested.'. . .

The notes have been set down with a fine, careful pencil. The characters are beautifully formed. You look as though you'd like to copy the remarks. Mrs Hardy fetches you a sheaf of paper. Here are a few of the items you scratch off:

> The birthplace of T. H. was not a humble cottage; it was (and is) a low, but rambling and spacious house with a paddock and (till lately) large stablings.
> This is impertinent.
> Primary school 8th to 10th year only – see *Who's who.*
> He knew the dialect as a boy, but was not permitted to speak it

– it was not spoken in his mother's house, but only when necessary to the cottagers, and by his father to his workmen, some 6 or 12.
First to London & the suburbs, then from place to place – Somerset & the Rhine, etc., then Sturminster-Newton, then London several years, then Wimborne. 3 or 4 months every year to London for nearly 30 years, in flats & houses rented for the season. . . .

The talk shifts around, somehow, to the teaching of English writing. Can writing be taught? Hardy thinks so. He wants to know why they don't teach the writing of verse. It's the best method of learning how to handle words and sentences he says, even if one's final object is the writing of clear and vivid prose.

In these days of inverted snobbery it is difficult to understand Hardy's extreme sensitivity about his humble background.
Roderick Haig-Brown (1908–76) was a grandson of Alfred Pope, twice Mayor of Dorchester and a senior member of the long established firm of brewers and wine merchants who today brew a 'Hardy Ale'. Hardy and Alfred Pope were in correspondence with each other as early as 1882 and there began a friendship which lasted until Hardy's death. Pope had eleven sons and four daughters serving in the First World War, and after the war Hardy wrote a foreword to A *Book of Remembrance* which memorialised their contribution to the war effort. In 1927 Haig-Brown emigrated to Canada and the following extracts are from his *Writings and Reflections* (Washington 1983):

Grandfather's respect for Hardy, at least in these later years, was unbounded – and to me surprising. He was more given to demanding than offering respect, and his judgments generally were material rather than intellectual or spiritual. But when he spoke of Hardy there was a tenderness in his voice that I can remember at no other time. When he went to visit Hardy, he went with ceremony, calling in advance to know if he might come, walking the distance from his own house to Max Gate, as though on a pilgrimage, and usually taking some member of the family with him. I went more than once, but the time I remember most clearly was in April of 1924, when I was sixteen . . .
I was awed and impressed, but neither observant nor perceptive. And I was probably the most inarticulate diarist who ever bothered to record anything. 'Sixth April 1924,' the small book says. 'Went to see Thomas Hardy with Grandfather. Had quite a good day for Sunday.'
At that time Grandfather was eighty-two, Hardy was eighty-four. Grandfather was to live to be ninety-two, Hardy to be eighty-eight.

Yet neither of them seemed to me then, or seem now in recollection, to be very old men. Both were spare and short, perhaps five and a half feet tall. Grandfather was the straighter of the two, with a brown face, dark-brown eyes, a straight, formidable nose and a neatly trimmed white beard, almost Spanish in effect. . . .

We had been invited to tea. I thought Max Gate, red brick hiding behind its high, red-brick wall and among the dark Austrian pines, rather an ugly house. But once inside, turning into the drawing room to the right of the small dark hall-way, everything was suddenly light and beautiful. This was a sunny April afternoon. The bright starched chintzes of chairs and sofas caught the sunlight and echoed it back to the pale walls and the pictures on them. The tea things shone and the second Mrs Hardy was concerned for Grandfather, while Hardy himself was easy and hospitable and quite talkative.

Through the short meal the two men talked the Dorset gossip I had listened to for so many years – who married whom and when, who was a Symons or a Sheridan, a Williams, a Lock, or a Foster, before she was married; whether old John Legh belonged to the Owermoigne, the Marnhull, or the Chilfrome branch of his family, and who was his mother. These things meant little to me, but to them they were full of meaning, summoning the ghosts of ancient scandals, the laughter of pretty lips, the bold lost eyes of Wessex men, who had adventured away from the land and never returned. This was the drama and life of the county through a hundred years and more, cleaned and carded to the warp and woof of the family names and place names; meaningless strands to outsiders, but a rich pattern of gloom or glory to those who understood . . .

Grandfather was not normally a considerate man, but I saw now that he was watching Hardy, whose enthusiasm had tired him a little. Mrs Hardy was hovering a shade anxiously in the background. Grandfather said his goodbyes, promising to come again very soon, and we went out into the sunshine of the April afternoon.

The works of great writers frequently appeal to composers and Hardy was no exception. As early as 1906 *Tess* had been turned into an opera by Baron d'Erlanger and only the President of the Immortals can be blamed for the volcanic eruption from Mount Vesuvius which took place on the evening of the first performance and brought it to a sudden close. It was subsequently performed at Covent Garden in 1909. On 28 July 1913 Hardy wrote to Sir Edward Elgar on the pleasure it would give him to 'do something together' (*CL* IV, p. 291). This was in response to a letter he had just received from Elgar suggesting that they should do a work together. Sadly, nothing came of this idea, probably because of the First World War and the death of Elgar's wife in 1920. One wonders what Elgar might have made out of Hardy's poetic lamentations for his dead wife.

Three composers visited Hardy in the 1920s: Rutland Boughton (1878–1960) on 11 June 1924, Arthur Bliss (1891–1975) on 12 December 1924, and Gustav Holst on 9 August 1927. They all wrote about their visits.

Rutland Boughton had made a name for himself as the organiser of the Glastonbury Festivals between 1914 and 1926. His most successful opera, *The Immortal Hour* (1914), produced one song which is still popular today. He read Hardy's poetic drama, *The Queen of Cornwall*, when it was published in 1923, and decided that it had possibilities as a libretto for another Glastonbury Festival opera. His article in *The Musical News and Herald* (15 February 1928, pp. 33–4) takes up the story:

> The only chance of making the play right for musical expression depended on the willingness of the author to reconsider it afresh from a point of view which he could scarcely be expected to appreciate, or on the existence of lyrics of his own which would exactly fit, verbally and emotionally, into those places where they are needed. An unlikely thing, but it happened all the same. I read again his poems from cover to cover, and discovered six poems which might have been written for *The Queen of Cornwall* itself. So I approached Hardy, asked if I might make a musical version of the play, if he would be willing for the extra lyrics to be interpolated, and for certain cuts to be made in the existing text. He suggested that I should call and consult him and, of course, he proved to be the generous and friendly artist one would have expected from the simple quality of his work. He accepted all my suggestions for the music-drama, and copied into my volume of *The Queen* those passages which he added subsequent to its first publication, in case they might be found suitable for the musical version also.
>
> Later on, when the first sketch of the music was finished, I visited him again and played much of it to him. His musical tastes were folkish, so he was felt near enough to my own work to enjoy the lyrical parts. For the rest he left it to me. During that visit his energy seemed unending; and a long drive, during which he pointed out some of the places and houses mentioned in his books, and referred to his characters as if speaking of real people, made it clear that the world he had created, beginning in realism, had to some extent passed over into the realm of vision. In the evening he brought out some old music in the hope that we might find a song suitable for the drunken choruses in *The Queen*. We were unsuccessful, and they had to remain wordless, as I could not induce him to write even four

lines of words, nor could the right sort of song be found elsewhere in his work.

His attitude to other artists was as perfect as one can ever hope to find. Bernard Shaw he spoke of as an artist who was too important and too gentle to be discussed. For Conrad and Galsworthy his feeling was scarcely less fine. For the younger men who visited him from time to time he had none but good words – for de la Mare, Drinkwater, and others; and he remembered with great happiness a visit from Daisy Kennedy, who had enchanted him with her playing on his own instrument, for I think he said he had played upon the fiddle in earlier life. The only shadow in his relations with other artists was caused by the fact that so many immature and incompetent people sent him their works, and asked for 'a few words of approval.' And it came out quite by accident that the reviewer who had described *The Queen of Cornwall* as a work of senility had previously sent Hardy what the old man said was 'a very unpleasant play,' in the hope of getting a push from the novelist's acknowledgement. In such cases Hardy said that he felt obliged to ignore the books sent; but that was as far as he would go in the direction of disparagement.

Hardy came to the Glastonbury Festival the following year to see our performance of *The Queen*, and again to Bournemouth in 1925 for the orchestral production which had been arranged by Sir Dan Godfrey. On each occasion his few criticisms were much to the point and never captious. Just as he had accepted Baron d'Erlanger's operatic setting, and an American film production of *Tess*, as things outside his sphere, so where the music and orchestra were concerned he left *The Queen* to my honour as an artist to do my best. On those points where our arts touched his judgments were what anyone would have wished – directed only to the future betterment of the production. When the musical version seemed to bring off a detail that was worth while – as in the swift nature of the climax, he was instant in his recognition and approval. Indeed, I think it may well be recognized by now that Hardy was something much greater than an artist. Here is an example of his quality. One of the cuts he allowed me to make entailed the complete sacrifice of the Prologue; and he frankly confessed that he had put it there for no artistic reason, but because without it one of the Hardy Players (for whom the play was originally written) would have been without a part. It seemed to him more important that a human being should have an opportunity for self-expression than that his work should be immune from the attack of petty reviewers – or even from his own attack as maker of the piece. Arising from that decent human attitude to art came the Prologue. Is the beauty of it any the less because its noble language and rhythm had a personal and not a dramatic origin? May it be that not until we get back to just such reasons for aesthetic activity shall we reawaken art to great life?

Of his personally retiring nature much has been said. We had experience of them [sic] also. At Glastonbury he failed to turn up on the day arranged, but at a later performance, just at the last moment, he and Mrs Hardy and Mr Cockerell came and preferred seats in one of the dressing-rooms which gave on to the back of the auditorium. Similarly at Bournemouth he got Sir Dan to hide him in a lime-light box, and at the end of the performance resisted all the clamour of the large audience who wished for a glimpse of him. The little tea-party which followed was my last sight of the old man, who was as blithe and ruddy and active as a winter robin. His simple nature was one more example of the statement of Shaw's, that 'greatness is merely one of the sensations of littleness.' There was no pose in Hardy. For him life was more important than art. His work is not a refuge from the woe of the world, but the battle-plain of a courageous spirit.

The visit to Glastonbury was on 28 August 1924.

Arthur Bliss's experience of tea with Hardy is described in *As I Remember* (London 1970, p. 85):

Musical memories can be quickly overlaid, and I found that to retain any footing in the changing musical scene I would have to work hard. But before starting on intensive work, I wanted to show Trudy [his wife] a little of England, so we set out to motor slowly through the West country. My brother, Howard, had for some time been a friend of Thomas Hardy, collecting with zeal what letters and manuscripts of his were available. Thanks to him an invitation came to us, as we went through Dorset, to take tea with Mr and Mrs Hardy at Max Gate.

When I was a student, I had set to music one of his poems 'The Dark-Eyed Gentleman' (CP 201) from *Time's Laughingstocks,* and I remembered how Stanford had angrily told me to take what he considered a most unpleasant poem away from his desk. It was difficult to equate this gentle little old man with the writer of the tragic novels and of the often ironical and pessimistic poems. True, his wrinkled apple-cheeked face told the tale of much experience, and his blue eyes were brilliantly penetrating; but his modest, absolutely natural manner towards his two unknown young guests was a surprise and an enchantment. He talked about the old instruments that he had heard as a young man in church services or at village dances, and which he has described in several of his novels. Hardy must himself have had some practical experience of music, for my brother once possessed his cello. As he stood in the evening light at his gate and said good-bye to us, my wife and I felt moved at having met the writer of the Wessex Novels face to face.

At tea Mrs Hardy had said 'If you are going in their direction you must meet our friends the Granville Barkers. I will ring them up and tell them.' So the next day we found ourselves invited there for lunch. No greater contrast in environment could be imagined. We arrived too early, and were told by the majestic butler that Mrs Granville Barker always worked at her writing, in bed, right on until lunch time, and had not yet dressed. Would we like to take a stroll through the gardens? This we did until our watches told us it was precisely one o'clock. The inside of the house was exquisite, and so seemed Mrs Granville Barker as she entered the dining-room with a brightly coloured cockatoo perched on her wrist. She was a gracious hostess but I longed to get Granville Barker himself to talk; after the easy natural atmosphere of Max Gate, we found the social formality rather stifling.

Gustav Holst sent his setting of Hardy's poem, 'The Homecoming' (*CP* 210), to Hardy in 1910, and in 1915 he wrote asking for permission to set yet another poem. There is a letter from Holst to Hardy (no date but believed to be about 1922) asking if he might call on him, but there appears to be no record of a visit at that time. Then on 4 August 1927 Holst wrote again asking for permission to dedicate a new orchestral composition, entitled 'Egdon Heath' to Hardy, and this was followed by the visit on the 9th. What we know about that visit is found in a letter to an American friend, Austin Lidbury, written from the Phoenix Hotel, Dorchester on 11 August. The text here is taken from *Gustav Holst: A Biography* by Imogen Holst (London 1938, pp. 126–7):

I fear that I shall not fulfil the delightful inscription you wrote in *The Story-Teller's Holiday* and write a scherzo.

But your gift of *The Return of the Native*, combined with a walk over Egdon Heath at Easter 1926 started my mind working, and I felt that according to my usual slow method I might write something in 1930 or thereabouts. However, a cable came last Easter from the New York Symphony Orchestra asking me to write something for them! With the result that my 'Egdon Heath' was half done by the end of July, and last Friday I started walking here from Bristol via the Mendips, Wells and Sherborne. I got here on Monday, and on Tuesday [9 August] I had an unforgettable lunch and motor trip with Thomas Hardy himself, who showed me Mellstock, Rainbarrow and Egdon in general. I've promised to go up Rainbarrow by night. He is sorry I'm seeing it in summer weather, and wants me to come again in November.

Do you like improbable true stories? Here is one. Hardy knows my Planets because he heard them on a gramophone belonging to T. E. Lawrence who was in camp on Egdon Heath in the Tank Corps! . . .

Hardy was never to hear 'Egdon Heath'. It had its first performance on 27 February 1928, little more than a month after his death. Florence attended the rehearsal and was deeply moved by Holst's tribute to her husband. His tribute has been followed by those of several other twentieth-century composers – Ralph Vaughan Williams, Benjamin Britten, Gerald Finzi, John Ireland and Alan Ridout among them.

Gertrude Bugler (1897–1992) and Norman Atkins (1899–1984) were two members of the Hardy Players who came together in 1924 to take part in the Society's production of Hardy's own dramatic adaptation of *Tess*. Gertrude played Tess, Norman was Alec, and they were both willing to talk about their memories of Hardy until death silenced them. Hardy was so impressed and moved by Gertrude as an actress that he became very fond of her, so much so that Florence became obsessed with jealousy. As Gertrude was fifty-seven years younger than he and was happily married with a young baby at the time, such an obsession was ridiculous. When I met Gertrude in 1980 she exclaimed, 'Hardy had two jealous wives and he knew it.' She added that Florence was a snob, deliberately cultivated the aristocracy and was surprised that after Hardy's death so many of her 'friends' came no more! Of course, Gertrude had every reason for disliking a woman who was capable of reprimanding her in the following terms for daring to call at Max Gate and asking first for Mr Hardy rather than for her, the lady of the house. 'As you must know this is a most extraordinary thing to do. In the first place all invitations to Max Gate, naturally come from me, as is the custom, and again it is not usual for any lady to call upon a gentleman. It is simply "not done"' (*Letters of Emma and Florence Hardy* p. 183). Her first public account of her memories of Hardy was probably in a talk 'Hardy at Max Gate' given on BBC radio and printed in *The Listener* on 29 June 1939, pp. 1375–6. It is from this that the following extracts have been taken:

> A great deal has been said and written, both during his lifetime and since his death, about the sad philosophy and pessimistic attitude to life of Thomas Hardy. But to me he was always a man of smiles and kindness; he was anything but the morose, grim, cynical man often

pictured, and if he sometimes emphasised the darker side of life he never forgot the sunshine of laughter. In 1913 I was asked to take the part of Marty South in *The Woodlanders*, one of the so-called Hardy plays. I had just left school and it must have been during these rehearsals that I first met Thomas Hardy. . . .

In 1921 the difficult task of adapting *The Return of the Native* was undertaken and this play, when produced, attracted the attention of the London newspapers, as those which preceded it had done. The critics were not always kind for there were those who thought Hardy's work beyond the power of the most skilful dramatist, though those of us taking part in these plays knew how much pleasure they afforded their great author. There was one very bitter criticism, and, feeling terribly sorry for myself and full of quite unnecessary indignation on his behalf, I asked T. H. what he thought about it. To my surprise, he was very amused and told me never to allow myself to become annoyed, for when opinions which differed were expressed, it really became more interesting and public interest was kept longer alive.

He said there had been a great deal of controversy when *Jude the Obscure* had been published, and how pleased and interested he had been about it at the time. He told me too, that there had never been a real Eustacia Vye, but that when he was a young man a boy had been drowned in Shadwater Weir and he had seen him taken from the water; some curious trick of the light on the body had at first made him think that it was of a girl, and it was this incident which started the train of thought which led him to write *The Return of the Native*. . . .

It was in 1924 and the early part of 1925 that I was mostly at Max Gate. *Tess of the d'Urbervilles* had been dramatised many years before by Hardy himself and he now allowed the Hardy Players to use it. He cast the principal parts himself and he entrusted the name part to me. One Sunday afternoon, while the play was in rehearsal, arrangements were made to take some members of the cast to Wellbridge House at Wool and Mr and Mrs Hardy joined us.

Wellbridge House, standing on the River Froom, where Angel Clare and Tess spent their strange honeymoon, was once part of a fine manorial residence and the property and seat of a d'Urberville, but since its partial demolition, a farmhouse. And in that house, in the very room described in the book, Thomas Hardy and his wife watched the rehearsal of that intensely moving and fatal confession scene. After a later rehearsal, with the opening night not too far away, and his lines not yet fully committed to memory, one of the actors approached the author and said: 'Sir, have you any suggestions to make regarding my part?' 'Yes,' said Thomas Hardy quickly with a smile, 'yes, one – that you learn it.' . . .

For some queer inexplicable reason, I remember with extraordinary clarity my last visit during his lifetime. I can see him now, as I saw him then, sitting in a low chair, with his knees crossed and his hand idly resting on the head of Wessex, his wire-haired terrier. I sat on a stool near the window looking on to the drive. He was not a tall man, rather spare, quick in gesture and animated in conversation. He had a really happy smile and his expression was never austere or severe. . . .

Then we talked, I remember, of my meeting with Lawrence of Arabia and he told me something of his frequent visits to the house and said of Lawrence almost reverently, 'He is a very great man.'

He wondered how I should like playing with professional actors and how I could bear to leave my baby in other hands; he asked a number of very unusual questions about her and then, for a few brief seconds, he had forgotten my existence, and I saw before me the Thomas Hardy who had written *Time's Laughingstocks* and *Moments of Vision*, looking a little sadly and wistfully beyond the object on which his eyes happened to be resting, and instinctively I knew that it was one of life's little ironies that he had no child of his own. Usually Mr and Mrs Hardy said goodbye to me in the porch, but on that occasion – with something of the obstinacy of an old man – Mr Hardy insisted on seeing me to my car. We walked halfway down the short winding drive in silence, then suddenly he said: 'If anyone asks you if you knew Thomas Hardy, say, "Yes, he was my friend."' I never saw him again.

Norman Atkins (1899–1984), a Dorchester banker, was a member of the Hardy Players and came to prominence in 1924 when he was cast as Alec in that year's production of *Tess*. As a local man who had known the Hardys and visited Max Gate 'for tea' on several occasions, he was much in demand as a lecturer right up until his death. Meeting him first in the 1970s, I was much impressed by the retentiveness and objectivity of his memories of the past. Discussing the way in which so many of the local people were so unpleasant about Hardy, he told me once that his wife had been informed by a man that half the population were descendants of Hardy's illegitimate children, and that a cousin of his in Cranborne had been told that the 'Fleur de Lys' was the pub where Hardy's girl friend walked into the bar stark naked. Norman's own opinion was that many people in and around Dorchester had the idea that Hardy was writing about themselves in his novels and they resented this. The following are extracts from *Thomas Hardy and the Hardy Players* (Channel Isles 1980):

When at the end of the summer of 1924, I was asked if I would like to play the part of Alec d'Urberville in the coming production of *Tess*, I accepted the offer with enthusiasm. I was one of several young members of the Society [The Hardy Players], and as many of the other male members were middle-aged, it was felt that the cast of Alec should be given to a younger member, as more in keeping with the part. Very soon rehearsals were under way. . . .

Early in October I received a letter from Mrs Hardy inviting me to tea at Max Gate on the following Sunday afternoon to 'Meet and discuss with her husband the part of Alec d'Urberville.' I accepted by return of post. . . .

The front door was opened to me by a smiling Nellie, the parlour maid, who showed me into the drawing room where I was welcomed by Mrs Hardy whose conversation immediately put me at my ease. . . .

A few minutes later my host entered the room, a not very impressive figure, as he moved silently to his chair on the opposite side of the table from me. But when he was settled, and he sat very upright for a man of his 84 years, he looked most impressive, his was a face of great character and I felt that I was in the company of a man of distinction. . . .

My attention was constantly attracted by a beautifully executed bronze head of Thomas Hardy which stood on top of a tallboy in a corner of the room facing the fireplace. It seemed to be looking out of the shadows, for the room was inclined to be dark, caused no doubt by the tall trees that grew close to the house, the dark furniture and dark brown paint of the decorations. The head of the man sitting in front of me might well have been a replica of that bronze head finely chiselled in pale stone, and the comparison fascinated me. It was almost eerie in its effect. This sculpture by Maggie Richardson can now been seen in the Dorset County Museum.

I remember the China tea and the microscopic pieces of bread and butter of lace-like thinness which looked like a collection of pale yellow and brown postage stamps decorating the plate on which they were served; the home-made cakes on a three-tier silver cake-stand, and the embroidered table cloth.

Mr and Mrs Hardy ate but little and politeness forced me to do likewise, although my walk had provided me with a comfortable appetite, but at least it gave me an opportunity of studying my host and hostess in some detail.

Mr Hardy was short in stature (about 5ft 5in – 5ft 6in) and usually dressed in dark loose-fitting suits, his tie loosely knotted but in no way untidy. . . .

Very few of his photos do him justice, for he was definitely not photogenic. His portrait in academic robes by Bernard Griffin, a Dorchester photographer, and the drawing by William Strang, R. A., in the National Portrait Gallery give the best impression of him, as I remember him. ...

About the middle of October the entire cast was invited to Max Gate for an evening rehearsal in the drawing-room. Mr Hardy helped rearrange the furniture to give us space in which to act and was in one of his best moods, he was an entirely different man, but it was to Tess that he directed most of his animated conversation. Mr Hardy sat with his wife and watched our rehearsal, but made no comment or criticism of our work during the rehearsal.

A day or two afterwards I received a slip of paper on which were typed four or five suggestions for voice inflections of some of my words, sent by Mr Hardy for my guidance. This was the beginning of a little difference of opinion as to how Alec should be played. Mr Hardy seemed of the opinion that I was being too nice to Tess, and his paper suggestions bore this out. ...

At Mrs Hardy's invitation I again went to Max Gate to tea and on my arrival was received by her alone in the drawing-room. The subject of her conversation took me completely by surprise. While she fully appreciated the acting talents of her husband's 'stage heroine' she was most definitely put out by his obvious appreciation and friendliness toward the lady herself. She was also convinced that this was a matter of some comment amongst the Players themselves and that was most undesirable. Hence my personal invitation to Max Gate as being the only young male member of the Players suitable for an invitation!

I was completely at a loss for words – it was a bolt from the blue. Such a thought had never occurred to me, for having lived most of my life in a large town I had little experience of small town local gossip. It had seemed to me a perfectly natural reaction of an old man toward a young and attractive woman who so ably portrayed his heroines. So I shook my head and said how much I appreciated her invitations to the house and the matter was never referred to again. Unfortunately it rather spoiled the pleasure of my visits and I tended to withdraw into the background at general public gatherings.

Was this then the cause of my host's somewhat unconventional greeting at my first visit? Thomas Hardy was no fool and my sympathy was rather with him and I thought his wife was taking the matter far too seriously. She was then 45 years of age. ...

At the end of October Dr Smerdon (Angel Clare) called on me one Sunday morning in a state of great excitement. He had conceived the brilliant idea of arranging a rehearsal that afternoon at Wool Manor (the Wellbridge Manor of the play) and had obtained the consent of the then occupiers. He had invited Mr and Mrs Hardy, Gertrude Bugler and Harry Tilley to meet there, and he said that he would drive me over with his wife and that we had been invited to tea afterwards at Max Gate.

The rehearsal was only a short one and concerned the tragic 'confession scene' between Tess and Angel Clare on their honeymoon; and the subsequent meeting of Tess with Alec. The latter scene had been introduced into the play at this stage for production purposes and its location differed from that in the novel.

On arrival at Wool Manor, which then served as a farm house, we were invited into a fairly large room sparsely furnished and apparently not much used. The walls were bare, but the winter sunlight lit up the room as it struggled through the mullioned windows. A small table and chair were all the 'props' required to set the scene. . . .

I think we all sensed the significant atmosphere of the setting, especially Gertrude Bugler, and I doubt if she ever played that scene to better advantage or with more intense feeling. It was as beautiful as it was tragic, and it was played throughout without interruption.

Here was one of the world's most eminent men of letters in the late evening of his life, watching the heroine, whom he himself created, come to life in the very house of the scene which he had visualised. Undoubtedly she was the very incarnation of Tess Durbeyfield of the novel, and as he sat and watched he appeared to be deeply moved.

As Tess's last heart-rending sobs died away the little audience remained perfectly still and complete silence followed, broken only by the producer suggesting that Tess and Alec should play their scene. That is an experience I shall never forget. . . .

Before returning to Max Gate we looked at the pictures of the ancestresses painted on the wall of the landing on the first floor. (Unfortunately, time and possible neglect has so ravaged them that only one can be vaguely recognised as a portrait). As we surveyed these two ugly women, Mr Hardy, with a twinkle in his eye, turned to Gertrude Bugler and said 'I think you are rather like your ancestresses!'

I left the little group discussing their history. I had brought my camera with me and I was about to take a picture of the house, when Mrs Hardy and Mrs Smerdon came out of the porch and the former, noticing my camera, suddenly turned her back on me and disappeared into the porch again! Afterwards she apologised and hoped that she had not spoiled my picture, explaining that she had seen the camera and thought I was a press photographer waiting to take a picture of her husband – and Tess?

I can here mention that Mrs Hardy had a perfect horror of all press reporters and that she distrusted them absolutely... There may have been some misquotation or misinterpretation in the past, but so strongly did she feel on the matter that one felt almost sworn to secrecy on leaving the house. ...

It has been said that Hardy, having no children of his own, had little sympathy with them, but this is contradicted by the presence in his house in the 1890s for several months each year of Emma's young niece and nephew. Florence had a nephew, Thomas Soundy (1918–88) who was just seven years old when he stayed at Max Gate in 1925 for a few days. This memory of that time comes from *The Thomas Hardy Society Review 1977*, p. 75:

It was the occasion of my first visit to England from Canada. For days previous to the journey to Dorchester from Enfield, I had been carefully instructed repeatedly to 'be good', to such an extent that on the final drive to Max Gate from the station I was fast becoming quite terrified of whom I should meet. Immediately on our arrival, Aunt Florence left my mother to deal with the luggage in the hall, and whisked me upstairs and along a dark corridor leading to the study door. Instead of a 'monster' (to a five-year-old), out stepped a very kindly white-haired old gentleman with a beaming smile, saying 'Well, well, so this is little Tommy.' I shall never forget that kindly welcome and the gentleness to a small bewildered boy.

My memory of Max Gate in those days was of complete tranquillity, broken only by the sound of the ticking of the grandfather clocks of which Thomas Hardy was so fond. There were three: one in the passage-way leading to the kitchen, the other in the hall, and the other in the drawing-room. There was a little brass Cromwellian clock in the dining-room which had a most distinct chime and was a perfect time-keeper (it is now in the Museum). Every Monday morning after breakfast, Thomas Hardy would wind the clocks and check the time with his watch. After his death, a man from Dorchester would come weekly on a bicycle to check and rewind them. No one else was allowed to touch the clocks right up to the death of Aunt Florence.

The last recollection of Thomas Hardy (and this is somewhat dim) is of spending a seaside holiday on Brunswick Terrace at Weymouth. One sunny afternoon, Thomas Hardy and Aunt Florence came to tea with my grandparents (the Dugdales), who were staying there. Beyond the bustle of all the promenaders, the Home Fleet could be seen at anchor in Weymouth Bay. All I can recall of the grown-ups' conversation afterwards is how much Thomas Hardy had enjoyed sitting in the Georgian bay-window during the afternoon, and looking out on the scene at tea-time.

In spite of Florence Hardy's repeated complaints about the loneliness and seclusion of Max Gate it is remarkable how many people came 'to tea' and how, as Hardy grew older, there was no diminution in the flow of visitors. As has been previously pointed out, not everyone signed the Visitors' Book but, even so, it registers more than one hundred visitors in 1925. One who didn't sign it was a Mr R. Pakenham who wrote the following letter on 29 July 1985:

Dear Miss Keith,
 I read with interest that you had formed a 'T. E. Lawrence Society' and wonder how many of your members had actually met that legendary character. On Easter Sunday 1925 I was invited with my parents by adoption, the late Mr & Mrs E. R. Sykes, to tea by Mrs Hardy at Max Gate. I knew Thomas Hardy because I used to meet him on his morning walk east towards West Stafford when we lived at Lewell Lodge, West Knighton and as a boy I bicycled to Dorchester via Stafford with orders to the County Stores etc. One day he stopped me to show me a bird's nest by the railway bridge and thereafter I always stopped and talked to him, he was a very nice old boy.
 Anyway during tea I was sitting next to Hardy on the old high backed 'Pub Settle' he had at one end of the dining table listening to his description of the different ways cider was made in Devon & Dorset when the parlour maid came in and spoke to Mrs Hardy 'sotto voce' at the other end of the table. 'Nonsense, show him in, we are all friends here' said Mrs Hardy to the maid. With that a man was shown into the room dressed in a rather untidy khaki uniform. Of medium height, clean shaven with a rather pink and white complexion and a head of fair curly hair. He spoke to Mrs Hardy, nodded to the rest of us and walked round to the vacant space on the settle the other side of Hardy to me.
 As he sat down I took a good look at him and our eyes met briefly. It was those very blue penetrating eyes which impressed me. At 13 I knew nothing about T. E. Lawrence but when we left Max Gate the Sykes and a lady friend who was with us fairly burst into song and Mrs Sykes explained who he was and what he had done.
 It may be a long time ago and I am no longer young (73) but I was a quiet and observant child and that scene is as clear in my mind's eye as when it happened. Hardy said to me 'You don't mind if I talk to my friend' and I replied 'Of course not, Mr Hardy.'

Frederic Lefèvre (1889–1949), editor of *Les Nouvelles Littéraires*, and Yvonne Salmon, lecturer in French at Reading University who was working on a translation of *The Dynasts*, called on Hardy on 7 February 1925. Lefèvre's visit was as a representative of the Alliance Française and Hardy obviously found it difficult to refuse the request for a visit although Florence, replying on his behalf, pointed out that he had nothing special to communicate on the subject of the Alliance and this together with the troublesome journey might make them decide to give up the idea of a visit. Whatever they decided it was 'to be distinctly understood that no personal details observed at the interview were to be published by M. Lefèvre'. Although their engagements and the railway timetable allowed them less than two hours in Dorchester, Lefèvre managed to write a lengthy account of the visit which first appeared in *Les Nouvelles Littéraires* on 21 February 1925 and then in translation in *Living Age* 11 April 1925, pp. 99–103. Part of the interview is suspect as its source is without doubt Hardy's Apology to his volume of verse, *Late Lyrics and Earlier* which had been published in 1922. However, part of what he reports I have found nowhere else:

> I was received on the threshold by Mrs Hardy, who made me welcome in the most courteous terms, explaining that the master was delighted to receive one of those young Frenchmen whose affectionate admiration had so deeply touched him. Then we went into the salon, where a few moments later Thomas Hardy joined us. If my emotion was great, my surprise was assuredly no less.
>
> Thomas Hardy will be eighty-five next June, and I had hardly expected the amazing vitality that he displayed throughout our short conversation. He spoke first of his love for France, and what a disappointment it was to think that *The Dynasts* should have been translated into German before it was translated into French. When I said that there might still be time to get ahead of the Germans, and that I should be glad to try, he smiled. From Germany our talk passed to the war – an easy transition.
>
> 'I never can think without astonishment,' said he, 'that there are some people in different countries who dare to talk about the benefits of war. What nonsense, what stupidity! War is an evil thing, and can only breed evil. No one is justified in trying to make out that war has had a beneficial effect upon things aesthetic. I frankly do not understand that. Since war has diminished our human capital – and to what a degree – it has therefore diminished our intellectual (capital). Many young writers were killed, and I frankly do not see how their intellectual wealth can have found its way to those who survived.

'You ask about lessons of the war? Yes, but they cannot be utilised. There are no lessons of war. War is a fatality. It has nothing to do with either reason or intelligence. War is something irresistible. It seems to obey some kind of devilish determinism and when peoples go to war they do not make that ridiculous decision in order to follow the counsels of reason or to obey their intelligence. No development or perfection in either one or the other could stop wars, since neither reason nor intelligence has anything to do with supporting them. Perhaps tomorrow things will be otherwise, but I have no great confidence. I think rather that we are entering on a dark age whose port of entry was the abominable war we have just lived through.

'The Great War seems to me to weigh upon the world like a curse, and it has not yet borne its bitterest fruit. Does it not terrify you to think that, at the very hour when your poor land of France is smoking with the blood of millions of dead whom the peoples of the world left there, there are still those who in the newspapers of the whole world even now are talking about the next war – 'the next,' as they call it, in a kind of ghastly abbreviation? Is this not a cause for frank despair? . . .

'These visits that you are making to English writers can only be beneficial to the intellectual bond between the two peoples. But I do not see that anything can save the world from all the bloody follies in which for ten years it has sunk itself. Religion alone has any chance of success in bringing about this union of the people. By religion I mean the religious spirit, but at this moment religion is suffering such shocks, such transformations, that its capacity for action is curiously diminished. . . .

'I dream of an alliance between religions freed from dogmas. The religion which ought to be preserved if the world is not to perish absolutely and which we must achieve if the world is not to perish, an alliance of rationalism and religion, would be created by poetry. People are likely to forget that poetry, pure literature, and religion are three different names for one and the same thing. Poetry, pure literature, and religion are the visible points of the most authentic mental and emotional life, and I am happy to think that this religion without dogmas – in which, I think, we may see in advance the religion of the future and by which all of the modern world that can be saved will be saved – may find shelter for its meditation and its songs in the churches of today.'

'Just now,' said I, 'you showed a keen desire to see *The Dynasts* translated into French. Is that your favourite among your books?'

Mr Hardy smiled gently.

'I am especially fond of the little poems, which I am trying to make successful tomorrow and in the days that follow. Nevertheless, to speak frankly, I do have a weakness for that rather long-drawn-out work, and especially for the third part. If the whole thing were not to be translated into French, I should prefer to have the third part translated, because I think it superior to the other two. I imagine that the subject and the way in which I have treated it would not be too distasteful to the French public. One of my thoughts in writing the book was to show that in the Napoleonic wars England was not fighting the French people, but their Emperor.'

'It is not possible to escape from literary influences,' said Mr Hardy in answer to a question, 'but I think that the best are indirect, or, if I may employ a French phrase, *à retardement*. Thus, at the moment when I was carrying *The Dynasts* around in my mind, I had occasion to read *War and Peace* by Tolstoi, whose *Anna Karenina* I had just finished with keen interest. I had carefully kept from reading it hitherto because I thought the subject of the book and its orchestration too closely related to what I was trying to do myself. I have not read the French novelists for a long time, either. They are too fascinating, too enveloping, and their influence is bad for you. There is a certain number of English novelists who, I imagine, would not stand being translated into French, because they would find themselves in a land which knew them already, and the French would be surprised at the very considerable borrowing that had been made from them. I have read a good deal of Stendhal, especially his *La Chartreuse de Parme*. Today – I must seem very old to you – I am reading especially Corneille, Racine, and Hugo.'

Here Mr Hardy indulged in a smile of keen irony:
'Someone told me the other day that your young comrades are inclined to despise Hugo a little too much. Believe me, the reason is that they do not know him enough. Hugo is a good, great man, and I have a feeling that in saying that I am stating a too evident banality. After today he will defy the centuries.

'Yes, yes, I always read a good deal, and in the evening, when my poor eyes are tired, Mrs Hardy reads aloud to me. I have just been rereading *Hamlet*. I read hardly anything but poetry.'

Teatime had come, but by a delicate attention on the master's part Mrs Hardy offered us, instead of the traditional tea, French coffee, and in defiance of his doctor's orders Thomas Hardy took a cup and drank with us. (I may say in passing that it was in the salon of Max Gate that I drank the best coffee in England.) I asked Mr Hardy whether he had met many French writers.

'No,' said he, 'last year I met Romain Rolland. Once I just missed meeting Anatole France – a sudden sickness made it impossible.'

'Do you know,' said I, 'that sometimes you and he are opposed one to the other, and that a good many French writers think they find in your work a franker feeling for humanity, a more generous pity, and, in a word, a keener sense of the tragedy of every day?'

Thomas Hardy bowed his head with an almost bashful air and said:–

'Anatole France was a great artist. I have read his *Histoire comique*, which I do not find comic at all, by the way, but of a terrible irony. Have you anyone to replace him – have you any great men now? There is a terrible lack of them in England today; or if there are any, they have not revealed themselves.'

After the success of Hardy's dramatisation of *Tess*, performed by the Hardy Players in November 1924, there were plans to have a professional performance in London in 1925, and the first suggestion was that Gertrude Bugler should be Tess. However, Florence Hardy, overcome with jealousy and the fear that her husband might follow Gertrude to London, brought pressure to bear on Gertrude to refuse the invitation, and she did so. The part of Tess was then offered to Gwen Ffrangcon-Davies and the play opened in London in September and ran for 131 performances. Ffrangcon-Davies was not at all like Tess in appearance but she was a very able actress and made a success of the part. On 6 December almost the whole cast came to Max Gate and performed the play in the drawing-room. Margaret Carter, who was acting the part of Joan Durbeyfield, wrote to a friend and described the occasion. Part of her letter appears in *The Life*, pp. 462–3:

> Mr and Mrs Hardy behaved as if it were a most usual occurrence for a party of West-End actors to arrive laden with huge theatrical baskets of clothes and props. They met us in the hall and entertained us with tea, cakes and sandwiches, and Mr Hardy made a point of chatting with everyone....
>
> Mr and Mrs Hardy, a friend of the Hardys (Mr T. H. Tilley, who also gave me an account of the performance), and two maids who, in cap and apron, sat on the floor – made up our audience. I think I am correct in saying there was no one else. The room was shaded – lamps and firelight throwing the necessary light on our faces.
>
> We played the scenes of Tess's home with chairs and a tiny drawing-room table to represent farm furniture – tea cups for drinking mugs – when the chairs and tables were removed the corner of the drawing-room became Stonehenge, and yet in some strange way those present said the play gained from the simplicity.
>
> It had seemed as if it would be a paralysingly difficult thing to do,

to get the atmosphere at all within a few feet of the author himself and without any of the usual theatrical illusion, but speaking for myself, after the first few seconds it was perfectly easy, and Miss Ffrangcon-Davies's beautiful voice and exquisite playing of the Stonehenge scene in the shadows thrown by the firelight was a thing that I shall never forget. It was beautiful.

Mr Hardy insisted on talking to us until the last minute. He talked of Tess as if she was someone real whom he had known and liked tremendously. I think he enjoyed the evening. I may be quite wrong, but I got the impression that to him it seemed quite a proper and usual way to give a play – probably as good if not better than any other – and he seemed to have very little conception of the unusualness and difficulties it might present to us.

Gwen Ffrangcon-Davies wrote to me in 1984 and described Hardy as 'charming and with a trace of a puckish sense of humour.' Elsewhere she has written:

> I found that for once I was not acting but living the part. And when the great scene came where Tess, sure of her husband's love and understanding, confesses to him that she has been betrayed and had a child, I had a feeling of absolute reality. We were playing by firelight, a few candles our only illumination; no theatre devices, no need to raise one's voice, no audience even, just Angel Clare and Tess in that quiet room where their tragedy unfolded itself under their creator's eyes. When it was all over, Hardy said very little. He sat quietly in his chair, but his eyes were full of tears.

A. E. Filmer was the stage-director and producer of the London production, and he was responsible for changes which were made in the text of Hardy's play in order to make it more suitable for dramatic performance. Filmer described it as a 'theatrical impossibility'. He had a number of interviews with Hardy whom he describes as 'sweetness incarnate, his whole personality emanated gentleness. I do not remember any other so unlike the portraits of him ... when I had screwed up my courage to the point of making, with sincere humility, certain suggestions, he literally gave me *carte blanche*. He said, "Do exactly as you think fit" ...' (Edmund Blunden: *Thomas Hardy*, London 1941, pp. 170–1).

John Masefield (1878–1967), a poet who became Poet Laureate in 1930, was an acquaintance of Hardy from about 1911 when Masefield had presented him with the first of a number of books of verse. The Max Gate Visitors' Book shows Mr and Mrs Masefield to have been there at least four times in the 1920s and Hardy made at least two visits to

Masefield's home near Oxford. On Masefield's visit on 14 October 1921 he presented Hardy with a magnificent model of a full-rigged ship made by himself. It was addressed

> To Thomas Hardy, Poet,
> From John Masefield, poet.

Masefield was at Max Gate on 24 June 1926, and on 24 July 1926 wrote to a friend, 'You ask: does T. H. enjoy life? I should say that he enjoys it more than he ever did; far more; and really does now enjoy it, horrors and all. He gives me the impression of growing within however much he may be declining without. This is the main test of greatness anywhere...' (*Letters of John Masefield to Florence Lamont*, London 1979, p. 152).

In his autobiography, *So Long to learn* (London 1952, p. 221) Masefield described Hardy's talk as being 'like his work; full of anecdote, story and suggestion'. Hardy seemed to speak 'from inexhaustible ancestral memory... He had told a friend that he had material for another thirty years. He was in touch with a source that is undying...'

Virginia Woolf (1882–1941), the novelist and essayist, made the journey by rail from London and back on 23 July 1926 in order to see Hardy. She was accompanied by her husband, Leonard, and both signed the Max Gate Visitors' book on that day. Hardy had known Virginia's father well as Leslie Stephen was the Editor of *The Cornhill* at the time of the serial publication of *Far from the Madding Crowd* in 1874. The first letter from Hardy to Virginia in *Collected Letters* is dated 20 January 1915 (V, p. 76). She had written to him on 17 January thanking him for the lines he had written about her father in W. Maitland's *The Life and Letters of Leslie Stephen* (London 1906) and for his poem about Stephen, 'The Schreckhorn' (*CP* 264). In his reply Hardy describes Stephen as 'having a peculiar attractiveness for me.' On 20 May 1923 Virginia wrote to Hardy asking him to contribute something to *The Nation and Athenaeum* of which her husband had just become literary editor (*CL* VI, p. 196). Hardy refused her request, saying 'I have fallen into the sere and yellow leaf' (*CL* VI, p. 196, 20 May 1923).

Her description of the July 1926 visit allows us to see Hardy at the age of eighty-six through the eyes of someone who was herself a great writer, and it is sufficiently interesting in what it has to say and how it is said to justify reproducing most of it. The following is from *A Writer's Diary* (London 1954, pp. 89–94):

> At first I thought it was Hardy, and it was the parlour-maid, a small thin girl, wearing a proper cap. She came in with silver cake stands

and so on. Mrs Hardy talked to us about her dog. How long ought we to stay? Can Mr Hardy walk much etc. I asked, making conversation, as I knew one would have to. She has the large sad lack-lustre eyes of a childless woman; great docility and readiness, as if she had learnt her part; not great alacrity, but resignation, in welcoming more visitors; wears a sprigged voile dress, black shoes and a necklace. We can't go far now, she said, though we do walk every day, because our dog isn't able to walk far. He bites, she told us. She became more natural and animated about the dog, who is evidently the real centre of her thoughts – then the maid came in. Then again the door opened, more sprucely, and in trotted a little puffy-cheeked cheerful old man, with an atmosphere cheerful and business-like in addressing us, rather like an old doctor's or solicitor's, saying 'Well now –' or words like that as he shook hands. He was dressed in rough grey with a striped tie. His nose has a joint in it and the end curves down. A round whitish face, the eyes now faded and rather watery, but the whole aspect cheerful and vigorous. He sat on a three-cornered chair (I am too jaded with all this coming and going to do more than gather facts) at a round table, where there were the cake stands and so on; a chocolate roll; what is called a good tea; but he only drank one cup, sitting on his three-cornered chair. He was extremely affable and aware of his duties. He did not let the talk stop or disdain making talk. He talked of father: said he had seen me, or it might have been my sister, but he thought it was me, in my cradle. He had been to Hyde Park Place – oh, Gate was it. A very quiet street. That was why my father liked it. Odd to think that in all these years he had never been down there again. He went there often. Your father took my novel – *Far from the Madding Crowd*. We stood shoulder to shoulder against the British public about certain matters dealt with in that novel. You may have heard. Then he said how some other novel had fallen through that was to appear – the parcel had been lost coming from France – not a very likely thing to happen, as your father said – a big parcel of manuscript; and he asked me to send my story. I think he broke all the *Cornhill* laws – not to see the whole book; so I sent it in chapter by chapter and was never late. Wonderful what youth is! I had it in my head doubtless, but I never thought twice about it. It came out every month. . . .

He puts his head down like some old pouter pigeon. He has a very long head; and quizzical bright eyes, for in talk they grow bright. He said when he was in the Strand 6 years ago he scarcely knew where he was and he used to know it all intimately. He told us that he used to buy second-hand books – nothing valuable – in Wyck Street. Then he wondered why Great James Street should be so narrow and Bedford Row so broad. He had often wondered about that. At this rate, London would soon be unrecognisable. But I shall never go there again. Mrs Hardy tried to persuade him that it was an easy drive – only 6 hours or so. I asked if she liked it, and she said Granville Barker had told her that when she was in the nursing home she had 'the time of her life'. She knew everyone in Dorchester but she thought there were more interesting people in London. Had I often been to Siegfried's flat? I said no. Then she asked about him and Morgan, said he was elusive, as if they enjoyed visits from him. I said I heard from Wells that Mr Hardy had been up to London to see an air raid. 'What things they say!' he said. 'It was my wife. There was an air raid one night when we stayed with Barrie. We just heard a little pop in the distance. The searchlights were beautiful, I thought if a bomb now were to fall on this flat how many writers would be lost.' And he smiled, in his queer way, which is fresh and yet sarcastic a little; anyhow shrewd. Indeed, there was no trace to my thinking of the simple peasant. He seemed perfectly aware of everything; in no doubt or hesitation; having made up his mind; and being delivered of all his work, so that he was in no doubt about that either. He was not interested much in his novels, or in anybody's novels: took it all easily and naturally. 'I never took long with them' he said. 'The longest was *The Dinnasts* (so pronounced).' 'But that was really three books', said Mrs Hardy. 'Yes; and that took me six years; but not working all the time.' 'Can you write poetry regularly?' I asked (being beset with the desire to hear him say something about his books; but the dog kept cropping up. How he bit; how the inspector came out; how he was ill; and they could do nothing for him.) 'Would you mind if I let him in?' asked Mrs Hardy, and in came Wessex, a very tousled, rough brown and white mongrel; got to guard the house, so naturally he bites people, said Mrs H. 'Well, I don't know about that,' said Hardy, perfectly natural, and not setting much stock by his poems either it seemed. 'Did you write poems at the same time as your novels?' I asked. 'No,' he said. 'I wrote a great many poems. I used to send them about, but they were always returned,' he chuckled. 'And in those days I believed in editors. Many were lost – all the fair copies were lost. But I found the notes and I wrote them from those. I was always finding them. I found one the other day; but I don't think I shall find any more.

'Siegfried took rooms near here and said he was going to work very hard, but he left soon.

'E. M. Forster takes a long time to produce anything – 7 years,' he chuckled. All this made a great impression of the ease with which he did things. 'I daresay *Far from the Madding Crowd* would have been a great deal better if I had written it differently,' he said. But as if it could not be helped and did not matter. . . .

I wanted him to say one word about his writing before we left and could only ask which of his books he would have chosen if, like me, he had had to choose one to read in the train. I had taken *The Mayor of Casterbridge*. 'That's being dramatised,' put in Mrs Hardy, and then brought *Life's Little Ironies*.

'And did it hold your interest?' he asked. I stammered that I could not stop reading it, which was true, but sounded wrong. Anyhow, he was not going to be drawn and went off about giving a young lady a wedding present. 'None of my books are fitted to be wedding presents,' he said. 'You must give Mrs Woolf one of your books,' said Mrs Hardy, inevitably. 'Yes I will. But I'm afraid only in the little thin paper edition,' he said. I protested that it would be enough if he wrote his name (then was vaguely uncomfortable).

Then there was de la Mare. His last book of stories seemed to them such a pity. Hardy had liked some of his poems very much. People said he must be a sinister man to write such stories. But he is a very nice man – a very nice man indeed. He said to a friend who begged him not to give up poetry. 'I'm afraid poetry is giving up me.' The truth is he is a very kind man and sees anyone who wants to see him. He has 16 people for the day sometimes. 'Do you think one can't write poetry if one sees people?' I asked. 'One might be able to – I don't see why not. It's a question of physical strength,' said Hardy. But clearly he preferred solitude himself. Always however he said something sensible and sincere, and thus made the obvious business of compliment-giving rather unpleasant. He seemed to be free of it all; very active minded; liking to describe people; not to talk in an abstract way; for example Col. Lawrence, bicycling [motorcycling] with a broken arm 'held like that' from Lincoln to Hardy, listened at the door to hear if there was anyone there. 'I hope he won't commit suicide,' said Mrs Hardy pensively, still leaning over the tea cups, gazing despondently. 'He often says things like it, though he has never said quite that perhaps. But he has blue lines round his eyes. He calls himself Shaw in the army. No one is to know where he is. But it got into the papers.' 'He promised me not to go into the air,' said Hardy. 'My husband doesn't like anything to do with the air,' said Mrs Hardy.

Now we began to look at the grandfather clock in the corner. We said we must go – tried to confess we were only down for the day. I forgot to say that he offered L. whisky and water, which struck me that he was competent as a host and in every way. So we got up and signed Mrs Hardy's visitors books; and Hardy took my *Life's*

Little Ironies off and trotted back with it signed; and Woolf spelt Wolff, which I daresay had given him some anxiety. Then Wessex came in again. I asked if Hardy could stroke him. So he bent down and stroked him, like the master of the house. Wessex went on wheezing away.

There was not a trace anywhere of deference to editors, or respect for rank or extreme simplicity. What impressed me was his freedom, ease and vitality. He seemed very 'Great Victorian' doing the whole thing with a sweep of his hand (they are ordinary smallish, curled up hands) and setting no great stock by literature; but immensely interested in facts; incidents; and somehow, one could imagine, naturally swept off into imagining and creating without a thought of its being difficult or remarkable; becoming obsessed; and living in imagination. Mrs Hardy thrust his old grey hat into his hand and he trotted us out on to the road. 'Where is that?' I asked him, pointing to a clump of trees on the down opposite, for his house is outside the town, with open country (rolling, massive downs, crowned with little tree coronets before and behind) and he said, with interest, 'That is Weymouth. We see the lights at night – not the lights themselves, but the reflection of them.' And so we left and he trotted in again.

Also Mrs Hardy said to me 'Do you know Aldous Huxley?' I said I did. They had been reading his book, which she thought 'very clever'. But Hardy could not remember it: said his wife had to read to him – his eyes were now so bad. 'They've changed everything now,' he said. 'We used to think there was a beginning and a middle and an end. We believed in the Aristotelian theory. Now one of those stories came to an end with a woman going out of the room.' He chuckled.

Of the two Max Gate gardeners who provided material for the Monographs, the more important is Bertie Stephens (Monograph No. 6, 1963), who worked there from 1926 until just after Florence's death in 1937. William Weston (b. 1899) worked as a gardener for the Hardys for only four months in 1923 and 1924. In a letter to James Stevens Cox of 26 July 1968 (Monograph No. 53, 1969) he described Hardy as the most shy man he had known and mentioned that in spite of Hardy's reputation for meanness, 'he always paid me far above the rate'. He added that, 'One of the places in the garden was a sacred spot and nobody was allowed to tidy it up, this was a broken down old garden seat covered with brambles. Mr Hardy used to sit there with his first wife. The following paragraphs are from Bertie Stephens' monograph:

> The garden was often visited by a hare which somehow managed to get over the wall which surrounded it. It would eat the carrot tops

and do a great deal of damage to other growing plants. Wessex used to try and catch it but without any success, and Mr Hardy, when I told him of its visits and the destruction it caused, said: 'I do not mind it in the garden. They are animals, let them carry on.' He was very fond of animals and birds, and would never allow me to trap or shoot them however destructive they were to the fruit or vegetables. He insisted that I allow all birds to do as they liked in the garden. This attitude did not always please me, especially when some carefully cultivated fruit was destroyed. We netted the raspberries and strawberries to protect them against birds, but after Mr Hardy's death Mrs Hardy employed a builder to erect a permanent fruit cage for the purpose. This was a great improvement and a big saving of time for me. . . .

A path with shrubs on either side of it wound right round the garden and on most mornings after he had studied the weather, which he did every morning when the weather was good enough for him to leave the house, he would walk round this path and examine his favourite flowers and bushes. Again in the evening when the weather was good he made the same journey over the same path. Every Saturday morning it was my job to sweep this path and the one that led from the gate to the house. Hardy liked this done on a Saturday as then the paths were clean and tidy for any visitors who might arrive on the Sunday. He had several favourite spots in the garden, one was near the shrubbery beneath an apple tree down the bottom end. Daffodils, polyanthus, primroses, snowdrops and other flowers grew up through the grass there. He also liked to stand in the conservatory and look out and watch the birds in the pine trees near the green door in the wall which he used when he went out for his walks in the fields. Having tea in the conservatory was another of his enjoyments and there he would sometimes entertain his close friends to tea. . . .

When there were guests at Max Gate Mr Hardy would give me instructions to be very quiet and I had to creep about the garden like a little worm. No grass cutting could be done, nor any job that made the slightest noise. Mr Hardy would not allow his visitors to be disturbed. He wanted them to have complete quiet; that quiet which he himself always demanded of life, and that his wife saw that he got. . . .

In my mind's eye I can see him now, with his ragged old shawl around his neck and shoulders, peeping out of it, and shuffling round the garden with Wessex his only companion; a never-to-be-forgotten picture of an aged old gentleman who was still keenly interested in nature and still studying for his books.

1927 was the last full year of Hardy's life and on 2 June he was eighty-seven, yet the stream of visitors coming to see him showed no sign of diminishing. May O'Rourke, his secretary (see p. 188), records him as saying to Mrs Hardy about some visitors who were coming to see him. 'They want to see me at the eleventh hour and fifty-ninth minute.' The Max Gate Visitors' Book – and again it must be said that it is by no means a complete record – is signed by more than one hundred people between 11 March and 10 December, and among those who signed were Henry Newbolt, the Buchans, the Gosses, Sydney Cockerell, Llewelyn Powys, Siegfried Sassoon, the Masefields, Gustav Holst, the Galsworthys, and Henry Williamson. In addition to this there would have been visits from relations and local friends. The last signatures in the Visitors' Book are of four people who called on 10 December, less than a month before Hardy died. There could be no greater tribute to Hardy's willingness to meet those who wanted to see him, and to his hospitality.

John Buchan, author, and later as Lord Tweedsmuir Governor-General of Canada, and his wife and son called at Max Gate on 3 April 1927. His wife Susan, in *A Festschrift for Professor Marguerite Roberts* (Virginia 1976, pp. 46–7) recalled two anecdotes she had heard about Hardy:

> I can only recall one or two slight anecdotes about Hardy. Hugh Walpole told me that Hardy was persuaded to come to a literary party in London. He sat silent when the writers there discussed in detail their royalties, and their disagreements with their publishers while Hardy, the only world famous author there, sat oblivious to their talk – his thoughts seemingly far away from the financial and business side of literature. I think I am right in saying that when one of the writers asked him about his royalties he changed the subject politely as a matter of no interest. . . .
>
> We heard echoes of Thomas Hardy from Henry Newbolt, who was a distinguished poet and prose writer. He had kept in touch with Thomas Hardy for many years, and I remember Margaret Newbolt telling me of a strange episode when they stayed with the Hardys and his first wife. The then Mrs Hardy showed Lady Newbolt over the house – she paused before a grandfather clock and other good pieces of furniture, remarking, 'These were mine, Mr Hardy's family didn't have any furniture like this!'

As the Buchans left Max Gate, Hardy said to their schoolboy son, 'Sign this book please, you may be a famous man some day.'

On 2 June, Hardy's birthday, he and Florence drove for the day to Netherton Hall in Devonshire, the home of their friends, Helen and

Harley Granville Barker. In a letter written to Florence some months later, Mrs Granville Barker remembered the visit:

> There were no guests, just the peaceful routine of everyday life, for that last birthday here. Mr Hardy said to you afterwards, you told me, that he thought it might be the last, but at the time he was not in any way sad or unlike himself. He noticed, as always, and unlike most old people, the smallest things. At luncheon, I remember, one of the lace doilies at his place got awry in an ugly way, showing the mat underneath, and I saw him, quietly and with the most delicate accuracy, setting it straight again – all the time taking his part in the talk.
>
> In the afternoon we left him alone in the library because we thought he wanted to rest a little. It was cold, for June, and a wood fire was lighted.
>
> Once we peeped in at him through the garden window. He was not asleep but sitting, walled in with books, staring into the fire with that deep look of his. The cat had established itself on his knees and he was stroking it gently, but half-unconsciously.
>
> It was a wonderful picture of him. I shall not forget it. Nor shall I forget the gay and startlingly youthful gesture with which he flourished his hat towards us as, once in the motor-car, later that afternoon, he drove away from us.
>
> (*Life*, p. 471)

Another Frenchman visited Hardy on 3 July 1927. He was Georges Lasselin who was working on a book, *Le Couple humain dans l'oeuvre de Thomas Hardy*. It was published in Paris in 1928, after Hardy's death, under the pseudonym 'Pierre d'Exideuil,' and an English edition was published in the following year. The following passages are taken from Appendix II which might not have been included if Hardy had still been alive:

> Is Mr Hardy at home? The bell seems to die away in some distant world, in the heart of the heaths, in the wilderness of Egdon....
>
> The 'parlour' is empty when we both come in. Fairly large and simply furnished, the room is hospitable, comfortable and tranquil. Beneath the gaze of the pictures which recall to life some of the Wessex scenes enshrined in the master's work, one feels that everything in the room conspires to evoke an atmosphere.
>
> Mrs Hardy is the first to appear. She announces that her husband will be with us in a minute. Slightly built, his neck somewhat emaciated, with the worn, shuttered countenance of age, hermetically lined at the corners of his mouth, looking almost rustic in his brown

suit, the old man stands before us. His greeting is at once sober and cordial. For all his eighty-seven years he is alert and upright. His face is wrinkled, but fresh. The complexion mates well with those greyish-blue eyes of such piercing clarity. The curving aquiline nose confers upon the face an air of aristocratic aloofness, devoid alike of haughtiness and affection. . . .

'Yes,' says Thomas Hardy, 'nothing irritates me so much as the mania of those critics who want at all costs to find something autobiographical in my novels and to identify me, for instance, with the character of Jude or Stephen. I assure you that nothing is further from the truth. The elements from which I have derived the idea of a novel are often manifold, sometimes strange and incongruous. Imagination and invention play a greater role than people realise.

'I have often had recourse to the same method when describing the surroundings, amid which the incidents in my novels were staged. A single scene is frequently formed from the synthesis of several sites. It is thus made up of original features borrowed from a number of different spots. I carried out this task of recomposition almost involuntarily. . . . It was simply forced upon me.' . . .

He was evidently very anxious to know how France had fared since the war, to learn how the country looked with its features marred by invasion. Both he and Mrs Hardy seemed much impressed by the social changes noticeable in Great Britain since the years of blood. The master also spoke to me of his admiration for some of the prominent figures on the other side of the Channel. Among them was Anatole France, whom circumstances always prevented him from meeting, and we spoke of 'M. Bergeret's' books and of the reception at that time accorded to them. The slow agony of La Bechellerie proved to be a kind of apotheosis. It would seem that the public had subsequently veered round. Works like those of Marcel Proust provoked its curiosity in different matters, thus directing its favour, no doubt only momentarily, from other writers.

These oscillations of taste interested Mr Hardy. 'And Balzac?' he inquired. That compact structure, I explained, retains all its solidity. It stands like one of those temples, assured of the tribute of its worshippers, no longer dependent upon fits of enthusiasm or an occasional vogue. Did this move the master of Max Gate to reflect how his work would stand in twenty or thirty years' time, to try to envisage the damage wrought by the years? At least it seemed that his thought strayed from us for a moment, to follow in contemplation this line of development. . . .

The patriarch of English letters does not like lengthy periods. His sentences are short and in his voice there is that note which one always encounters among those who live in contact with the soil, less abrupt than the intonation of the Londoner or of the inhabitant of the great towns, a singing note, almost a note of folklore. . . .

Once we were assembled about the tea and the cakes dispensed by Mrs Hardy, the conversation became less gloomy. The writer made merry for a few minutes at the expense of the visitors who sought to force an entry into his retreat and to take snapshots of his flower-decked lawns, with a view to carrying away pansies which should transform the rare editions of his works into the semblance of a herbal.

His talk became quite racy in its animation when he described the tempestuous arrival of his friend Bernard Shaw in a car worthy of an ambassador, coming all triumphant from Weymouth, where he had occupied the king's room in the best hotel.

It was now time to take leave. When should we next see Mr Hardy? We know that he approves of the way in which we have tried to study his work, without seeking to link it closely with biographical notes, the material for which he has always refused to supply. There is a note of encouragement which we do not deserve in the poet's farewell. The master expresses the hope that our labours will receive their reward.

But we also take with us some flowers from the garden of Max Gate, pink and mauve sweet-peas and some white roses. I shall always see the last gesture of farewell, brief but cordial, which Hardy bestowed upon me. It was in very truth farewell.

In the BBC radio programme of 19 February 1955, Llewelyn Powys (1884–1939), brother of John (see p. 50), said , 'What no-one ever realises about Thomas Hardy is that he was a happy man.' In considering this remark we should bear in mind that Llewelyn's acquaintanceship was mostly based upon the last twenty years or so of Hardy's life . . .

In his article in the *Virginia Quarterly Review* (Winter 1939, pp. 425–33), Llewelyn describes a visit to Max Gate in 1919. Florence was a 'dark, nervous woman, of an awkward carriage, who possessed an odd distinction of her own. As I stood by her side in that room emptied of its company I received a draught of romantic melancholy the strength of which I have never forgotten.' He continues:

Six years passed before I saw Mr Hardy again. I had been living during this time in New York City. . . . The necessity of paying the monthly rent of my hall bedroom in Waverley Place (into which the sun shone only by reflection from the factory opposite) often put me to my shifts and, on the occasion of one of these crises, the idea came to me of writing of a short article about Hardy for *The Dial*

[March 1922, pp. 286–90]. In this article I was indiscreet enough to allude to a conversation I had had with him, which seemed to me to be of general literary interest. He had confided to me after tea during my last visit to Max Gate that he remembered as a boy a family of saddlers living in the nearby village of Broadmayne whose name was Keats, and he told me, as John Keats's forebears had been saddlers, he had often wondered whether this Dorset family could not have been relations of the poet – a surmise that appeared to receive support from the fact that the features of some of the members of the Broadmayne saddlering family had, he had often thought, a remarkable facial resemblance to those of the author of 'Endymion'. Indeed, he told me that he had sometimes indulged the fancy that Keats might have actually walked over those downs to visit these west-country cousins during those days when, on his voyage to Rome his ship, because of bad weather, was driven to take shelter in Lulworth Cove, where was composed the famous last sonnet with thoughts of the hills, stars, and sea so characteristic of this particular Dorset locality.

As ill luck would have it, my essay fell under the all-seeing eye of Amy Lowell, who was just then collecting material for her biography of Keats. And what must she do but bustle off to Max Gate to harass Mr Hardy with a cross-questioning after the manner of one who wants facts rather than fiction and has a mind to sift all evidence to the bottom! It was not until I had returned once more to Dorset with my American wife, Miss Alyse Gregory, that the full effect of this awkward solecism was felt by me. My brother John, as was his custom, had written to ask whether he could pay his summer visit to Max Gate and on this occasion bring with him my brother Theodore. Just before the two of them left East Chaldon a letter arrived from Mrs Hardy complaining of my ill conduct in having published in *The Dial* an intimate communication that had never been intended for literary use. . . .

Relationships were eventually restored and Llewelyn paid a final visit to Max Gate on 9 July 1927, which is also described in the *Virginia Quarterly Review*:

> Not long after this Mrs Hardy invited Miss Gregory and me to tea at Max Gate. The visit remains one of my happiest memories. Hardy appeared to have forgiven and forgotten our estrangement. We talked together freely on many matters. He insisted that the correct name for the cliff on which we lived was White Nose and not White Nore or White Nothe, all of which names are to be read upon maps. 'The

name of the cliff is White Nose and if you stand and look at it from Weymouth Esplanade the reason for its being so named becomes clear. It is like a human nose, like Wellington's nose.' He was particularly anxious to learn, and it was so characteristics of his mind, deep sinking always to the simplest facts of life, how we managed to get on for water in so remote a place. I explained that the government had built large cisterns for the storing of rain water from the roofs. The idea pleased him and he declared that the rain water was more wholesome for drinking purposes than spring water. Horses, he said, will always choose the water of the foulest pond that has had the sun and air upon it rather than that of the purest fountains that jet up from the earth. 'Water that has stood a while is good for the bots [a disease caught from the botfly],' the old man concluded. We mentioned, I remember, Frank Harris. I told him I had been reading *The Man Shakespeare* and found the book penetrating in certain ways, though I was repelled by the style. How could he, for example, use the objectionable word 'smutty' in connection with Ophelia? Hardy sympathized with this resentment. He concluded the subject by remarking that Frank Harris had the gruffest voice of any man he had ever heard speak, an observation to which I could acquiesce, well remembering how Harris, after having driven me back to my Waverley Place lodging, had boomed out at the top of his voice, so that all the street had heard him: 'It will all come out in the wash' – a remark that referred to the approaching publication of his *Lifes and Loves*. Hardy spoke also of the degrading influence of blood sports and told me that he believed that the feeling of the general public towards animals was far more sensitive than it had been in his childhood. Even on the farms the labourers were now not so brutal. He recalled, as a young man, remonstrating with a carter for flogging his mare and receiving the answer: 'But she bain't no Christian.' I remember telling Hardy that a pair of ravens was still to be seen frequenting the precipitous walls of our great sea promontory. In his boyhood he said these birds were much more common and he had often observed cottage people bless themselves as the dolorous fowls flew over their chimneys in the village of Bockhampton.

When we rose to leave, he walked with us to the white gate and it was here that I said good-bye to him for the last time.

J. C. Squire (1884–1958) was editor of the *London Mercury* which published a number of Hardy's poems in the 1920s. He was at Max Gate on 4 August 1922, 25 August 1925, and 24 August 1927, and the following are excerpts from his *Sunday Mornings* (London 1930, pp. 289–300):

Thomas Hardy is dead, in his eighty-eighth year: one of the most illustrious of that band, Origen and the others, of whom he said himself that they 'burned brightlier toward their setting day.' (*CP* 660) That little bird-like body was active until it was at last stricken by this winter's cold; and the eyes in the weather-beaten old face still twinkled with humour and curiosity. At eighty-seven he could still throw his head back and laugh with a youth's gaiety; still course briskly round his garden (a little cosmos) chattering about its Roman remains and the signatures of German prisoners on the shed-door. Only last summer he made a speech. No blanketed mumbling in the chimney-corner for him. And his heart to the last was as young as his will; no faculties decayed save the purely physical, and even those were preserved beyond the normal . . .

And how could he always remember, except when (he wrote a curiously moving poem about this) he looked at the deep wrinkles around the eyes that were the windows of his eager mind? The world was still of inexhaustible interest to him; for all his love of gossiping about the past, he was still curious about the present and future, and would discuss all manner of projects, whether for preserving the world's peace or the amenities of rural England, and still delighted to hear the latest personal news from the town whose roar he had left behind. He never grew satiated with experience; one of his latest poems was inspired by the noise and the lights of a motor-car going past his house at night (*CP* 715); it would not surprise one to find that he had left behind him poems about television and the wireless, both as stimulating to the poetic imagination, as capable of being linked with universal beauty and mystery, as the most consecrated objects of traditional song. With undiminished curiosity he retained a marvellously undiminished sensibility; his heart never lost its quick responsiveness and the horn never came over his eyes; custom inured him to no cruelty, nor did the long battering of life lessen his capacity for love or pain. The boy of seventy years ago had not felt more acutely spring's freshness or autumn's grief, brooded with more luxury over the memorials of vanished years, lost himself more utterly in the visionary red of the robin's breast, or the slaty light of wet roads, pitied more spontaneously the victims of man's brutality or Fate's, than this old man of nearly ninety. To the end he was capable of forming new friendships and anxious to read new books. . . .

My own last glimpse of him I shall always especially cherish as it was the best, leaving a picture which embodies the very essence of Hardy the English countryman and Hardy the unexhausted old man. It was at the end of last August. Knowing it would give him pleasure, I brought with me a splendid and celebrated singer of sea-shanties and traditional songs – Mr John Goss. From lunch till tea we had music. First there were the Dorset folk-songs. The old man took great delight in supplying alternative versions remembered from his youth, and whenever there was a refrain Hardy's light but vigorous old voice joined in, whilst his hand beat the air to the time. 'Well, well, well!' he chuckled, tears of pleasure in his eyes, as each old favourite appeared. One thing led to another; long-neglected music books of the mid-Victorian age were sent for; we carolled 'The Mocking-Bird' and other such sentimental ditties. I thought of all the poems he had made on such themes – of William Dewy and 'the old bass viol' (CP 36), of the Argyle Rooms and 'the deep Drum-polka's booms' (CP 165), of the dead dances he so much loved to recall, with names like 'The Full [New]-Rigged Ship' (CP 227). He was steeped in the social history of England and of his countryside.

Ellen Glasgow (see p. 112) made another visit to see Hardy on 2 September 1927:

> In London, in 1927, I had hesitated whether or not I should go down to Dorchester. 'I shouldn't go, if I were you,' Hugh Walpole had said to me. 'I haven't seen him since the war, but I hear he is much changed.'
> Still I hesitated, but in the end, I wrote to Mrs Hardy, and I received, by return post, a cordial note asking me to stop for tea when we were motoring by Dorchester. She wrote that Hardy had been ill, but he was now much better, though he was able to see very few visitors. And she added: 'How kind of you to remember our dear old Wessex. He died of old age just three months ago. Somebody has given us a Persian kitten, but it can never fill the place of Wessex in our hearts.' Few incidents have given me a more vivid sense of the relentless passage of time. Only a short while before, I had seen Wessex as a puppy, and now, after so brief a period, he was dead of old age.
> There were two other guests, the Tomlinsons, father and son, at Max Gate that afternoon in 1927, and the conversation was more general. But Hardy himself had not changed. He was still gentle, considerate, with a poetic fire in his glance when he spoke of something that moved him. They had a handsome blue Persian kitten, but he told me he missed Wessex more and more. 'Wessex was so fond of the wireless,' he said, 'that I used to get up early in the morning and come downstairs to turn it on for him.' And, presently, he took me out into the garden, and showed me the little grave where Wessex was buried.

Henry Williamson (1895–1977), West Country writer and novelist greatly admired Hardy's work and called on him on 31 October 1927. His account of that visit is found in *Goodbye West Country* (London 1937, pp. 271–3):

> The first author I called on was Hardy... Having knocked at the door I resisted an impulse to run away. A smiling maid opened the door. The following dialogue was uttered.
>
> 'Can I see Mr Hardy?'
> 'Have you an appointment, sir?'
> 'I'm afraid not. I think I'd better go.' ...
> 'Perhaps I'd better tell Mrs Hardy, sir. Will you wait a minute?'
> I waited, resisting a score of pulls to run away.
> 'Mrs Hardy says she will see you, sir, for two minutes.'
> 'Really, I think I should go.'
> 'Mrs Hardy is expecting you.'
> Entering, I noticed a drawing of Shelley by the fireplace.
> 'I'm afraid my husband cannot see anyone just now; he is resting.'
> 'I quite understand. I called only for a moment –'
> Mrs Hardy was nervous. While she talked the toe of her right shoe moved about; she sat in a chair, one leg crossed over the other. I was very nervous; babbled about having come to shake the hand of Hardy, who had written the finest pages of English country life detail, while I had written a book about an otter which I wanted to ask permission to send him. I must go.
> 'Must you go so soon? I think I should tell Mr Hardy you are here.'
> 'Oh no, I must go. I wouldn't know what to say to him.'
> 'He is resting; I'll see if he can see you. Just two minutes...' ...
> 'Mr Hardy will come down, but only for two minutes.'
> A little man came into the room, dressed in a dark suit. We were shaking hands. The lines of his small face were wisdom itself. He was from another world. He sat so quiet and afar, asking me about my book, while I walked about the room and reeled off names to prove I was justified in calling to see him – John Fortescue, John Galsworthy, J. C. Squire, Edward Garnett, Walter de la Mare, all had said my book about an otter was what I knew it was. Conscious of the stream of immodesty falling in my words, I said I knew he would see it as I saw it, and so I had come specially to ask him to accept a copy. I must go. But I must sign her visitors' book before I went, said Mrs Hardy. Look, she said, opening the large pages. This man came from Chicago, and here's a Chinaman who called last week. With a hand shaky and triumphant, I scrawled my name, and prob-

ably, the barn-owl outline. I must go. There was no hurry, murmured Mrs Hardy. Did I know Bude, asked Hardy, saying he was there in 1864. Wasn't otter-hunting cruel, asked the same quiet voice, with the bird-like glance of wisdom. I said I did not like it; but had tried to write a book without that not-liking in it. He nodded, and I got up, and shook his hand, and murmured something about Keats and Coleridge – having lived alone for so long, in a detachment of life, I had a different standard of life from the normal – while tears fell from my eyes and I hurried away.

I sent a copy of the vellum *Tarka*, one of the unsaleable 100 copies published by 'Mr Williamson, Bookseller at the Sign of the Owl, Georgeham, North Devon,' and later Mrs Hardy wrote to the publisher whom she knew, that Hardy wanted his opinion quoted in an advertisement, in the words, 'A remarkable book.' She wrote also that he had told her that in one of Hudson's books was a description of Hudson coming to Max Gate to call on Hardy, walking about outside for half an hour, then failing to go in. Hudson died, not having met Hardy. Therefore, said Hardy, he was doubly glad the author of *Tarka* had come to his door.

The last five names in the Max Gate Visitors' Book for 1927 all signed it on 10 December 1927, only one month before Hardy died. Of Harry Wiley of Chicago, who adds to his signature that he is the grandson of 'Edward Cox,' nothing is known. Thomas Bucklin Wells was Chairman of the American publishers, Harper & Brothers, who were Hardy's American publishers and who had been hoping to get permission for Siegfried Sassoon to write a biography of Hardy. He came on this visit with his wife and with Henry Tomlinson and his wife, Florence. Tomlinson (1873–1958) was a novelist and writer of whom Hardy had 'a high opinion... as a writer of English prose, not to speak of his other capabilities'. (CL VII, p. 24) The Tomlinsons had a house at Abbotsbury, near Dorchester, and Florence wrote to them on 25 November 1927 (*Letters of Emma and Florence Hardy* pp. 252–3) saying that they would 'be most delighted to see you and Mrs Tomlinson, and also Mr and Mrs Wells, whenever you are able to come'. She added, 'TH is fairly well, but he feels very tired today, for no reason apparently, which always rather worries me.' Hardy died on 11 January 1928. Subsequently the somewhat hysterical Florence was sufficiently unbalanced to regard the visit of the Tomlinsons and the Wells as partly responsible for Hardy's death because of the strain this had put upon him. Her annoyance was partly the result of Tomlinson having published an article, 'Hardy at Max Gate', in the *Saturday Review of Literature* on 11 February 1928. She said that he had observed 'the evidences of old age – and then calmly cabled them off to America for money, while he was lying dead here'. (*Letters of Emma and Florence Hardy*, p. 272). This article was repeated and revised in *Out of Soundings* (London 1931). The following are extracts from his *Thomas Hardy* (New York 1929, pp. 13–18):

> A meeting with Hardy was comforting to self-esteem. He was venerable, he was indeed already a legend; his great epic which placed him next to Shakespeare was published over twenty years ago; yet all that seemed rather odd, too, because the little old man himself, as he entertained us, might have been the youngest and most innocent of us all. He appeared content to talk of the habits of owls, and of the signs of the weather, of local inns and queer characters, and of the strangeness of hearing in Dorchester by wireless telephony the dancers' feet when an orchestra was playing at a London festival. Trivial life interested him. Little things amused him. Little things, you could see, often had for him a significance which a clever listener failed to grasp. Hardy was a simple man....
>
> Mrs Hardy always knew how to keep out intrusions such as easterly winds. Her house was as warm and comforting that evening as a quiet heart. The old man, brisk and youthful, showed us where we should sit to get the benefit of the fire. There was a lazy smoke-coloured Persian cat – appropriately named Cobweb – who stretched and yawned, and was an assurance of the ease and rightness of the time and place.... Some who met him might say that you would not have known Hardy for a poet. Perhaps that is because the younger poets frequent the town, and are so often seen and heard. We get to think that a poet should resemble the pattern of a poet. Hardy did not. He resembled in no particular way any other poet you may have met. He might have been a retired solicitor of the country town, pursuing keenly in his leisure several hobbies, finding cheerful entertainment in the fact that his house was on the side of a patrician graveyard of the Romans, and that when gardening he sometimes turned up relics; that there were signs nearby that men unknown had a grove for their god long before Caesar came; startling you with the remark that Robert Louis Stevenson, when he saw him last, was sitting in your chair, admitting strangely then, for a man of his years, that he read poetry nowadays and very little prose, but that he enjoyed the prose of Sir Thomas Browne and Lamb, and preferred Sterne to Swift. It would not be odd, but quite in keeping, that a retired solicitor should have a shrewder knowledge of men and women than a fashionable novelist. His interests turned quickly with any change of the conversation. He would give you a rum story of a dog, and you had to admit it was stranger than your own anec-

dote; so very strange indeed that you fell silent, wondering what on earth the clue to the mystery could be.

Yet when Hardy was in repose his face was that of a seer. There was no doubt then, no need to wonder what special privilege had admitted him to so intimate a knowledge of his fellows. That little man, with wisps of soft grey hair resting on the collar of his tweed jacket, for his hair would grow long at the back, blue-eyed, with a masterful nose that turned slightly from the straight, whose raised and questioning eyebrows pushed furrows up his forehead to the bald and shapely head, had with his life work taken the place in English literature next to Shakespeare; and it was always easy for me to feel that there was the very man.

There are three varying recollections of Hardy's death, the first written by Florence and published in her *The Later Years of Thomas Hardy* (London 1930), the second read by Dr E. W. Mann, the Hardy family doctor on the BBC 1955 radio broadcast, and the third that of the maid, Ellen Titterington, on p. 154. The two-volume biography of Hardy supposedly written by Florence was soon recognised as almost entirely Hardy's own work, only the last two chapters having been written by Florence, probably with help from James Barrie, Sydney Cockerell, E. M. Forster and others. Here is her account of Hardy's last day:

He had a better night, and in the morning of January 11 seemed so much stronger that one at least of those who watched beside him had confident hopes of his recovery, and an atmosphere of joy prevailed in the sickroom. An immense bunch of grapes arrived from London, sent by a friend, and this aroused in Hardy great interest. As a rule he disliked receiving gifts, but on this occasion he showed an almost childlike pleasure, and insisted upon the grapes being held up for the inspection of the doctor, and whoever came into the room. He ate some, and said quite gaily, 'I'm going on with these.' Everything he had on that day in the way of food or drink he seemed to appreciate keenly, though naturally he took but little. As it grew dusk, after a long musing silence, he asked his wife to repeat to him a verse from the *Rubaiyat of Omar Khayyam*, beginning

Oh, Thou, who Man of baser Earth –

She took his copy of this work from his bedside and read to him

Oh, Thou, who Man of baser Earth didst make,
And ev'n with Paradise devise the Snake:

> For all the Sin wherewith the Face of man
> Is blacken'd – Man's forgiveness give – and take!

He indicated that he wished no more to be read.

In the evening he had a sharp heart attack of a kind he had never had before. The doctor was summoned and came quickly, joining Mrs Hardy at the bedside. Hardy remained conscious until a few minutes before the end. Shortly after nine he died.

An hour later one, going to his bedside yet again, saw on the deathface an expression such as she had never seen before on any being, or indeed on any presentment of the human countenance. It was a look of radiant triumph such as imagination could never have conceived. Later the first radiance passed away, but dignity and peace remained as long as eyes could see the mortal features of Thomas Hardy.

Michael Millgate in the textual notes to his edition of *The Life and Work of Thomas Hardy* by Thomas Hardy, tells us that the typed drafts of this final chapter had originally read at the end of the penultimate paragraph above: 'Hardy remained conscious until a few minutes before the end, when a few broken sentences, one of these heart-rending in its poignancy, showed that his mind had reverted to a sorrow of the past.'

Here is the beginning of Dr Mann's broadcast:

> I was the Hardy family doctor for several years prior to his death in January, 1928.
>
> He was seldom ill and required very little medical attention until just before Christmas 1927, when he caught a chill and was confined to bed. At first, his illness seemed to run a normal course, except for the extreme weakness which I suppose one might expect in a person over eighty. After a couple of weeks, as he didn't seem to be gaining strength, a medical specialist from Bournemouth was called, in consultation. For a short time Hardy seemed to improve a little, then on January 11th I was paying my usual evening visit and sitting in his bedroom with his wife, Florence Hardy, and her sister, Miss Dugdale – who was a trained nurse – he was telling me about a book called *Possible Worlds* by J. B. S. Haldane, which he was reading, but found too deep! Then all four of us were talking rather light-heartedly about how we would celebrate when the patient was able to get up and come downstairs, when suddenly there was a short sharp cry and Hardy complained of acute pain in his chest, and in spite of everything that we could do, he became more and more breathless and after two or three minutes, he passed on.

On the next and following days there was great discussion as to where the burial should take place. His widow felt as he belonged so much to Dorset, the funeral should be in Stinsford, the family burying ground, but Sir James Barrie, a great friend of the family thought it ought to be in Westminster Abbey. Finally, the Vicar of Stinsford suggested that the heart should be removed for burial in the family grave and the remains cremated for burial in the Abbey. This was agreed to by the widow and when the necessary permission was obtained, my partner and I removed the heart and placed it in a casket for burial in Stinsford, and later the remains were taken to Woking for cremation.

The last memories of all that end this strange, eventful history are contributed by those who attended Hardy's two funerals. The cut-out heart was buried on 16 January in the 'most hallowed spot on earth', as Hardy described it, Stinsford churchyard, while in London at the same time the cremated remains of his body were given a public burial in Westminster Abbey. What a poem Hardy could have written about this! And what irony that Hardy who wanted a quiet life and would have appreciated a quiet death was buried with such an uproar and such a controversy about the butchering of his body. However, there was something symbolic about the two ceremonies, one in Hardy's much-loved ancient parish church in the heart of his Wessex, the other in the 'pomp and circumstance' of Westminster Abbey at the heart of a London with which Hardy had a love-hate relationship. The continual tension in Hardy's life between his humble birth and his middle-class life are well illustrated here.

One comment on the Stinsford funeral came from Teresa Hardy, his cousin, and is found in Monograph No. 12:

It was Miss Teresa Hardy (aged eighty-four), Thomas Hardy's cousin, who had been most strongly against the Abbey burial. She told a reporter for a popular newspaper of the day:

'I am grieved that they are going to take poor Tom away from London. He wanted, I know, to lie with his own folk in the churchyard yonder.

'Poor Tom. He was a clever boy, but I never thought he would take to writing, and did not like it when he did. Writing, I think, is not a respectable way of earning a living.

'I am quite sure he did not find all his queer characters hereabouts. He must have discovered a good many of them when he went to London.'

In Monograph No. 14 a local resident, Dorothy Meggison, had this to say:

> On the day of Thomas Hardy's funeral I was walking down Bowling Alley Walks, Dorchester, when I heard an old Dorset character say to her companion as they passed me:
> 'And when day of Judgement be come, Almighty, 'e'll say, "Ere be 'eart but where be rest of 'e?"
> The Dorchester people rather resented the removal of Hardy's heart and the separate burials of heart and body. They considered it sacrilegious.

The chief mourner at the Stinsford funeral was Hardy's brother, Henry. He was dead before another year had passed.

Bertie Stephens, the Max Gate gardener (see p. 226), in Monograph No. 6 describes in some detail the funeral day at Stinsford. Subsequently Hardy's clothes and many of his papers were, like his body, committed to the flames. Here is the gardener's description of that:

> Within a week or so of Hardy's death there was a grand clearance of his clothes, and masses of letters and other papers from his study. I was given the task of burning his clothes and bundles of newspapers on a bonfire in the garden. Mrs Hardy stood by the whole time and watched, presumably to ensure that nothing escaped the flames. All was burnt in her presence except a scarf which she gave me for my use. Mrs Hardy herself burnt, on another bonfire, baskets full of the letters and private papers that I had carried down from the study to the garden under her supervision and watchful eye. She would not let me burn these, but insisted upon doing it herself, and after all the papers had been destroyed, she raked the ashes to be sure that not a single scrap or word remained. It was a devil of a clear out. I never knew so much stuff come out of a room or such a burn up. My impression was she did not want any of the letters or papers to be seen by anyone and she was very careful to destroy every trace of them. I had wondered when she was burning them what had been among the papers. Had they not been private I should have had them with the clothes and newspapers on my bonfire. Whether she was destroying them on her own initiative or carrying out the wishes of her late husband I never knew, and the world will never learn what went up in flames on that 'bonfire day.'

That this should happen was completely predictable.

Westminster Abbey was full of dignitaries and good and not so good writers. The pall-bearers were two politicians (Stanley Baldwin and

Ramsay MacDonald), and six writers (Barrie, Galsworthy, Gosse, Housman, Kipling and G. B. Shaw). Arnold Bennett complained bitterly to the press about the way tickets for the Abbey funeral had been distributed and the absence of any member of the Royal Family. This was the end of any hope he might have had of a knighthood. William Rothenstein decided to paint a picture of the scene but both Housman and Barrie were so difficult about this that he abandoned the idea. According to Blanche Patch, G. B. Shaw's secretary, in her *Thirty Years with G. B. S.*, Kipling did not want to meet Shaw and 'shook hands hurriedly and at once turned away as if from the Evil One'. Hannen Swaffer in the *Daily Express* (17 January) described it as 'a funeral without tears' because Hardy was eighty-seven and his work was done. 'The floor of Poets' Corner was covered with a purple carpet edged with white, and nearly in the centre, not much more than a foot long and six inches across, was the oblong hole intended for the urn.'

Bernard Shaw's wife, Charlotte, in a letter to T. E. Lawrence thought that the service was 'very beautifully sung', that Kipling looked 'sinister' and that the clergy were 'full of worldly pomp and disdain'. Bernard Shaw complained that, 'As we marched, pretending to carry the ashes of whatever part of Hardy was buried in the Abbey, Kipling, who fidgeted continually and was next in front of me, kept changing his step. Every time he did so I nearly fell over him.'

Charles Morgan was 'indignant at the cutting out of his heart and the disposal of his body. And yet. . . . Would he have refused Abbey burial? More powerfully even than other artists he had a desire for recognition and a sense of having been neglected and spurned. He told me, with outstanding naivety, that he was glad *Tess* had been filmed because the film would call attention to the book. He never altogether transcended the mood of *Jude the Obscure*. His honorary doctorate at Oxford meant much to him. Abbey burial might well have appealed to him as one of the more triumphant of Life's Little Ironies.' (*Selected Letters of Charles Morgan*, London 1967, p. 201).

Virginia Woolf's entry in her diary for 17 January is interesting more because of what it tells us about her and her friends than for anything that it says about Hardy who surely would have smiled at the self-centred coldness revealed:

Yesterday we went to Hardy's funeral. What did I think of? Of Max Beerbohm's letter, just read; or a lecture to the Newnhamites about women's writing. At intervals some emotion broke in. But I doubt the capacity of the human animal for being dignified in ceremony. One catches a bishop's frown and twitch; sees his polished shiny nose; suspects the rapt spectacled young priest, gazing at the cross he carries, of being a humbug; catches Robert Lynd's distracted haggard eye; then thinks of the mediocrity of X; next here is the coffin, an over-grown one; like a stage coffin, covered with a white satin cloth; bearers elderly gentlemen rather red and stiff, holding to the corners; pigeons flying outside, insufficient artificial light; procession to poets corner; dramatic 'In sure and certain hope of immortality' perhaps melodramatic. After dinner at Clive's Lytton protested that the great man's novels are the poorest of poor stuff; and can't read them. Lytton sitting or lying inert, with his eyes shut, or exasperated with them open. Lady Strachey's slowly fading, but it may take years. Over all this broods for me some uneasy sense of change and mortality and how partings are deaths; and then a sense of my own fame – why should this come over me? and then of its remoteness; and then the pressure of writing two articles on Meredith and furbishing up the Hardy. And Leonard sitting at home reading. And Max's letter; and a sense of the futility of it all.

T. E. Lawrence was serving in the RAF in India at the time Hardy died. It is right that he should have the last word because of their mutual admiration and affection. Here is an extract from Lawrence's letter to Florence of 16 April 1928:

One thing in your letter pleases me very much: you say you have failed him at every turn. Of course you did: everybody did. He was T. H. and if you'd met him or sufficed him at every turn you'd have been as good as T. H. which is absurd: though perhaps some people might think it should be put happier than that. But you know my feeling (worth something perhaps, because I've met so many thousands of what are estimated great men) that T. H. was above and beyond all men living, as a person. I used to go to Max Gate afraid, & half-unwillingly, for fear that perhaps it would no longer seem true to me: but always it was. . . .

He will defend himself very very completely, when people listen to him again. As you know, there will be a wave of detraction, and none of the highbrows will defend him, for quite a long time: and then the bright young critics will rediscover him, & it will be lawful for a person in the know to speak well of him: and all this nonsense will enrage me, because I'm small enough to care. Whereas all that's needful is to forget the fuss for fifty years, and then wake up and see him no longer a battle-field, but part of the ordinary man's heritage.

(*The Letters of T. E. Lawrence of Arabia*, London 1964, pp. 592–3).

Index

A.E.H. 61
Academy, The 52
Adams, Katharine 146
Adventures of a Novelist (Gertrude Atherton) 26
Aeneid, The 29
Aeschylus 97
Afternoon Neighbours (Hamlin Garland) 196
Ainsworth, Wm H. 110
Aldeburgh 30, 31, 73, 76, 80, 88
Allen, Grant 73
Alma-Tadema, Sir L. 21
Amaryllis at the Fair 148
America 201
Animals 51, 63, 64, 76, 78, 79, 87, 112, 120, 227, 233
Anna Karenina 219
Anthologies 141
Archer, William 65–71
Architecture 20, 22, 36, 63, 67, 116, 165, 190
Arnold, Matthew 97, 169
As I Remember (Arthur Bliss) 207
Asquith, Lady Cynthia 159–62
Athenaeum, The 154
Atherton, Gertrude 26
Atkins, Norman 209, 211–15
Australian at Weymouth, The 118
Authors and I (Charles L. Hind) 52
Autobiography with Letters (Wm Lyon Phelps) 63
Autograph hunters 101, 135, 147, 161

Backward Glance, A (Edith Wharton) 25
Baldwin, Stanley 242
Ball, Private R. L. 113
Balzac, Honoré de 230
Baptism 135
Barker, Harley & Helen Granville 62, 82, 166, 201, 208, 229
Barnes, William 1, 10, 22, 78, 128, 161, 169, 171, 176, 189, 192
Barrie, James 121, 122, 127, 153, 159, 162, 181, 196, 198, 224, 239, 241, 243
Bath 165

Beauchamp's Career 94
Beerbohm, Max 126, 162
Beethoven 120
Bennett, Arnold 121, 132, 149
Benson, A. C. 105, 130
Bergeret, M. 230
Besant, Sir Walter 38
Best of Friends, The (Katharine Adams) 146
Binyon, Lawrence 97
Black and White 38
Blanche, J. E. 143
Blathwayt, Raymond 38
Bliss, Arthur 205, 207
Blomfield, Sir Arthur 9, 20, 116, 202
Blundell, Weld 83
Blunden, Edmund 130, 170–2, 178, 221
Blythe, Samuel G. 131
Book of Women's Verse 140
Bookman, The 47, 162
Bookman's Letters, A (Robertson Nicoll) 47
Borgognone, Ambrogio 21
Boughton, Rutland 205
Bowker, Richard 12, 13
Braddon, Mary 95
Bradley, Rose M. 60
Brennecke, Ernest 200–3
Bright, John 149
British School, The 2
Brooke, Rupert 82, 158
Broughton, Rhoda 96
Brown Owl, The (Ford Madox Ford) 29
Browne, Sir Thomas 238
Browning, Robert 75, 97, 114, 115
Buchan, John & Susan 228
Bugler, Gertrude 200, 209–11, 214, 220
Bury, John 149

Cakes and Ale (Somerset Maugham) 89
Cambridge University 82, 104
Campbell, Mrs Patrick 52
Carlyle, Thomas 42
Carter, Margaret 220
Cassell's Saturday Journal 36
Cave, John 193

Cecil, Lord David 162
Celebrities and Simple Souls (Alfred Sutro) 50
Censorship 40, 43, 49, 96
Chambers's Journal 3, 36
Change 166, 177
Changes and Chances (H. W. Nevinson) 76
Chapman and Hall 96
Chaucer 142
Chiaroscuro (Augustus John) 199
Chekov, Anton 121, 139
Chesterton, G. K. 45, 163
Children of the Ghetto, The 43
Christ Church College (Cawnpore) Magazine 14
Christ's Hospital 171
Cider 135
Clarke, G. H. 172
Clodd, Edward 47, 60, 65, 72, 73, 75, 88
Cock, Revd Albert 167
Cockerell, Sir Sydney 62, 106, 146, 178, 228, 239
Coleridge, Mrs S. 52
Coleridge, S. T. 171
College of Sarum St Michael 3
Collins, Lottie 159
Collins, Mr H. Shobbrook 3
Collins, Vere H. 136–44, 157, 172
Conrad, Joseph 128, 172, 198, 206
Corelli, Marie 95
Corneille, Pierre 219
Cornford, Frances 82, 141
Cornhill Magazine 8, 10, 31, 146, 222, 223
Cosmopolis 107
Cox, James Stevens 3
Crabbe, George 130
Craigie, Mrs P. 96
Critic, The 35
Critics and reviewers 43, 71, 77, 81, 87, 129, 136, 149, 171, 179
Crome, John 54

Daily Chronicle 57, 122
Daniel Deronda 17
Dante 15
Darwin, Charles 82
Daudet, Alphonse 95
de la Mare, Walter 62, 97, 162–4, 166, 169, 206, 225
de Vere, Aubrey 22
D'Erlanger, Baron 204, 206

d'Exideuil, Pierre (Georges Lasselin) 18, 229
Dial, The 232
Dialect 34, 71, 86, 124, 133, 136, 169, 202
Dickens, Charles 42, 139, 175, 197
Dolman, Frederick 41
Donne, John 128
Dorset County Chronicle 2, 149
Dorset County Museum 44
Dorset Year Book, The 2, 102
Douglas, Sir George 16, 31
Douglas Library Notes 173
Drama 42, 84
Dreiser, T. 202
Drinkwater, John 62, 206
Dugdale, Eva 153

East Lynne 96
Edward, Prince of Wales 62, 120, 124, 192, 195
Egoist, The 110
Elgar, Sir Edward 204
Eliot, George 8, 13, 17, 43, 114
Ellis, Henry Havelock 18
Ellis, Stewart M. 109
Elton, Lord Godfrey 184–8
Emerson, Ralph W. 63
Encounter 113
English Illustrated Magazine, The 101
Ervine, St John 180
Evan Harrington 94
Evans, Evelyn 98

Felkin, Elliott 113
Festschrift for Prof. Marguerite Roberts 228
Fielding, Henry 72
Filmer, A. E. 221
Fisher, Dr F. B. 14, 15
Fitzwilliam Museum, The 106, 178
Flaubert, Gustav 95, 113
Flecker, J. E. 186
Flower, Newman 62, 174–7
Flurried Years, The (Violet Hunt) 88
Ford, Ford Madox 29, 103
Forster, E. M. 115, 166, 167, 169, 184–8, 224, 239
Fortnightly Review, The 109
Forty Years of Spy 34
France, Anatole 219–20, 230
Ffrangcon Davies, Gwen 145, 200, 220–1

Frazer, Sir James 72
Frith, William 11, 12
From the Angle of 88 (Eden Phillpotts) 119

Gale, Dolly 154
Galsworthy, John 120, 122, 138, 141, 166, 172, 206, 228, 243
Garland, Hamlin 195–9
Garnett, Constance 139
Garnett, David 111
Garnett, Edward 139
Garnett, Richard 139
George III 92, 170
Gibbs, Armstrong 129
Gibson, Wilfrid 97
Gifford, Gordon & Lilian 47
Gissing, George 47, 49, 197
Gittings, Robert 29, 86
Glasgow, Ellen 112, 235
Glastonbury Festival 205–7
Gleanings in Prose and Verse (George Douglas) 17
Godfrey, Sir Dan 206–7
Godwin, William 116
Goethe, J. W. 79, 114
Golden Bough, The 72
Goldring, Douglas 103
Goodbye to All That (Robert Graves) 133
Goodbye West Country (Henry Williamson) 236
Gorki, Maxim 77
Goss, John 235
Gosse, Edmund 12, 25, 47, 105, 106, 107, 126, 228, 243
Gosse: A Literary Landscape 107
Grand, Sarah 43, 95
Grant, James 111
Graphic, The 22
Graves, Robert 131, 133, 183–6
Gray, Thomas 188
Great Victorians, The 172
Green, Julia 3
Griffin, Bernard 213
Grove, Lady Agnes 77
Gustav Holst, A Biography 208

Haig-Brown, Roderick 203
Haldane, J. B. S. 240
Half Hours with Living Writers 141
Hamlet 219
Handbook to the Wessex Country of Thomas Hardy 54

Hankinson, Charles James (aka Clive Holland) 74
Harding, Ernest 3
Harding, Louisa 3
Hardy, Admiral Sir Thomas 78, 92
Hardy, Augustus 104
Hardy, Emma (first wife) 5, 12, 14, 23, 24, 26, 32, 38, 41, 47, 48, 50, 53, 73, 91, 92, 98, 105, 108, 126, 129, 163, 177, 188, 189
Hardy, Florence (second wife) 1, 9, 23, 49, 73, 85, 86, 109, 144, 146, 161, 163, 167, 174, 182, 190, 196, 199, 204, 209, 214, 220, 223, 231, 239, 242
Hardy, Henry (brother) 165, 242
Hardy, James (uncle) 4
Hardy, Jemima (mother) 14, 135
Hardy, Kate (sister) 48, 49
Hardy, Mary (sister) 3, 49, 104, 141
Hardy, Teresa (cousin) 241
Hardy, Thomas (father) 14, 164
Hardy Players, The 84, 98, 122, 206, 212
Harper Bros. 12
Harper's (New Monthly) Magazine 10, 12, 13
Harris, Frank 233
Harte, Bret 10, 197
Hartmann, Karl 169
Harvard University 198
Harvey, Montague 16
Hawker, Revd R. S. 171
Hawkins, Aileen 193
Heavenly Twins, The 43
Hedgcock, Frank 90, 91, 96, 137, 143
Henley, W. E. 18
Henniker, Florence 41, 58, 65, 109, 166
Hibbert Journal, The 31
High Stoy Hill 177
Hill, Vernon 170
Hind, Charles Lewis 52
Hinton, Eric Austin 168
History 58, 92, 130, 197
Hobbes, Thomas 185
'Hodge' 35, 38
Holland, Clive (*see* Hankinson)
Holst, Gustav 129, 205, 208–9, 228
Homer 183
Homer, Christine Wood 47
Horizon 184
Housman, A. E. 60, 65, 98, 111, 243
Housman, Laurence 61
Hudson, W. H. 237
Hugo, Victor 42, 219

Human Pair in the Work of Thomas Hardy, The 18, 229
Hume, David 70
Hunt, Violet 88
Hurden, Fanny 163
Huxley, Aldous 226

I Look Back (Arthur Compton Rickett) 87
Ibsen, Henrik 65, 75
Ilchester 165
Ilminster 165
Imagination 42, 79, 113
Immortal Hour, The 205
Impenetrable Wall, The (Ellen Glasgow) 113
Independent, The 44
Irving, Henry 10

James, G. P. R. 110
James, Henry 10, 95, 148
James, Seumas and Jacques 101
Jefferies, Richard 148
Jeffreys, Judge 79
Jeune, Mary, (later Lady St Helier) 24, 25, 89, 159
John, Augustus 72, 199
John Inglesant 148
John O'London's Weekly 125, 194
Johnson, Lionel 170
Jones, Ebenezer 172
Jonson, Ben 141, 143
Journals of Arnold Bennett, The 121
Just As It Happened (Newman Flower) 174

Kant, Immanuel 114
Katherine Mansfield & Other Literary Portraits 154
Kaye-Smith, Sheila 111
Keats, John 180, 232
Keeble, Lady L. 83
Kenilworth 111
Kennedy, Daisy 206
Kipling, Rudyard 79, 243
Kipps 94

La Fontaine's Fables 183
Lacey, Charles 2
Ladies' Home Journal, The 41
Lamb, Charles 88, 160, 238
Language 71, 115, 128
Lasselin, Georges (Pierre d'Exideuil) 229

Last, Isaac 2
Later Life and Letters of Sir Henry Newbolt, The 98
Lawrence, T. E. 62, 150, 151, 153, 164, 167, 172, 182–4, 186, 199, 209, 211, 216, 225, 244
Lea, Hermann 2, 47, 54
Leaves from a Life (Jane Panton) 10
Lefèvre, Frederic 217–20
Letters of Emma and Florence Hardy 199, 209, 237, 238
Letters of George Gissing, The 49
Letters of John Masefield 222
Letters of Lawrence of Arabia, The 182, 244
Lidbury, Austin 208
Life and Letters of John Galsworthy, The 120
Life and Letters of Leslie Stephen, The 222
Life of Thomas Hardy (Brennecke) 200
Lilly, Marjorie 144
Listener, The 160, 162, 209
Literature 75, 137
Literary World (Boston) 8
Living Age 217
London Mercury, The 46, 233
Lowell, Amy 232
Lowndes, Mrs Belloc 88
Lulworth Castle 83
Lyceum Club 86
Lynton, Mrs Lynn 29

Macaulay, Thomas 128
McCarthy, Desmond 72
McCarthy, Lillah 82
MacDonald, Ramsay 243
Macmillan 5, 23, 61, 138, 148, 158
Macmillan, Alexander 61
Macmillan, Sir Frederick 61
Macmillan, Harold 61
Manchester Guardian 74
Mann, Dr E. W. 154, 239, 240
Mansfield, Katherine 154, 156, 158
Mardon, Vera 122
Marmion 183
Married Love 194
Marriott-Smith, Sir H. 181
Marsh, Edward 184
Martin, Henry 149
Mary Rose 160
Masefield, John 82, 97, 141, 166, 172, 186–7, 221–2, 228
Massingham, Harold 122

Massingham, Henry 122
Master of Ballantrae, The 95
Maugham, Somerset 89
Media 41, 71
Meggison, Dorothy 242
Meliorism 70, 173
Mellstock Choir, The 122
Memories (Desmond McCarthy) 72, 73
Memories (C. K. Paul) 10
Memoirs of a Bookman, The (James Milne) 80
Memories of Fifty Years (Lady St Helier) 24
Men and Memories: Recollections 1872–1938 (Wm Rothenstein) 54
Meredith, George 10, 47, 50, 65, 77, 94, 96, 99, 108, 110, 114, 116, 127, 140, 148
Mew, Charlotte 141, 161
Mightier than the Sword (Ford Madox Ford) 29
Millgate, Michael 1, 240
Milne, James 57, 80
Milton 82
Montgomery, R. 128
Moore, George 163
Morley, John 148
More Changes, More Chances (H. W. Nevinson) 76
Morgan, Charles 178–80, 243
Morgan, Brig-Gen J. H. 177
Morris, William 38
Moule, Revd Henry 4
Moule, Horace 9
Moulton, Louise Chandler 35
Mummers' Plays 85
Murray, Prof. Gilbert 88
Murry, John Middleton 62, 154–8
Music 52, 77, 120, 123, 129, 130, 135, 207
Musical News & Herald, The 205
My Autobiography and Reminiscences (Wm Powell Frith) 11
Myself and My Friends (Lillah McCarthy) 83

Napoleon Bonaparte 79, 92, 182
Napoleon, Louis 78
Nation, The 100, 121, 122, 222
National and English Review, The 91
Nelson, Horatio 88
Nevinson, Henry Woodd 76, 77
New Quarterly, The 10, 72
New Review, The 28

Newbolt, Sir Henry & Lady Margaret 98, 228
Nichol, Robertson 47
Nicholson, Nancy 135
Nietzsche, F. W. 169
Nobel Prize 131
Novel 45, 64, 65, 78, 81, 149, 222, 226, 230
Noyes, Alfred 168

O'Connor, Thomas P. 26
O'Rourke, May 188–92, 228
Observer, The 132
Odes and Other Poems 50
Old Delabole 119
Old Huntsman and Other Poems, The 125
Old Mortality 110
Old St Paul's 110
Omar Khayyam Club 47
Opie, Mrs I. 32
Order of Merit 134
Ouida 95
Out of Soundings (Henry Tomlinson) 238
Oxford 78, 83, 134, 138, 178, 184–7
Oxford Book of English Verse, The 78

'P' 1
Pain, Barry 43
Pakenham, R. 216
Pall Mall Gazette, The 34
Pall Mall Magazine, The 66
Panton, Jane 10
Parker Wm. M. 146
Patch, Blanche 243
Patten, Leonard 102
Paul, Charles Kegan 10
Payn, James 148
Pearmain, Miss 3
Pessimism 70, 88, 101, 109, 127, 132, 136, 148, 163, 167, 173, 179, 182, 209
Peveril of the Peak 111
Phelps, Wm Lyon 63
Philadelphia Home Journal 41
Phillips, Dorothy 194
Phillpotts, Eden 56, 118
Pitt-Rivers, General 77
Places 37
Poe, Edgar Allan 51
Poems and Ballads (Swinburne) 117, 201
Poetry 83, 87, 93, 112, 115, 117, 118, 123, 127, 130, 135, 136, 140, 147, 157, 168, 174, 195, 201, 203, 218, 224

Poets Laureate 116
Politics 22, 202
Pope, Alfred 203
Porter, Harold 131
Portrait of Barrie 160
Portraits from Life (Ann Thwaite) 109
Portsmouth, Lady 24, 114
Possible Worlds 240
Powys, John Cooper 50, 232
Powys, Llewelyn 4, 52, 228, 231
Procter, Mrs Anne 114, 115
Proust, Marcel 230
Publishing 45, 46, 140, 143, 148, 158
Pugin, A. W. N. 171
Purdy, R. L. 36

Quarterly Review, The 28
Queens' College, Cambridge 9
Queen's College, Oxford 184
Queen's Doll's House Library 172

Rabelais Club 10
Rabelais, F. 184
Racine, Jean 95, 219
Random Recollections of an Old Publisher (Wm Tinsley) 7
Raverat, Gwen 82
Reade, Charles 13
Reader, The 76
Reading (Hardy) 73
Real Conversations (Wm Archer) 66
Religion and the Church 75, 135, 136, 178, 218
Remembrance, An Autobiography (H. J. Massingham) 122
Rhys, Ernest 34
Richardson, Maggie 212
Richardson, Samuel 67
Rickett, Arthur Compton 86
Robinson, Mabel 23
Rolland, Romain 219
Ross, Robert 126
Rothenstein, William 153
Royal Society of Literature 99
Rubaiyat of Omar Khayyam, The 117, 239
Ruskin College 78

St Juliot Church 5
St Paul's Cathedral 77
Saintsbury, G. E. 149
Salisbury Training College 3
Salmon, Yvonne 217
Salome 65

Salt, Meriel, Lady 194
Sassoon, Siegfried 87, 125, 139, 162, 166, 170, 172, 186, 224, 228, 237
Saturday Evening Post, The 131
Saturday Review, The 28, 237
Savile Club 13, 127
Schopenhauer, A. 169
Scott, Sir Gilbert 20
Scott, Sir Walter 32, 42, 81, 99, 110, 183
Scottish Cavalier, The 111
Scribner's Magazine 3
Second Mrs Hardy, The 86
Selected Letters of E. M. Forster, The 166
Selected Letters of Charles Morgan, The 243
Seven Pillars of Wisdom, The 153
Shakespeare, William 10, 95, 114, 127, 141, 143, 179, 186, 238, 239
Sharp, Evelyn 75
Sharp, William 27
Shaw, Charlotte 243
Shaw, G. B. 121, 122, 149, 181, 206, 231, 243
Shelley, P. B. 17, 116, 128, 186
Sheltering Tree, The (Netta Syrett) 85
Short stories 42, 93
Shorter, Clement 74, 75, 90
Shorthouse, J. H. 148
Siegfried Sassoon's Diaries 130
Siegfried's Journey 128
Smedley, Constance 90
Smith, Sydney 94
So Long to Learn (John Masefield) 222
Society of Authors 38, 191
Some Recollections (Emma Hardy) 5
Sophocles 70, 97, 114
Soundy, Thomas 215
South Lodge (Douglas Goldring) 103
Spencer, Herbert 140
Sphere, The 90, 133
Spy cartoon 34
Squire, J. 46, 132, 140, 233
Stanford, Charles 207
Stendhal 219
Stephen, Leslie 222
Stephens, Bertie 226–7, 242
Sterne, Laurence 238
Stevens, E. J. 84, 122
Stevenson, Mrs Fanny 17
Stevenson, R. L. 12, 17, 95, 110, 121, 238
Stinsford Church 104, 117, 241
Stoker, Bram 62

Stonehenge 57–60
Stopes, Marie 194–5
Strachey, Lytton 244
Strang, William 72, 155, 213
Sunday at Home 1
Sunday Mornings (J. C. Squire) 233
Sutro, Alfred 50
Swaffer, Hannen 243
Swift, Jonathan 238
Swinburne, A. 38, 97, 116, 117, 201
Symons, Arthur 60, 65
Symons, Rhoda (née Bowser) 65
Syrett, Netta 86

T.P.'s Weekly 26, 90
Talks with Thomas Hardy at Max Gate 1920–1922 (Vere Collins) 136
Tarka the Otter 237
Tate and Brady 178
Tchaikovsky, P. I. 77
Tennyson, Alfred Lord 75, 97, 116, 138
Thackeray, William 14, 139
The Man Shakespeare 233
Thirty Years with G.B.S. 243
Thomas, Edward 97
Thomas Hardy (Blunden) 178
Thomas Hardy (Tomlinson) 238
Thomas Hardy: A Bibliographical Study (Purdy) 36, 57
Thomas Hardy and the Hardy Players 211
Thomas Hardy as Man, Writer and Philosopher (R. E. Zachrisson) 132
Thomas Hardy on Stage (Keith Wilson) 84
Thomas Hardy: Penseur et Artiste (F. Hedgcock) 90
Thomas Hardy Society Review, The 144, 215
Thomas Hardy's Universe (E. Brennecke) 200
Thomas Hardy's Wessex (Hermann Lea) 54
Thornycroft, Agatha & Hamo 25, 26
Thwaite, Ann 105, 107, 109
Tinsley, William 7
Tite, Sir William 9
Titterington, Ellen 149–54, 239
Tolstoy, Leo 75, 219
Tom Jones 72
Tomlinson, H. M. 235, 237
Tomson, Rosamund 44
Treves, Sir Frederick 79, 181
Trollope, Anthony 139
Tupper, Martin 128, 129
Tynan, Katherine 27

Untermeyer, Louis 202

Victorian Age in Literature, The 45
Vincent, Ellen 130
Virginia Quarterly Review, The 231–2
Voss, H. L. 164–6

Wagner, Richard 147
Waley, Arthur 115
Walpole, Hugh 228, 235
War 65, 70, 127, 136, 155, 168, 172, 177, 178, 182, 201, 217–18
Ward, Mrs Humphry 95
Ward, Leslie 34
Warren, Sally 2
Washington Square 95
Watts-Duncan, Theodore 47
Weir of Hermiston 121
Wells, H. G. 62, 94, 121, 122, 125, 132
Wells, Thomas B. 237
Wessex University 167
West, Rebecca 62, 125
Westminster Gazette, The 41
Westminster Review, The 18
Weston, William 226
Wharton, Edith 25
What Maisie Knew 95
Wilde, Oscar 65, 94, 95, 130
Wiley, Harry 237
Williamson, Henry 228, 236
Willis, Irene Cooper 23, 73
Wilson, Keith 84
Window in Fleet Street, A (James Milne) 58
Windsor Castle 110
Women 35, 36, 96, 108
Women Novelists 95
Wood, Mrs Henry 95
Woodhall, Norrie 193
Woolf, Leonard 121, 222
Woolf, Virginia 121, 125, 167, 222–6, 243–4
Wordsworth, William 51
World, The 19
Writers' Diary, A (Virginia Woolf) 222
Writing methods 14, 22, 45, 106, 118, 128, 148, 189, 230
Writings and Reflections (R. Haig-Brown) 203

Yates, Edmund 19
Yeats, W. B. 98–100
Young Man, The 41
Youriévitch, S. 175

Zachrisson, R. 131
Zangwill, Israel 43

WORKS BY HARDY

Novels

Desperate Remedies 7, 9, 43, 108, 179, 202
Under the Greenwood Tree 7, 8, 10, 13, 37, 92, 93, 111, 185
A Pair of Blue Eyes 7, 8, 10, 92, 141
Far from the Madding Crowd 7, 8, 10, 13, 17, 23, 39, 77, 84, 93, 111, 180, 222, 223, 224
The Hand of Ethelberta 10
The Return of the Native 7, 9, 10, 12, 40, 85, 93, 149, 176, 197, 208, 210
The Trumpet-Major 16, 33, 66, 84, 94, 197
A Laodicean 63
Two on a Tower 63
The Mayor of Casterbridge 12, 22, 24, 93, 114, 197, 225
The Woodlanders 12, 14, 61, 93, 177, 210
Tess of the d'Urbervilles 28, 31, 33, 38, 43, 72, 77, 78, 81, 84, 89, 93, 94, 96, 120, 132, 133, 142, 145, 179, 180, 193, 199, 204, 210, 220, 243
Jude the Obscure 18, 25, 28, 50, 53, 78, 81, 83, 86, 96, 133, 185, 187, 188, 210
The Well-Beloved 194, 195

Short Stories

Wessex Tales 61

Poetry

Wessex Poems 54, 62
Time's Laughingstocks 82

Satires of Circumstance 142
Late Lyrics and Earlier 171, 173, 217
The Queen of Cornwall 62, 205, 206
Collected Poems 138, 140, 154, 157
The Dynasts 31, 62, 74, 77, 79, 82, 93, 97, 110, 112, 127, 134, 138, 140, 162, 168, 169, 173, 182, 197, 217, 218, 224

'An Ancient to Ancients' 130, 234
'And There was a Great Calm' 128, 173
'At the Word "Farewell"' 140
'The Blinded Bird' 112
'The Bride-Night Fire' 136
'The Convergence of the Twain' 128
'The Dark-Eyed Gentleman' 207
'Friends Beyond' 163, 235
'The Homecoming' 208
'The Last Signal' 128
'Near Lanivet' 140
'Nobody Comes' 234
'On an Invitation to the United States' 174
'One We Knew' 235
'A Poet' 132
'Reminiscences of a Dancing Man' 235
'The Schreckhorn' 222
'A Sunday-Morning Tragedy' 31
'The Temporary the All' 168
'To Louisa in the Lane' 3
'A Trampwoman's Tragedy' 82
'Without Ceremony' 155

Other Works

'The Poor Man and the Lady' 5, 61, 103
'How I Built Myself a House' 3, 9, 36, 163
'The Dorsetshire Labourer' 12, 38
'Candour in English Fiction' 28